SITTING BULL'S BOSS

Above the Medicine Line
with James Morrow Walsh

SITTING BULL'S BOSS

Above the Medicine Line
with James Morrow Walsh

Ian Anderson

Heritage
House

Copyright © 2000 Ian Anderson

Canadian Cataloguing in Publication Data

Anderson, Ian, 1930-
    Sitting Bull's boss

    ISBN 1-895811-63-5

    1. Walsh, James Morrow, 1840-1905. 2. Sitting Bull, 1834?-1890.
3. Northwest, Canadian—History—1870-1905.* 4. North West Mounted
Police (Canada)—Biography. I. Title.
FC3216.3.W34A52 2000   971.2'02'092   C00-910911-0
F1060.9.W34A52 2000   .

First edition 2000

We acknowledge the financial assistance received through Heritage
Canada's Book Publishing Industry Development Program and the British
Columbia Arts Council.

Cover and book design by Darlene Nickull and Emily Jacques
Edited by Rodger Touchie and Emily Jacques

HERITAGE HOUSE PUBLISHING COMPANY LTD.
Unit #108 - 17655 66 A Ave., Surrey, BC V3S 2A7

Printed in Canada

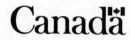

Acknowledgments

In addition to support staff at the Glenbow Museum and RCMP Museum I wish to thank Bonnie Burke, curator, Brockville Museum, and volunteer staff Brenda Foss and Brian Porter. Special thanks also to cartographer Cathy Chapin, and Merv Ahrens for information provided on the Dawson Route.

The author wishes to particularly acknowledge the additional research undertaken by Rodger Touchie, Heritage House's publisher, whose Mountie father I was privileged to meet almost 50 years ago in the course of RCMP duty. Rodger's extensive research has enlarged the scope of this work and made it a better book.

Contents

Foreword

The year 2001 marks the 125th anniversary of one of the defining moments in the history of the North American west. During the summer of 1876 the great Sioux nation and its brotherhood of allies faced a surprise attack by U.S. cavalry forces under the command of George Custer. The resounding Sioux victory that day was but one result in a war they had no chance of winning.

While the battle itself and its dominant personalities, Custer, Sitting Bull, Crazy Horse, and Gall, have been portrayed endlessly in various printed and cinematic renditions, a subtler story played itself out over the next five years.

Students of frontier history know that it is impossible for a single book to capture the nuances of Native American life during an era when an expansionist U.S. government was devoted to a policy of aboriginal containment. Likewise, no single writer has depicted the ambitions and complex relationships of the military men—the bluecoats of the U.S. and the redcoats further north in the new land called Canada.

Ian Anderson has explored a fascinating niche in the story of the west with this tale of two men thrust by chance into the same drama. They first met in a remote area only miles north of the U.S. border, and in their years together they faced circumstances more reminiscent of a Shakespearean tragedy than the western epics depicted in cowboy movies. Somehow a mutual trust and loyalty evolved where it had no right to flourish. Starvation, political hypocrisy, and lifelong enemies were always close at hand, but as Ian Anderson shows, the bond between Sitting Bull and James Walsh was never broken.

* * *

As a young man, Ian Anderson, born in Australia, was drawn to the land of Walsh and Sitting Bull. By then Walsh's North West Mounted Police was known as the Royal Canadian Mounted Police and Ian immigrated to Canada intent on being among the five percent of applicants then accepted into the force. Clad in the scarlet tunic recognized around the world, proud of his new home and career, Ian was further inspired during an assignment that took him to the force's museum in Regina, Saskatchewan. There, behind glass, was the original uniform of one of "The Original Nine," Inspector James Morrow Walsh.

Canada has never been a land to celebrate its heroes—there are few statues of pioneers in its magnificent parks. Even in Walsh's day, his deeds and observations resulted in more news coverage in Chicago and New York than they ever received in Ontario. But history has documented that he managed an almost unfathomable achievement during his first six years as a NWMP officer.

When author Ian Anderson penned more than a half-dozen western novels in his *Scarlet Riders* series for Zebra Books in the 1980s, Walsh was only part of the backdrop for Ian's collections of mounted fictional protagonists. Now James Morrow Walsh stands front and centre, where heroes should be.

Prologue

The Medicine Line

In 1818, negotiators from Great Britain and the United States drew an arbitrary line to define their new realms in western North America. These were the great central plains, a land that up until then had been the domain of roaming buffalo and of Native peoples who often migrated with the herds. None of these original inhabitants took part in the convention that would shape their destiny. A new political boundary along the 49th parallel of latitude separating U.S. states and territories from lands administered by Great Britain stretched from Lake of the Woods to the Rocky Mountains. The Oregon Treaty, signed 28 years later, extended the white man's line all the way to the west coast of the continent.

The immediate effect upon Native people of the U.S. plains and Canadian prairies was unsettling. By the 1860s an image of Washington's "Great White Father," harsh and relentless in his ambitions, had incited the Indian warriors of the west. Buffalo hunters, whisky traders, wagon trains of settlers, and the long-knifed bluecoats of the U.S. Cavalry continued to infringe upon the traditional hunting grounds. Meanwhile, to the north, a land ruled by the "Great White Mother" remained less altered, less invaded. The Mother, the northern tribes said, was a chief who led her people with compassion, truth, and understanding. The distinction between Father and Mother was clear, and what separated them was an invisible wall understood only by the "white world" that had descended upon them. With time this boundary became both a curse and salvation to Native peoples on both sides. Most importantly in the 1870s to the Sioux, the Cheyenne, the Arapaho, the Crow, and other

From 1872 to 1874, boundary commission crews marked the 49th parallel from Lake of the Woods west to the "Stony" Mountains (the Rockies) to distinguish the lands governed by the "Great White Father" from those tended by the "Great White Mother." This ox train is seen leaving the commission depot at Long Creek (northeast of Fort Buford, southwest of Fort Ellis).

tribes it was a force that could stop the ruthless bluecoats in their tracks. They called it the "medicine line."

For the Sioux nation and other tribal groups in this area, the medicine line, intangible and undefended, would come to prove its protective power time and again, but after the end of the Civil War it was unscrupulous white men who took advantage of its status. By 1870, the U.S. cavalry had established enough forts and gathered enough manpower to police the territories of Dakota, Wyoming, Montana, and Idaho. North of the medicine line there was no law enforcement, and whisky traders from Montana flourished.

While Washington advocated expansion, extolled a "manifest destiny," and prepared to celebrate its national centennial, government north of the medicine line was far less advanced. Until 1870 the area was divided into Rupert's Land, ruled by the Hudson's Bay Company (HBC), and the North-Western Territory, under British jurisdiction. In that year, the federal government of Canada purchased

Rupert's Land from the HBC and the North-Western Territory was transferred officially from Britain to the new Dominion. The small province of Manitoba was created to encompass the Red River settlements around Fort Garry, and along with the remaining land, renamed the North-West Territories, was governed by a lieutenant-governor of Manitoba who in turn reported to Canada's governor-general (Queen Victoria's representative) in Ottawa. Or, rather, ignored by Ottawa. It was only after ceaseless rumours of unethical traders, and eventually a blatant massacre of Indians by white traders in the Cypress Hills, that the Canadian prime minister saw fit to form the North West Mounted Police. In 1874, a new sense of order was about to be established above the medicine line.

Below the line, new disorder was erupting. In 1875, almost a decade after the end of the Civil War, an inevitable clash of the proud Sioux nation and the U.S. authority it had come to despise was drawing nearer.

Summer Solstice, 1876

The high sun of midday baked the blood-soaked torso of the Sioux chief as he limped back toward the shadow of his Enemy. The Enemy stood tall and still—a symbolic tree, carefully chosen, suitably adorned in red, blue, green, and yellow by the Sioux's brethren. The blood of the Sioux chief, his scarlet blanket, had seeped from 100 wounds inflicted along the length of his arms and shoulders by the weapon of his attendant, Jumping Bull.

Again the 46-year-old man raised his head, half-blinded by a day of constantly staring skyward. His body bobbed only slightly as he struggled to maintain the motions of dance that had carried him through the night.

Finally, as the warm sun rose to its highest point and the solstice of summer was upon him, the resolute chief collapsed in exhaustion. The priests and the few old men who had performed the Sun Dance in their own time looked on as the prone body of the great leader of the Hunkpapa band lay in the dust before them. Hours passed.

That evening the chief, once again conscious, sat stoically and told the assembled council of his vision and the victories that awaited the Sioux and Cheyenne nations. His resolve was inspiring, but this message was not without warning. "Covet not the spoils of war," he warned. "Fight only to preserve our land." Slowly he raised his head and stared beyond his audience toward the black hills. Beyond, he knew, lay the battlefields.

Heeding their spiritual leader, the many tribal chiefs broke camp and led their people westward toward Greasy Grass, the river that whites called Little Bighorn. Still weak from the Sun Dance ordeal, but concealing his pain, Sitting Bull rode with them.

The First Encounter

In 1877, the disaster of Little Bighorn, the misfortunes of General Custer, and the blood of the 7th U.S. Cavalry were still forefront in frontier memories when the *Fort Benton Record* printed a headline about "Sitting Bull's Boss," a phrase that seemed unfathomable. "Boss," the editor called him. Who could such a man be?

Only a year earlier, those words had clearly fit the aspirations of an ambitious George Armstrong Custer. The overconfident bluecoat and 264 soldiers of all ranks within his command were annihilated beside the Little Bighorn River, Montana Territory, on Sunday, June 25, 1876. This slaughter and the shocking success of what most whites saw as a primitive enemy had thrown the west into turmoil. Following the cavalry's defeat, fear, loathing, suspicion, and endless rumour abounded as the threat of Sitting Bull and his war chiefs remained. There wasn't a settler west of the Mississippi who didn't want to believe that Sitting Bull had a "boss." The idea of the great man and his Sioux nation meekly taking orders from any white was beyond comprehension. Yet the newspapers said it was true!

In the article below the three words, the depiction was sketchy. The boss was a redcoat, north of the medicine line, where the tribal chiefs had taken 5,000 Sioux. He had ridden into the Sioux camp with a small escort. No long-knives, no visible fear—only his reputation and his word. His name was James Morrow Walsh.

Chapter 1

Sitting Bull's Vision

If I were an Indian, I often think, I would greatly prefer to cast my lot among those of my people who adhered to the free open plains rather than submit to the confines of reservation; there to [receive] benefits of civilization with its vices thrown in without stint or measure.

George A. Custer, *My Life on the Plains*, 1874

The Yankee press had called Lieutenant-Colonel George Armstrong Custer the "boy general," Union Army hero of the Potomac, but a decade later, at age 36, his Civil War reputation had faded. Ill-chosen words and an irrepressible vanity had put him in a political doghouse. Esteem was important to this soldier, and Custer hoped to regain it on the frontier with a glorious victory over the rebellious Sioux and their Indian allies.

In late June 1876, Custer and his 7th United States Cavalry Regiment left Fort Lincoln on the Missouri River as part of a two-pronged attack force directed into the Montana Territory under the command of Brigadier-General Alfred H. Terry. The force of 925 soldiers, scouts, and some Indian allies was marching down the Rosebud and Bighorn rivers towards a large body of Sioux, Cheyenne, and other Plains Indians that the government had ordered onto reservations six months earlier. Brought together by their common enemy, a camp of over 1,000 tepees gathered around their spiritual chief, Sitting Bull. Cavalry reconnaissance had them concentrating somewhere near the Little Bighorn and Rosebud rivers. A second Terry command, 450 troops strong under Colonel John Gibbon, approached the Indian stronghold along the Yellowhead River from Fort Ellis in the west.

The Bighorn Campaign

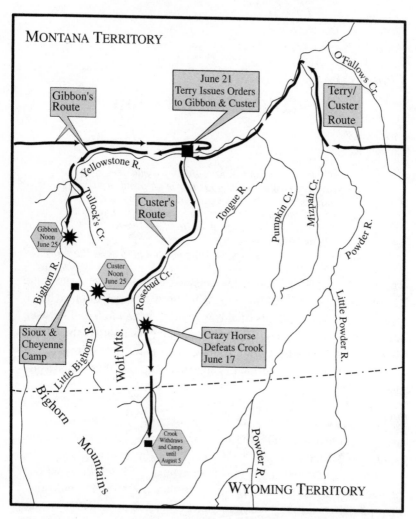

Troop movements of the three cavalry forces targeted at the Sioux nation in June 1876. After Crazy Horse defeated General George Crook at the Battle of the Rosebud on June 17, Crook was unable to deliver the southern assault force intended to help Custer and Gibbon rout the Sioux.

At the same time, a third military column of over a thousand cavalry and 250 Shoshoni and Crow recruits under Brigadier-General George C. Crook, deemed by Civil War hero William Tecumseh Sherman to be "the greatest Indian-fighter the army ever had," marched along the Bozeman Trail from Fort Fetterman, Wyoming. Crook, fresh from campaigns against the Apaches in Arizona, moved northwards, intent on driving the Sioux into the twin arms of Terry's southward-advancing force. In a textbook war these three co-ordinated columns would act in a pincer-like movement. The Sioux and allied chiefs had read no textbook.

General Terry, his troops converging from both east and west along the Yellowstone River, met on June 21 aboard the steamer *Far West* at the confluence with Rosebud Creek. Terry ordered Custer to move southwest up the Rosebud, turn west to the Little Bighorn, then push back down the Little Bighorn toward Gibbon. Gibbon would retrace the Yellowstone to the mouth of the Bighorn River and turn south toward the Little Bighorn. If possible, Terry ordered, Custer should wait for Gibbon so the two cavalries could attack the Indians from opposite flanks. If either Custer or Gibbon were forced to fight, it was to be a holding engagement while waiting for support to arrive. Then the colonels would act together. Custer and Gibbon were instructed to maintain contact with each other by courier. General Terry himself followed Gibbon's march, bringing up slower-moving infantry and Gatling guns.

Although half of Custer's 7th Cavalry was green troops, he was confident they could handle anything they might encounter. Accordingly, he turned down Gibbon's offer of four troops of the 2nd Cavalry and the Gatling battery. Even though the Gatling guns fired over 250 rounds per minute at 900 yards, Custer argued they would slow his advance. His real motives may, however, have been personal. Custer had incurred Washington's displeasure over his allegations that graft was a common practice at army posts. As a result he was anxious to make amends and distinguish himself in the field to regain favour. There were also suggestions that the ambitious fading star was keen to adorn himself with renewed glory for political purposes.

Into the fourth week of June, Custer set a gruelling pace as they marched southwest, pushing tired men and horses relentlessly up the Rosebud. In the meantime, unbeknownst to General Terry, General Crook with 1,300 men had clashed with the Sioux chief Crazy Horse and his warriors farther along the Rosebud on June 17. Crook had

Warlords of the Western Plain

William T. Sherman,
Military Commander,
U.S. Army
"They all have to be killed or maintained as a species of paupers."

Ulysses S. Grant, *President & Chief Commanding Officer*
"Settlers and emigrants must be protected, even if the extermination of every Indian tribe is necessary to procure such a result."

General George Crook, *Commander, Department of the Platte*
"The American Indian commands respect for his rights only as long as he inspires terror in his rifle."

Lieut.-General Philip Sheridan,
Commander, Division of the Missouri.
Speaking to Custer before attacking a Cheyenne village:
"Kill or hang all warriors and bring back all women and children."

In 1840 the U.S. government established a permanent Indian Country on the Great Plains of the American Midwest. The chiefs were assured the land would be forever theirs. This proved a shallow promise as politicians proclaimed their "Manifest Destiny." After January 31, 1876, any Indians still off the reservations in this territory were deemed to be hostiles, in a state of war with the U.S. army. General Philip Sheridan, with the blessings of the army's overall commander William Tecumseh Sherman, set into action a plan that would use soldiers from various cavalry units to pursue the enemy. In ensuing months, and relentlessly for the next two years, the armies of Commanders Sheridan, Alfred Terry, George Crook, John Gibbon, and Nelson Miles would battle the Sioux nation and its allies. Only one general failed to survive the campaign—George Armstrong Custer.

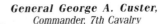

General George A. Custer,
Commander, 7th Cavalry
"We see him as he is, a 'savage' in every sense of the word ... whose cruel and ferocious nature far exceeds that of any wild beast of the desert ..."

"The army is the Indian's best friend."

Brig.-General Alfred Terry,
Commander, Department of the Dakota. On Custer's plea to be reinstated to command the cavalry, May 7, 1876: "Custer, with tears in his eyes, begged my aid. How could I resist?"

Colonel John Gibbon
Commander, Fort Ellis, Montana
"Now Custer, don't be greedy, wait for us."

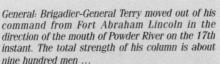

General: Brigadier-General Terry moved out of his command from Fort Abraham Lincoln in the direction of the mouth of Powder River on the 17th instant. The total strength of his column is about nine hundred men ...

Brigadier-General Crook will move from Fort Fetterman with a column about the same size.

Colonel John Gibbon is now moving down north of the Yellowstone and east of the mouth of the Bighorn with a force of about four hundred ...

I have given no instructions to Generals Crook or Terry, preferring that they should do the best they can under the circumstances ... hostile Indians in any great numbers, cannot keep the field as a body for a week, or at the most ten days ...

I presume the following will occur: General Terry will drive the Indians towards the Bighorn valley and General Crook will drive them back towards Terry; Colonel Gibbon moving down on the north side of the Yellowstone, to intercept if possible such as may want to go north of the Missouri to Milk River.

Lieutenant-General P. H. Sheridan in a letter to General W.T. Sherman May 29, 1876

Colonel Nelson A. Miles
"Everybody hopes the Indians will return to their agencies, which would surely be a great accommodation to us and spare us much embarrassment."

Indian Chiefs of the Western Plain

Sitting Bull, *Hunkpapa Sioux spiritual leader*

"I feel sorry that too many were killed on each side, but when Indians must fight, they must."

"The life my people want is a life of freedom. I have seen nothing that a white man has ... that is as good as the right to move in this open country."

Sitting Bull's surrender song (composed in 1881):

*"A warrior
I have been.
Now
It is all over
A hard time
I have."*

The wife of Spotted Horn Bull recalling the state of the Sioux village at Little Bighorn when Custer attacked:

"We women wailed over the children for we believed that the Great Father had sent all his men for the destruction of the Sioux. From across the river I could hear the music of the bugle and could see the column of soldiers turn to the left, to march down to the river to where the attack was to be made. All I could see was the warriors of my people. They rushed like the wind through the village, going down the ravine as the women went out to the grazing-ground to round up the ponies. It was done very quickly. There had been no council the night before—there was no need for one; nor had there been a scalp-dance: nothing but the merry-making of the young men and the maidens. When we did not know there was to be a fight, we could not be prepared for it. And our camp was not pitched anticipating a battle. The warriors would not have picked out such a place for a fight with white men, open to attack from both ends and from the west side. No; what was done that day was done while the sun stood still and the white men were delivered into the hands of the Sioux ...

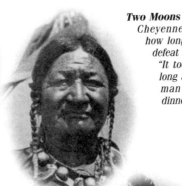

Two Moons
Cheyenne Chief, on how long it took to defeat Custer:
"It took about as long as a hungry man to eat his dinner."

Gall
Hunkpapa War Chief who joined Sitting Bull in Canada
"One man held the horses whle the others shot the guns. We tried to kill the holder ... we scared the horses down the coulee where the Cheyenne women caught them."

Spotted Eagle
"I was born an Indian and it is as an Indian I wish to live and raise my children. The white man's ways do not work well for us; we sicken and die." — Cypress Hills, 1877

Crazy Horse, War Chief of the Lakota Sioux (no photo has ever been verified). Speaking before his famous Battle of the Rosebud with the forces of General Crook's army, June 17, 1876:
"Come on Lakotas, it's a good day to die. Hoka hey!"

Although Sitting Bull was the respected spiritual leader of the Sioux nation, the warrior chiefs were more responsible for the battlefield victory at Little Bighorn. It was Sitting Bull's fellow Hunkpapa, Gall, who was the leading chief at Little Bighorn. Another Hunkpapa, Rain-in-the-Face, would later brag that he had cut out the heart of George Custer's brother, Tom. Two Moons led his Cheyenne brothers into hand-to-hand combat to avenge the unprovoked assault of his village four months earlier by Colonel J.J. Reynolds (under General Crook's command). The Sans Arcs were led by Spotted Eagle and the Ogalalas by Crazy Horse (who was adamant that he never be photographed). In all, 1,500 lodges representing a dozen non-treaty tribes were gathered beside the Little Bighorn River at the time of Custer's attack.

Rain-in-the-Face
reputed to have killed General Custer's brother.

been repulsed and fallen back. Crazy Horse had then gone north down the Rosebud and through the Wolf Mountains to Little Bighorn to join his allies—Sitting Bull, Gall, Rain-In-The-Face, and others.

At dawn on the morning of Sunday June 25, Custer and several of his officers joined a Crow scout standing atop a ridge between the Rosebud and the Little Bighorn rivers. To their west, park-like grassland, dotted with stands of pine, fell away to the Little Bighorn. Along the river valley below they saw signs of a massive camp of Sioux and Cheyenne among the cottonwoods. Custer's chief scout, an Arikara named Bloody Knife, expressed his concern. There were too many Sioux down there, he said.

Looking down toward the big Sioux camp in the valley, Custer expressed concern that the Indians would escape or only fight long enough for their women and children to flee the camp. Then, when they were safely gone, the warriors too would run. Despite General Terry's orders to wait until Gibbon's column arrived, Custer decided to attack immediately. Glory was at hand and he wanted a quick, decisive victory to go to his 7th Cavalry alone.

Custer divided his regiment into three columns. Major Marcus Reno with three companies—approximately 122 officers and men—was ordered to follow a creek leading down to the Little Bighorn, cross the river south of the Sioux, then proceed along the west bank to attack the Indian camp at its upper or southern end. Three companies under Captain Frederick W. Benteen were to follow, sweep out west of Reno and watch for Indians fleeing from the camp, and, if circumstances allowed, attack the camp from the western flank. Custer led the third column of five companies, marching parallel to Reno on the east side of the river for much of the way. Custer then planned to go beyond the camp, cross to the west side of the river, and strike the perimeter while Benteen struck from the west and Reno drove down the centre. One company under Captain McDougall was to follow Custer's main column, escorting the pack train carrying the regiment's ammunition and supplies. As he issued his orders, Custer did not know Colonel Gibbon's location. There had been no courier contact in days.

At the crossing of the river, Reno's column quickly ran into resistance and never got close enough to the upper end of the camp to press an attack. They did manage to kill the two wives and three children of Sitting Bull's war chief, Gall, thus earning his undying hatred. The column was met by heavy fire from the Sioux, and after fighting back from the cover of cottonwoods for a short while, Reno and his men retreated, recrossing to the east side of the Little Bighorn. A third of their number were killed, wounded, or missing in the retreat. They were soon joined by Benteen who, not having seen any fleeing Indians, had returned east toward the battlefield. On his way back he witnessed Reno's retreat and joined those forces. Together the survivors retreated further to a bluff, where they dismounted and held off repeated attacks by the Indians.

Unaware of this disarray, Custer's troops marched the entire length of the Indian camp before attempting to cross the river and attack the camp from the north. The pace of Custer's force proved easy to measure from the Sioux perspective on the western bank, and their first assault was quickly driven back from the river. The outwitted soldier and his column sought high ground, and with Companies E and F he retired to what history would name Custer's Hill. There Custer made his famous last stand. A short distance away on Calhoun's Hill, named after Custer's brother-in-law and subordinate, Companies C, I, and L were foiled in an attempt to join Custer. Gall, burning to revenge the loss of his family, and Crazy Horse led their warriors against the two hills, overrunning one, then the other. The soldiers were in desperate straits as rapid firing heated their single-shot Springfield carbines, causing the cartridges to jam in the breeches. In the end, all they had to fight with were their rifle butts and revolvers.

In all, Custer and 264 officers, men, and attached civilians of his command had been wiped out. Many were Civil War veterans. There was even one Canadian, Lieutenant William W. Cooke, Custer's adjutant, who had served with the United States Army since Civil War days.

America stood aghast. In the eyes of the American public, it was a massacre—a bloody massacre. In Washington the hawks cried out, and with the Senate's and military commander William T. Sherman's blessing, General Philip H. Sheridan, commander of the Military Department of the Missouri, stripped every army post between the Canadian border and Texas, assembling a powerful military force to strike back at the Sioux and Cheyenne. Sheridan aimed to give the hostiles a lesson they'd never forget.

To inflict that lesson, Sheridan established a very specific target: the chief of the Hunkpapa Sioux, who held the respect of all. Sitting Bull was the mystic visionary who had drawn together the various Lakota bands and their Cheyenne allies and melded them into a mighty league. Although he had only played an indirect part in the battle, his was the name soldiers and settlers alike most associated with the Indian victory at the Little Bighorn. Gall, Crazy Horse, Two Moons, and Spotted Eagle were all forces to reckon with, but Bull was the "big medicine" the army most eagerly sought to conquer.

Chapter 2

Redcoats on the Prairie

*It seems to me that the best Force would be Mounted
Riflemen, trained to act as cavalry, but also
instructed in the Rifle exercises. They should also
be instructed, as certain of the Line are, in the use
of artillery, this body should not be expressly
military, but should be styled* Police, *and have the
military bearing of the Irish Constabulary.*

Sir John A. Macdonald, *Commission of Inquiry*, 1873

James Walsh's introduction to Native ways had come at an early age. In
fact his favoured sport as a young man came not from the traditions of
his Irish ancestors but from the pastimes of the region's aboriginals.

At the time of Confederation in Canada on July 1, 1867, 27-year-
old James Walsh was one of the new nation's leading lacrosse players.
Lacrosse, a game originated by the Algonquin tribes, was first observed
by French missionary Jean de Brebeuf in the mid-1600s. Two centuries
later the game had gained popularity with non-Native athletes from
the Ottawa Valley through to northern New York State. In 1869 Walsh
captained the Prescott, Ontario, team when it defeated opposing sides
from Montreal, Ottawa, Kingston, Toronto, and Buffalo, New York, to
rank as the continent's best.

James Morrow Walsh was born at Prescott, Upper Canada, May
22, 1840, the first of nine children for ship's carpenter Lewis Walsh
and Elizabeth Morrow Walsh. Although an indifferent student, he
excelled at athletics, being handy with his fists and a notable runner
and swimmer. He was a keen cricketer and excelled at soccer and
canoeing. At age twenty he also found time to captain the Prescott
Fire Brigade.

Walsh was less successful in his choice of occupation, at least for a time. As a young man he tried several things—selling dry goods in a local store, working in a machine shop, training as an engineer on the railroad. All left him restless. Attracted to soldiering and eager to widen his experience, Walsh enrolled in the Kingston Military School, excelling in gunnery and cavalry, graduating with honours in 1862. As fate would have it, the head of the school of gunnery at Kingston was Colonel G.A. French, the man who would lead him to the Western frontier. That summer, adding to his reputation as an adventurer, Walsh and a friend ran the treacherous rapids of the St. Lawrence River from Prescott all the way to Montreal.

Then in 1866, Fenians—members of a secret Irish revolutionary movement founded in the United States to overthrow British rule in Ireland—began making raids into the British colony beyond the American border. Canada quickly sought militia volunteers to fight them off. Answering that call was a turning point in James Walsh's life. Soldiering was in his blood: his Irish ancestors had fought under the Duke of Wellington during the Napoleonic War. Commissioned a lieutenant in the 56th Grenville Regiment, he saw action against the raiders, earning praise from his superiors and promotion to captain. A ramrod-straight five feet nine inches tall, he suited a military uniform; he looked like a soldier, and carried himself like one. Men respected James Walsh and responded to his direct manner. There was something about him, something that suggested he was destined for more than mere ordinary. In 1868 Walsh left Kingston's School of Cavalry as an officer after receiving a first-class certificate. Dated February 1869, the certificate included the Cavalry Commandant's assessment: "He is the smartest and most efficient officer that has yet passed through the Cavalry School. He is a good rider and particularly quick and confident at drill. I thoroughly recommend him to the notice of the Adjutant General."

Perhaps stimulated by the outbreak of the Métis-led Red River insurrection in 1869, Walsh continued his education in Toronto. After gaining his first-class certificate from the Militia School of Gunnery in June, Walsh joined Colonel Garnet Wolseley's announced military expedition of 450 British regulars and 800 Canadian militia that was to proceed west to suppress the rebels. However, while serving as ensign and acting adjutant he came under the spell of eighteen-year-old Mary Elizabeth Mowat of Brockville. They married on April 19, 1870, five weeks before the Red River Expedition started its three-month journey to

Manitoba. Walsh, no doubt torn between two loves, settled into family life in Prescott. Later that year James and Mary's first and only daughter, Cora, was born.

Marriage only delayed the inevitable, however. Though Walsh took over management of Prescott's North American Hotel, army life was still in his blood. He formed a local militia and as a part-time major commanded the Prescott Cavalry.

In May 1873, Parliament passed a bill calling for a "Police Force in the North-West Territories." The force of mounted rifles was to travel westward

The original crest of the NWMP paid tribute to both the fast-disappearing buffalo of the west and the nation's bilingualism.

to the wild, unsettled plains of the great prairie. There it would plant the British flag over the lands recently acquired from the HBC and Britain— the North-West Territories. This new force would establish law and order among the warring Indian tribes and protect them from the unscrupulous activities of American whisky traders who had escaped U.S. jurisdiction by moving north of the 49th parallel. One of these traders was John J. Healy, an entrepreneur and former sheriff, whose northern outpost, Fort Whoop-Up, was one of the most notorious. The force's mandate was to penetrate the heart of Blackfoot country, clean out Fort Whoop-Up and other whisky-trading forts, and put a stop to the illegal liquor trade with the Indians. Canada's prime minister, Sir John Alexander Macdonald, wanted as "little gold lace, fuss and feathers as possible" in the new force. Well aware of the broad contempt felt for American soldiers in the west, Macdonald foresaw a non-military force. He did not want a crack cavalry regiment, simply an efficient police, built along the lines of the Royal Irish Constabulary, to enforce the law in a rough-and-ready country. It was to be a civil body under military discipline, trained and equipped to fight if it had to, but its purpose was clearly to keep the peace and, in the words of its motto, "maintien le droit"—uphold the right.

That summer Walsh caught wind of the impending formation of the police force. Thirsting for a life more stimulating than Prescott could

Six years into his first term as Canada's prime minister, Sir John A. Macdonald was infamous for both his procrastination and his attraction to alcohol. Only eighteen days after appointing George French to head the NWMP, Macdonald ended an extended drinking binge by announcing to the House of Commons on November 5, 1873, that he was resigning. Although he would lose the next election, he would not be gone for long.

offer, he let it be known in Ottawa that he was interested in a position in the proposed force.

Walsh's brief military record served him well. The 30-year-old Walsh and a few like him bided their time through the summer while "Old Tomorrow" procrastinated. The prime minister's nickname came from his reluctance to leap into action and his propensity for crawling into a bottle of port, made worse by the trials of leadership.

Canada in 1873 was already a political juggling act of British and French ideals and new demands from the west. Manitoba had become Canada's fifth province in 1870, but concerns for peace and security remained after the infamous Métis rebellion was quelled. Then the colony of British Columbia was induced to join as the sixth province in 1871, with promises of a national rail link to connect it to the country's capital in Ottawa.

The United States formally recognized Canada's existence in the 1871 Treaty of Washington, and a boundary commission began marking the border as far west as the Rockies. For a brief moment, Canada's future looked bright.

Two years later, "Old Tomorrow" was running out of time. He could no longer ignore two commissioned studies that warned of pending disaster unless a militia was sent west. Protection for settlers and railway builders was an absolute necessity, and the unfulfilled promises made to the West Coast citizenry were now breeding impatience.

In desperation, British Columbia had gone so far as to send its premier to Ottawa as a Member of Parliament. This obstinate if articulate man bore the unlikely name of Amor de Cosmos and he reminded Canada's Tory government of its promises daily. Sir John was driven further to drink. James Walsh waited patiently for the clamour to yield his desired result. Finally in August, after word of a heinous massacre of Assiniboine people near a whisky fort in the Cypress Hills reached Ottawa, Macdonald started the wheels rolling.

Hewitt Bernard, deputy minister of justice, established a budget for the force. Sub-constables and constables would be paid 75 cents to a dollar per day—a small stipend for the task that lay ahead. Further details of the Cypress Hills massacre crossed Macdonald's desk in September when a telegraph arrived from Alexander Morris, lieutenant-governor of Manitoba. A gang of wolf hunters had killed 36 Assiniboines at the hills, just north of the U.S. border. Delay no longer an option, the prime minister wrote to the governor general, "If anything went wrong the blame would lie at our door."

James Walsh was appointed a North West Mounted Police sub-inspector on September 25, 1873, along with eight other officers. At a salary of $1,000 per year, Walsh was assigned responsibility for recruiting able-bodied horsemen of sound character, aged 18 to 40. They were to be of good health and literate in English or French. Of the nine officers'

On October 3, 1873, Commanding Officer James Walsh issued the following memo to members of his "A" Troop command. The next day they embarked from Collingwood to begin the long trek west.

The C.O. requests that the men will abstain from too free use of intoxicating liquors.

While he is no advocate for totally abstaining still it will be his duty to report to the Commissioner on his arrival at Stone Fort any cases of drunkenness that may be brought before him.

All having received certificates of good moral character they should bear in mind that if they abuse them, it reflects not only on themselves but also on their sources who vouched for them.

The C.O. wishes it to be distinctly understood that this memo, is intended more as a request than as a warning.

The C.O. hopes that in passing through the country the men will bear in mind that this is not a mere volunteer military Force which has only to obey orders but that each man will be able to at any time to be called upon to Exercise his own judgement & trusts that by their conduct they will show themselves worthy of the trust placed in them.

By order

appointments, three might be considered political. Nephews of both the prime minister and Justice Deputy Bernard, plus one strong Tory supporter, filled a third of the appointments made.

Walsh was selected to lead the first NWMP recruits into the west. He was ideal for the task—strong-featured, determined-looking, soldierly, direct, firm, decisive, a born leader of men. On October 1, as officer in command of "A" Troop, James Walsh left Ottawa with a contingent of one non-commissioned officer (NCO) and 32 men en route to Toronto. One trumpeter was discharged for drunkenness and eight new recruits joined the ranks at Prescott. They included Walsh's younger brother, William, and three sons of a retired naval officer, Elmes Steele of Simcoe County. The most prominent of this trio, Samuel Benfield Steele, who had already been west as a nineteen-year-old recruit in the 1870 campaign to crush the Métis rebellion, was appointed by James Walsh as his second NCO before the train reached its final destination at Collingwood. There the hastily formed contingent boarded the steamer *Cumberland* and crossed Lakes Huron and Superior, destined for Prince Arthur's Landing (now Thunder Bay), 1,000 miles from Walsh's home. The worst lay ahead as they disembarked in morning darkness on October 8 and started their march at 7:30 a.m. They would travel in wagons over muskeg road and rely on dilapidated "teakettle tugs" to barge them upstream along the tortuous 545-mile Dawson route that led to the stone walls of Lower Fort Garry.

The route was named for surveyor Simon J. Dawson, who had defined the trail in 1858 and remained responsible for maintenance fifteen years later. Dawson had boasted that even in early October, "passengers were sent in six days from Thunder Bay to the Northwest Angle of the Lake of the Woods." Walsh's was the first of three troops to make this arduous trek during that month, and Sam Steele quickly became his right hand due to his knowledge of the route. The series of lakes, rivers, and twenty portages across mosquito-infested bogs was the same path the Wolseley expedition had taken to reach the Red River country three summers earlier to put down Louis Riel's Métis insurrection. Since then, despite Dawson's claims, the trail had deteriorated badly, with many ferryboats and shelters abandoned.

The second day of "A" Troop's journey from Thunder Bay began early. Walsh started a four-hour march at 2 a.m. only to spend the next 24 hours idly awaiting the Lake Shebandowan steam tug. Once underway, the tug towed an armada of barges and small boats the length of the lake to the first of the twenty portages. For another four

The Stone Fort at Lower Fort Garry in 1872, one year before Major James Walsh led the first NWMP recruits through its gate. This former Hudson's Bay Company supply post was twenty miles north of Winnipeg on the Red River.

days the NWMP recruits encountered swamps, snowstorms, rapids, and more ferry delays. Arriving at Fort Frances nearly spent on October 14, they found the provisioning station empty and marched two miles westward to the Rainy River. After being delayed a day near Lake of the Woods and stranded on the lake itself for two hours, Walsh's patience was at an end. Ferryman George Dixon long remembered Walsh calling him "a Goddamn black-hearted villain." The worst of the trail was now behind them, and a week later they arrived at Fort Garry down the Red River from Winnipeg. They had completed the 1,500-mile trip from Collingwood with but a single injury when Private John Todd managed to shoot himself in the arm. Todd was sent to the hospital in Fort Garry, and the next day, October 22, Walsh and his men drifted north down the Red River and finally arrived at Lower Fort Garry, the Stone Fort, after three weeks of hard slogging, their spirit largely intact. The *Winnipeg Manitoban* reported, "Judging from the first detachment, the Mounted Police are a fine body of men."

On November 3, Lieutenant-Colonel Osborne Smith, Deputy Adjutant-General of Militia, who had been appointed temporary commissioner of the NWMP in the North-West Territories, swore in each recruit. Ranks were formalized and the North West Mounted Police

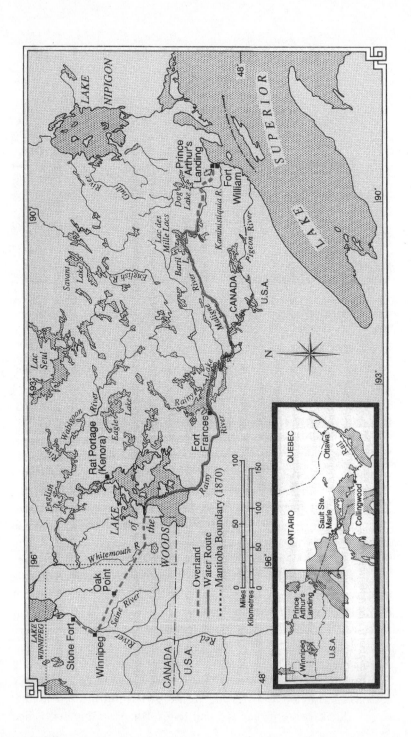

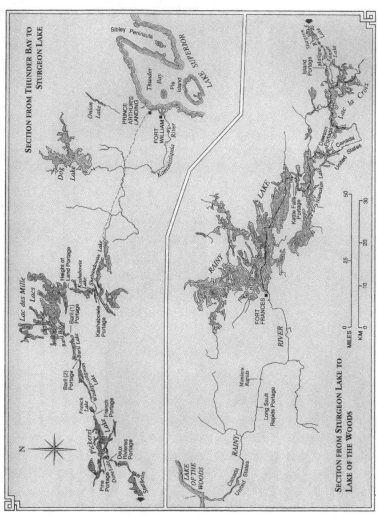

SECTION FROM THUNDER BAY TO STURGEON LAKE

Sibley Peninsula

Thunder Bay

Pie Island

LAKE SUPERIOR

Onion Lake

PRINCE ARTHUR'S LANDING

FORT WILLIAM

Kaministiquia River

Dog Lake

Lac des Mille Lacs

Height of Land Portage

Kashabowie Lake

Shebandowan Lake

Baril Bay

Baril (1) Portage

Kashabowie Portage

Baril Lake

Baril (2) Portage

French Lake

Windegoostigwan Lake

French Portage

Pickerel Lake

Deux Rivières Portage

Pine Portage

Doré Lake

Sturgeon

N

SECTION FROM STURGEON LAKE TO LAKE OF THE WOODS

Sturgeon Lake

Island Portage

Maligne R.

Tanner Lake

Lac la Croix

Dawson Portage

Namakan Lake

Canada

United States

Kettle Falls Portage

RAINY LAKE

FORT FRANCES

RAINY RIVER

Manitou Rapids

Long Sault Rapids Portage

LAKE OF THE WOODS

Canada

United States

MILES 0 10 20 25 50
KM 0 30

In 1873 the Dawson route (shown above) provided an all-Canadian trail to the fledgling province of Manitoba. Made famous by Colonel Garnet Wolseley's Red River Expedition three years earlier to quell the riotous Métis, the trail, which connected Lake Superior with the settlement at Fort Garry, Manitoba, had deteriorated significantly by the time the NWMP arrived. Maps to the right detail the most challenging part of the portage trail from Prince Arthur's Landing to Lake of the Woods. (Maps courtesy of Cathy Chapin, Lakehead University Geography Department, and The Beaver.)

James Morrow Walsh (inset), seen here at a later point in his NWMP career, can fairly be called "the original Mountie." It was he who led the first detachment of recruits out of Ontario and onto the western prairie, beginning one of the most fascinating policing adventures in world history.

A younger Walsh? Perhaps. National Archives of Canada records identify the portrait (right) only as Mr. Walsh. Although the resemblance to verified photos (inset) is obvious, this could be a younger brother.

effectively came into existence. The second and third contingents of the new police force arrived within the next ten days, until eventually 150 men were at the Stone Fort. By early 1874 they had been formed into three 50-man troops, undergoing a rigorous course of training. James Walsh performed the duties of acting adjutant, acting veterinary surgeon, and riding master. Sergeant-Major Griesbach was in charge of foot drill, and Sergeant-Major Sam Steele took on the task of breaking in the horses.

It may not have worried Walsh that 150 recruits were pitifully few for the task ahead, but it certainly worried his commanding officer. Lieutenant-Colonel George Arthur French was on loan to the Canadian government from England's Royal Artillery and was formally appointed to head the NWMP on October 18, 1873, after the first troops had already started the journey west to Fort Garry.

French faced other worries besides a possible shortage of manpower. The Tory government and Sir John A. Macdonald were besieged by scandal over bribes received from Sir Hugh Allan in exchange for receipt of the transcontinental railway charter. The deputy minister of justice

While in command of the Kingston Military School, George French had released some of his charges, including Sam Steele, to join the NWMP. French knew that he would see these men again once his new position at the head of the North West Mounted Police was made public.

French brought strong opinions, sometimes ill-conceived, to his leadership role. Ultimately the west would leave more of a mark on him than he left on it.

was reluctant to make any commitments amid the instability, and the plight of the new NWMP commissioner was hardly noticed. When Macdonald resigned on November 5, it was unclear what level of support the NWMP would gain from the new government. Colonel French decided the political quagmire of Ottawa surpassed anything the Canadian prairie could offer. On December 1 he boarded a train that would take him to Fargo, North Dakota, en route to Fort Garry and his first meeting with the force he now commanded.

Two days after arriving at the Stone Fort, French wrote Justice Deputy Bernard of his findings: "The officers generally are a good lot of fellows, the men are also." He estimated that only 10 percent of the recruits were ill-chosen and destined to be discharged. French then set about planning the spring expedition, selectively seeking the advice of politicians, administrators, and even the astronomer of the boundary commission. Either through over-confidence or lack of vision he ignored the most important source available to him. William Hallet, the commission's chief scout, could have told French what the great prairies held in store.

On his return east in February, French pressed Ottawa for more men. Accordingly, the first three troops were joined by another three, consisting of 201 men, 16 officers, and 278 horses, which left Toronto on June 6 and travelled by train to Fargo, North Dakota. They met their counterparts from Fort Garry at Dufferin, on the west bank of the Red River just north of the Dakota border, where they all went into advanced training. James Walsh, promoted to inspector, commanded one of the six troops. The spring march became a summer march.

Chapter 3

The March West

*I doubt if any expedition ever undertook a journey
with such complete faith and such utter ignorance.*
Sir Cecil E. Denny, *The Riders of the Plains*, 1905

Among his charges, Major Walsh inherited the NWMP's youngest member. Frederick Augustus Bagley was a strapping fifteen-year-old who passed his medical, lied about his age, bragged about his horsemanship, sought the blessings of his family, then headed west to Dufferin with the 1874 recruits. Bagley's diary would become one of the more entertaining accounts of the Mounties' earliest days.

The assembly at Dufferin, and Fred Bagley, trumpeter, were tested almost immediately. Hail, lightning, relentless thunder, and a herd of stampeding horses brought chaos late on June 21. With tents torn asunder, men huddled together through the night. Bagley wrapped himself in a water-soaked blanket. For Fred, morning reveille came in the form of Sam Steele. "You go with Major Walsh," Steele said, pointing at Bagley.

Near midnight, after covering 100 miles that day, Walsh returned to camp with 80 horses and a spent fifteen-year-old. Bagley was asleep in his saddle when Walsh steered the boy off his mount and carried him to a tent.

Days later Inspector James Walsh watched Sub-Constable Bagley leading a new horse towards the corral. He knew young Bagley was up to mischief but he also knew the immediate value of a good horse. Walsh hid his amusement while Bagley explained his good fortune in finding the mount. "They hang horse thieves where we're heading," was all he said, but his message was clear. Fred Bagley had "found" his last horse.

A red-coated column of 275 North West Mounted policemen, 120 oxen with carts, and 30 Métis drivers left Dufferin on July 8 with great anticipation. Their immediate mandate was to seek out the whisky-trading

Fred Bagley, seen here after more than a decade of service, originally joined the NWMP march west for a short-term adventure. It was 14 years before he saw home again (as a staff sergeant) and 25 years before he retired as an officer at age 41. At a NWMP reunion almost 50 years after the event, he met the ex-constable whose horse he had "borrowed" at Dufferin.

devils who were known for maltreating the Indians to the west. They left behind a small detail of men at Lower Fort Garry, and French had earlier deployed a detachment of fifteen redcoats to Fort Ellice, a Hudson's Bay Company post on the Assiniboine River.

Within weeks, enthusiasm had surrendered to reality. Even the sturdiest horses were badly weakened from crossing vast stretches of arid country without proper food or water. On August 3 another violent storm ravaged the campsite. Artist Henri Julien called the military tents that were their shelter a "fraud." By the time they sighted their first buffalo one month after leaving Dufferin, French had lost ten horses, and his column straggled over miles behind him. At this point the men were victims of a disorganized quartermaster (who also happened to be Prime Minister John A. Macdonald's nephew). A chance meeting with a group of Métis buffalo hunters provided them with a much-needed store of pemmican. Supplies had dwindled quickly and rations of flour were not enough to sustain the troops. Everyone from Walsh and fellow officers down to junior trumpeter Fred Bagley savoured the chewy mix of buffalo bits and fat.

Henri Julien, an artist with Canadian Illustrated News, *was invited by Colonel French to join the epic march. His earliest sketches featured the chaos at Dufferin and the fury of a prairie thunderstorm. Julien and his trusted mount, Old Rooster, returned to Montreal in October 1874.*

Major James Macleod, the assistant commissioner and second in command to French, was concerned for the horses as well as the men. He managed to secure 30 tons of oats from the boundary commission after a three-day return trip to their camp at Wood Mountain.

By late August the march had reached Strong Current Creek (now Swift Current), and another river crossing slowed their progress. The next week they covered only 30 miles as road-building became a prerequisite.

Rain, mud, boredom, and the tedious pace sapped morale. Then midway through the morning march on September 2, the treeless prairie horizon took on a new look. Like a burnt umber mirage, the rolling hills began to move. Suddenly Major Walsh urged his horse out of the ranks following Colonel French and rode toward the brown mass. "Buffalo!" he cried out, and the hunt was on.

✳ ✳ ✳

Two months and 700 miles out from Dufferin in the "Great Lone Land," Colonel French was a wiser but chagrined man. The 34 eastern horses

A timely encounter with the buffalo herds likely saved numerous lives as Colonel French's ill-conceived supply priorities left both men and horses in dire straits less than two months into the march. Julien captured the conditions of an unforgiving trail as French's hand-picked mounts fell victim to a waterless prairie (below).

he had selected to lead the march had fared poorly compared to the mongrel mustangs most of his officers favoured. French had also lost two of his six inspectors due to strenuous arguments and insubordination over the Colonel's ill-conceived load allocations and the choice of horses. One, Theodore Richer of "F" Troop, had walked out of camp threatening to expose French for incompetence. In general, however, fallout among the recruits was surprisingly small. They were men of good character and education. More than half claimed military service in Canada or other parts of the British Empire. Most were British or Canadian born, with a few Americans, a Frenchman, a German, and a Bohemian among them. The average age of the officers was 31, of NCOs and men, 25.

French reckoned he was 83 miles shy of Fort Whoop-Up at the fork of the Belly and Bow rivers, but his guide had never been beyond this point, and a new man in camp named Moreau had yet to earn French's trust. The Colonel would not see the Bow River before facing his most serious challenge. The humourless commander was as much disliked by his men as his second-in-command was cherished. The men had concluded that French was out of his element, but it was obvious that Major Macleod, James Walsh, Sam Steele, and a handful of others had found theirs.

On September 8, Colonel Arthur French's pompous style got the best of him. In a fit of rage he ordered two sentries into irons, accusing them of stealing biscuits during the night. There was little evidence, and French's command seemed extreme. All present were shocked by the outburst until Major Macleod stepped forward. A trained lawyer, Macleod quickly sought to ease the tension. Refusing the order he said, "Sir, you can't do that. Our regulations give you no authority for such a course of action. It is very clear." He spoke firmly, and when French persisted, Macleod added, "I'm sorry, sir. I can't allow this to happen."

Both men stood silent, an awkward sense of mutiny hanging in the air. After allowing French a respectful silence if he had a retort, Major James Macleod saluted and returned to the morning duties.

Chapter 4

Taking Fort Whoop-Up

> *Macleod and the inspectors [came] to the unanimous*
> *agreement that it would be best if Colonel French*
> *returned as fast as possible to Manitoba.*
> Cruise and Griffiths, *The Great Adventure*, 1996

Cold and hunger were constant enemies in early September. Fred Bagley wrote in his diary on September 10 of "B" Troop's refusal to leave camp without breakfast. Walsh's troop had gone without dinner the night before. Much of their trail had been burned over by prairie grass fires, so natural feed for the animals was hard to come by. During the day, Colonel French seemed confused about where they were and where they were going. He sent parties in various directions searching for forts, Indians, rivers—anything that might help establish exactly where he was.

Two days later he presented a new strategy. With winter approaching, French was now thinking of shelter, a place to survive, and in his diary the notorious and elusive Fort Whoop-Up took on a new façade. "It is principally a trading post of the firm Baker & Co. of [Fort] Benton, highly respectable merchants who do not sell whisky or spirits." This convenient assessment (the new scout Moreau, distrusted only days earlier, seems the only possible source of this new perspective) left French free to set new orders. The Colonel assembled Macleod and his inspectors to announce his plans.

Weak horses and sick men would go north to Fort Edmonton. Others would return to forts farther east in Manitoba, and a final contingent would build a fort along the route to Fort Benton, in Montana Territory, where supplies could be obtained.

The column reached the junction of the Bow and Belly (South Saskatchewan) rivers. It was here that French expected to find the centre of the whisky trade, Fort Whoop-Up. But all he discovered were the crumbling remains of three long-deserted log cabins. There were fewer of his command with him now; 2 officers and 21 men of "A" Troop had struck out northwest at La Roche Percée for the HBC's Fort Edmonton, a post on the North Saskatchewan River, and 14 sick or incapacitated men had been sent to Fort Ellice or left at a "cripple camp" along the way.

Mystified by the absence of Fort Whoop-Up, Colonel French sent scouting parties west and north along the two rivers to find it. Inspector Walsh, "B" Troop, and the remainder of "A" Troop were ordered to ride 200 miles north to join "A" Troop at Fort Edmonton.

The scouting parties returned two days later, reporting no sign of Whoop-Up. French's chief scout, Pierre Leveille, also advised him there was no suitable food west or north. He convinced French that it would be impossible for Inspector Walsh and his men, because of the poor condition of their horses, to reach Fort Edmonton. The commissioner sent a rider to overtake Walsh, ordering him to return and follow the bulk of the command south. Their new destination consisted of three hills rising out of the prairie some 60 miles away. Leveille called them the Trois Buttes, or Sweetgrass Hills, just below the border in Montana Territory. There they would find good grazing and water, but French's real attraction to the southerly route was possible contact with civilization. A hundred miles farther south lay Fort Benton, head of navigation for the Missouri River sternwheelers. It was the only centre for hundreds of miles where he could replenish supplies. French also knew there was a telegraph office there, where he could wire Ottawa a report on his progress.

Four days later, French and his four troops made camp at the westernmost of Trois Buttes. Two more days passed before Inspector Walsh and his men caught up to them, six of the troops' horses having died from exhaustion and starvation. In spite of their discipline, the camp was a sorry site, summed up in Fred Bagley's diary: "The sentry on the Commissioner's tent in rags, and with gunny sacks wrapped around his feet."

September 22 was Bagley's sixteenth birthday, but all of the men got a present they accepted with a sense of relief. Colonel French left their camp for the last time. Diarist James Finlayson wrote, "He left here with the best wishes of the men. That he may never come back."

French and Macleod left camp and rode south to Fort Benton. Accompanying them were two other officers, six men driving empty

Fred Bagley and Old Buck were part of the deployment that travelled to Swan River, Manitoba, under Colonel French. Bagley's mustang lived to age 32. This photo was sent to Bagley before Old Buck's life was humanely ended in 1898.

wagons, and, to Bagley's dismay, his horse, Old Buck, which the Colonel had commandeered. They reached Fort Benton at noon on the third day, after crossing the winding Teton and Marias rivers eleven times.

Benton was a fort in name only. All that remained of the old stockade were a few rotting logs. In the 1830s it had been the principal trading post on the upper Missouri of J.J. Astor's old American Fur Company and later that company's successor Pierce Chouteau and Company. In 1862 Chouteau's river steamers had unleashed a new mob of whites on the territory as a short-lived gold rush took hold. By September 1874 it was a wide-open town in one of the wildest and least-civilized parts of the American west. It was used to seeing buffalo hunters, plainsmen, mountain men, trappers, miners, cattlemen, wolfers, squaw-men, soldiers, drifters, Indians, river men, gamblers, and just about anyone else likely to be found in the west. On one side of its main street was a row of false-fronted buildings and a variety of frame and ramshackle structures of various sizes and shapes—trading stores, hotels, saloons, greasy spoon restaurants, a doctor's office, banks, music halls, gambling dens, one barbershop, a bath house, billiard parlours, and a blacksmith's shop. Facing them on the other side of the street was the steamboat landing, lapped by the muddy waters of the Missouri, where tall-funnelled river steamers, with large

After the rude awakening the journey had brought, Colonel French lapped up the hospitalities extended at Fort Benton by Isaac Baker and Charles Conrad of I.G. Baker Company. They provided supplies and introduced scout Jerry Potts to French.

oblong plates fastened to the wheelhouses or the upper deck railings bearing their names, docked along the levee.

The main street bustled with activity. Covered wagons rumbled along to the accompaniment of bullwhackers cussing as they cracked their whips over the backs of their stubborn teams. Grim-faced horsemen clattered by, hard eyes flitting over everything around them. Tinny music razzed from dance halls, laughter and raucous shouts erupted from the saloons, a pistol exploded sharply from somewhere down the street.

Traders Isaac and George Baker, proprietors of the I.G. Baker Company, welcomed Colonel French and Major Macleod. Upon learning the red-coated Mounted Police officers' purpose, Isaac Baker told them Fort Whoop-Up was located at the junction of the Belly and St. Mary's rivers, not the Bow and Belly.[1] Isaac Baker recommended a local Métis named Jerry Potts should the officers need a guide. Isaac Baker and his employee Charles Conrad also let them know the

---

[1] The Belly and Oldman rivers come together 28 miles west of the Bow-Belly junction, and modern maps carry the name Oldman east of that point. This section of river was known as the Belly in the 1870s. What was then St. Mary's River is now officially the St. Mary.

The above-ground graves of the Blood Nation and other tribes that shared the practice were a common sight on the prairie. These stood near the Belly River, a reminder to NWMP recruits that they had entered a new and strange land.

company could supply them with anything they might need, anything at all. French accordingly entered into a contracting arrangement with the Baker Company, which went on to supply the force for many years.

At the telegraph office, Colonel French received instructions from Ottawa that he was to take two troops back northeast to Swan River, the proposed site for the capital of the North-West Territories, and establish Mounted Police headquarters, leaving the remainder of the force in the far west, where they were to set up a post and stamp out the illegal whisky trade.

Leaving Major Macleod at Fort Benton to complete arrangements for supplying the remaining three troops, Colonel French returned to the international boundary and took "D" and "E" Troops northeast toward Swan River.

A few days later, Major Macleod left Fort Benton to meet up with "B," "C," and "F" Troops north of the border. Accompanying him was his new scout, the slope-shouldered, bow-legged Jerry Potts, son of a Blood woman and a Scottish-born Missouri River trader. About 37—he wasn't sure of his exact age—Potts was a valuable acquisition for a wage of 90 dollars per month. He spoke the Native languages and knew the country intimately on both sides of the border. Potts went on to serve the Mounted Police for the next 22 years. Also riding with

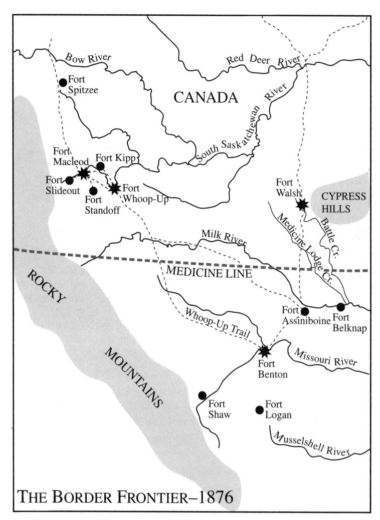

Jerry Potts knew the prairie lands from the outposts north of Fort Macleod and the Cypress Hills south to the U.S. Army forts of the Missouri River and Montana Territory.

them was Charles Conrad, a Virginian veteran of Stuart's cavalry during the Civil War and the Fort Benton manager of the I.G. Baker Company, who was going along to supervise supply arrangements for the force. With supply wagons in tow they crossed Powder Flat and the Milk River.

At Trois Buttes, James Walsh and his fellow troop commanders had benefited from the much-needed rest. Macleod and Potts now led the

Mounties back across the "medicine line" toward the convergence of the Belly and St. Mary's Rivers. Scout Potts quickly proved his worth by leading them to a campsite with spring water and plenty of firewood. At dawn the men woke from a fitful sleep, disturbed by an incessant rumble, to find themselves surrounded by a sea of buffalo. Intent on avoiding a stampede, Potts insisted that they holster all weapons. Quietly he led his column of redcoats for half a day through rolling fields of brown fur.

James F. Macleod was a 33-year-old practising lawyer until he joined the Wolseley expedition in 1870. Respected widely for his judgment and fairness, he would serve the west both as NWMP commissioner and as a member of the NWT Supreme Court. He is shown here at a later point in his NWMP career.

* * *

From the height of his saddle, tall and lean Major Macleod, lawyer, soldier, and gentleman from Bowmanville, Ontario, looked down at the large grey fort standing ominously silent on a grassy tuft of land along the river below. His eyes lingered on the two bastions, from one of which flew a flag resembling the Stars and Stripes.

This was the main reason he and the three troops behind him had trekked all this way—here stood John J. Healy's elusive Fort Whoop-Up.

Macleod reached to the binocular pouch on the back of his shoulder belt and pulled out a pair of field glasses. A taciturn Jerry Potts sat on his cayuse beside him. Behind, Inspector Walsh rode at the head of "B" Troop, together with "C" Troop under Inspector William Winder, and "F" Troop under Inspector Paddy Crozier. Already they had been given the order to load weapons, and now they anticipated the next order: dismount and deploy for advance. It was October 9, a little more than three months to the day since the column, now only half its original size, had marched out of Dufferin. A bright sky spread wide above them with a thin stretch of white cloud drifting across it. The air was bracingly clear. A good day for a fight.

Fort Benton whisky traders had no qualms about raising their own version of the Stars and Stripes over Fort Whoop-Up before they heard the redcoats were coming. There was no one but a caretaker left when the NWMP arrived.

In addition to John Healy's residence and five other dwellings, Whoop-Up housed two stores, a blacksmith, stables, and a warehouse. Two cannons were strategically positioned to discourage any uprising.

John J. Healy was a legendary Fort Benton entrepreneur who made Fort Whoop-Up his northern whisky outpost in 1870, after a showdown with a band of wolfers who called themselves the Spitzee Cavalry. He operated out of Whoop-Up for three years unobstructed, but abandoned it before the redcoats arrived.

Later, as sheriff of Fort Benton, he refused to co-operate with the NWMP when they sought his assistance.

In 1877 Healy would represent the Fort Benton Record at Fort Walsh when General Terry sought a meeting with Sitting Bull.

Raising the glasses to his eyes, Macleod studied the fort in closer detail. Afternoon sunlight danced on the sparkling waters of the St. Mary's River where it flowed into the Belly just beyond the fort. Huge grey cottonwood logs formed a stockade standing 12 feet high and 100 yards long on all sides, loopholed for riflemen inside to hold off any attackers. Buildings inside backed onto the stockade, with doors and windows looking in on a square. The fort was well sited for defence, the two rivers forming a junction just beyond, protecting it from attack on three sides. Defenders within had clear views all around; it was impossible to approach the place unseen. Even the tops of the stone chimneys were built for defence, with iron bars fitted across to keep out attacking Indians. The fort was too far away for marksmen on the rising ground above to fire down into it. Out front stood two ancient cannons, but despite their antiquity they looked threatening enough. The two main gates were open, swinging outward, not inward as with most frontier forts. To the right of the gates were three small wickets through which Indians pushed the buffalo skins they traded for the white man's rotgut firewater.

Walsh and the others waited while Macleod considered his next move. They were approximately 60 miles north of the international boundary, in the heart of Blackfoot country. Potts had told Macleod the fort was empty, that buffalo hunters had warned J.J. Healy and his whisky traders that a column of men wearing red coats was approaching, The scout said the whisky traders had then pulled out back across the boundary line. But Macleod wasn't so sure. Potts could be wrong. Macleod knew all too well the rumours about the whisky-trading forts the Montana men had built north of the Canadian line: that the forts—particularly Whoop-Up—contained dozens of well-armed men, as many as a hundred, who had vowed they'd fight any British force that rode up and tried to oust them rather than give up their lucrative whisky trade with the Indians. Macleod had read accounts by such men as Colonel Patrick Robertson-Ross, whom the government had sent west to do a reconnaissance and who had talked to Hudson's Bay Company traders farther north. He had also read the words of a Wesleyan missionary, Reverend John McDougall, who'd come to live with the ferocious Blackfoot and set up a missionary station in the foothills of the Rocky Mountains. According to McDougall, outlaws could be waiting in the fort for the police to ride down. Even if there were only a few well-armed, experienced gunmen, they could inflict dozens of casualties among the police. Macleod wanted to save his men for future battles. He had heard there was not just one whisky-trading fort in Canadian territory, but six!

Macleod ran his field glasses over the fort again. No sign of movement. Not a sound carried up to them. Nothing but the noise of the wind sweeping across the prairie grasslands. Anyone down below would be aware of the nearness of the police. They would be able to see them clearly enough. Scarlet tunics were bright, conspicuous against the dun-coloured prairie—too conspicuous.

Macleod set worries about the colour of their coats aside and turned to putting Fort Whoop-Up out of business. He signalled Inspector Winder to join him. "No sign of any movement down there, Mr. Winder," Macleod said when the inspector reined in beside him, "but I'm not taking any unnecessary chances with the lives of our men. Position the guns and mortars so you can lob shells down there in case those infernal whisky runners are hiding and try to give us any trouble. We'll blow that damned fort of theirs to Kingdom Come if we have to."

"Very good, sir." Winder's "C" Troop included the artillery component Colonel French had insisted the column haul along from Manitoba—two muzzle-loading nine-pounder field guns and two brass mortars.

While Inspector Winder returned to his troop, Macleod called over his shoulder. "Mr. Walsh!"

"Sir!" Walsh replied, legging his horse forward and pulling in beside the major.

"Send out scouting parties to scour those ridges and gullies we'll have to pass on the way down to the fort," Macleod said, pointing to

William Winder was—along with Macleod, Walsh, and six others—one of the original "Nine," the first group of Mounted Police officers appointed September 25, 1873 at the Stone Fort. Macleod relied heavily on him as a most trusted officer during their years together at Fort Macleod.

several ridged ravines lining the slope leading to the flat below. "Make sure there aren't any gunmen hidden down there waiting to ambush us."

Walsh nodded. "Very good, sir." He wheeled his horse around and trotted back to his troop, detailing half of the men into several scouting parties, then sitting in his saddle anxiously watching as they carried out their assignments at the same time as "C" Troop's gun crews manoeuvred the two nine-pounders and the mortars into position.

When the guns were positioned and the scouting parties had reported the ridges and gullies clear, tension among the troops' officers and men increased. Any second now they anticipated the order to advance. Instead they saw Macleod and Jerry Potts urge their horses down the slope toward the fort.

Walsh and the others watched breathless, taken by surprise at their major's unexpected action. It was an agonizing several moments. Every second they anticipated a fusillade of shots would shatter the stillness and topple their popular commander and scout from their saddles.

Moments later, Major Macleod and Potts reached the fort. Reining in their mounts in front of the open gates, they swung down and walked through the gates into the enclosure. Still no sound. Left hand grasping the hilt of his scabbarded sword to hold it steady at his side, Macleod strode over to the nearest door, raised his right hand, and hammered. Nothing happened.

Jerry Potts grunted from behind him. "Smoke."

Turning, Macleod cast his eyes to where Potts inclined his head. A thin wisp of smoke rose from the stone chimney of the next building.

Macleod marched boldly over to it and pounded on the heavy door with his fist. Still nothing happened. He pounded again, harder this time. Then the door swung open. An unkempt, grey-bearded man stood beside it, his eyes widening as he took in the tall figure in gold-braided scarlet tunic and white helmet standing in front of him.

"I'm Major Macleod of the North West Mounted Police."

A slow grin spread across the man's face. Then he stood aside to make way. "Well, come on in, Major. Been expectin' you. Heard you was a comin'."

In a large room behind him were two middle-aged Native women, a wooden table, four crude chairs, three tin cups on the table, a bearskin rug on the floor, and a crackling fire burning in a stone fireplace.

"Are you in charge here?" Macleod asked the grey-bearded man.

The man nodded. "Reckon I am, Major. Name's Akers, Dave Akers." His grin widened. He made a half-hearted effort to straighten his shoulders. "I'm a military man, too ... leastwise I was, back durin' the war 'atween the States."

"I've heard there's liquor in this place," Macleod said. "Liquor for trading to the Indians. That's against Canadian law."

Akers shook his head. "Ain't no liquor for tradin' to no Indians here, Major."

"Well, we'll search the place, if you don't mind," Macleod said politely but firmly, making it clear he intended to search the place whether Akers minded or not.

"Don't mind the least, Major. Search all you want." Akers waved his arm toward the room behind. "Anyways, you're welcome to stay for supper. We got buffalo steaks." He flicked his head over his shoulder. "An' vegetables out back. Reckon we can rustle up some canned peaches, too."

Leaving Inspector Winder's "C" Troop on guard up on the prairie above, Macleod signalled Inspectors Walsh and Crozier to bring "B" and "F" Troops down to the fort, which they then searched from top to bottom. Out by the rear stockade was a vegetable garden. Ponies grazed on the river flats farther off. Three or four dogs prowled around the enclosure. Discoloured grass outside the stockade showed signs of dozens of circles, indicating Indian lodges had stood there. But the only liquor they found amounted to a few cupfuls, enough for Akers' personal use.

Jerry Potts was right. Buffalo hunters had indeed warned the whisky traders of the approach of a column of red-coated horsemen, and the whisky traders had pulled out for the American border, taking their liquor with them. The Fort Whoop-Up liquor trade had come to a sudden and uneventful end.

From Fort Whoop-Up, Jerry Potts led Macleod and the three troops northwest across rolling grass plains. With their first mission accomplished, uppermost in everyone's minds was the need to build winter quarters. The last thing they wanted was to be caught exposed on the open prairie with blizzard winds sweeping down on them.

From ridges and high spots they could see the dark green mass of foothills rising out of the prairie farther west. Beyond them by some 60 to 70 miles, a long glittering line of snow-crowned mountains thrust their jagged peaks against the blue sky—the Rocky Mountains. It was a sight that mesmerized the men from the east, a sight none of them had set eyes on before they reached these far western plains.

The journey continued over a land of intense loneliness, endless distance, and sheer solitude. This was a world of grass and sky and mountains. It was as though they were the only humans out there in that vast landscape—they and the Indians they couldn't see but knew were all around them.

They passed herds of buffalo grazing their way across the plains, seemingly impervious to the approach of colder weather. Overhead, flights of wildfowl streamed southward to escape the coming winter. As if to remind the men of this, occasional bursts of snow flurries whirled around them, obscuring the surrounding countryside. Scattered in the grass wherever they looked, bleaching skulls and skeletons of buffalo lay, mute testimony to the hunting skills of the inhabitants of this wild land.

Apart from a few friendly Indians and occasional Métis, they had hardly seen anyone since leaving Dufferin. Macleod's journey to Fort Benton had been the lone respite. The "Great Lone Land" had lived up to its name. But now that they were moving deeper into Blackfoot country, the column of policemen glanced around uneasily as they rode on, looking for the Indians some expected they'd have to fight. Some had read novels about scalp-crazed Indians who galloped over the western plains attacking white men. Occasionally they'd see a lone Indian watching them from a distant hilltop. The sight of those Indians—whom the redcoats assumed were the fierce Blackfoot—chilled some to the bone. Others, buoyed by the prospects of untold adventure, thirsted for action. They'd missed out on a fight at Fort Whoop-Up. Maybe they'd get one from the Blackfoot.

Macleod thought differently. He wanted to make peace with the Blackfoot, not fight them.

Three days, but only 28 miles, from Fort Whoop-Up, Jerry Potts led them to a sweeping stretch of plain interrupted by a valley and a river, fringed by tall cottonwoods, that flowed from the Rocky Mountains.

"Ol' Man's River," Potts said.

Macleod assessed the setting below. The river—Old Man's, or Crow Lodge as the Indians called it—offered an endless supply of good water for both men and horses. The cottonwoods along the banks would provide timber for building and firewood. Grass growing on broad meadows on the river flats could be cut, dried, and used as hay for the horses. Buffalo grazing on the prairie grasslands, as well as deer and elk frequenting the river brushlands, would be a plentiful source of meat. It was also close enough that they could watch for whisky runners who might return to Fort Whoop-Up, intent on resuming their liquor trade.

Macleod decided it was here he would await the supply wagons that trailed their march. By sunset the column's tents were spread over a stretch of grassland beside a wide sweep in the river. The next day the Major watched as young Cecil Edward Denny, at the time a 23-year-old sub-inspector, led the transport wagons into camp. Years later Sir Cecil wrote in his memoirs:

> We arrived at the Old Man's River the fourth day ... Here we found the force comfortably settled in camp on the south side near a heavy growth of woods extending for miles up and down either bank. We had a hearty welcome, glad to be at our journey's end. The location chosen looked beautiful to us after the long and weary march. And beautiful indeed it was, with the lofty barrier of snow-draped peaks to the west, the timbered range of the Porcupines to the north, and the Old Man valley as far as the eye might reach, lined with sheltering woods. Buffalo in bands dotted the prairie to the south.
>
> Our tired horses and oxen, freed at last from the wearing drag, grazed unworried; the many tents of the force gleamed white among the trees. The scene was one of peace and loveliness: the atmosphere homelike and restful. I was glad to learn that our stay here was to be permanent. A log fort was to be built at once; indeed, the men had already started to fell cottonwood trees for logs."

James Walsh and the officers staked out ground lines for the fort while parties of men dug trenches, and others stood tree trunks upright to form a twelve-foot-high stockade for the outer walls. Still others chinked spaces between the logs with clay. They hauled stones and small rocks from the river to build fireplaces and chimneys. Crossbeams piled over with sod formed the roofs. The I.G. Baker Company bull train hauling doors, windows,

(Copy.)

J. F. McLEOD to N.-W. Telegraph Company, Dr.

Dec. 2, 1875. To 22 messages to Bernard, Ottawa,		....	$5 08
" 15, " " 12	"	"	.... 3 18
Jan 24, 1876. " 13 "	Morris, Fort Garry,.		.... 5 12
" 24, " " 13 "	Bernard, Ottawa,		.... 3 37

$16 75

(Gold, $15.23.)

Certified.

JAMES F. McLEOD

Paid by check, 1621; Feby. 24th, 1876.

(Signed)   J. A. B.

—

Fort McLEOD, 31st December, 1876.

NORTH-WEST MOUNTED POLICE: In account with J. G. Baker & Co, Dir

To building barrack at Bow River $2,476 00
" extra expense incurred by locating post by Captain
Brisebois further from timber than agreement with
Col. McLeod 1,000 00

$3,476 00

My returns show only 8,520 feet closed in, which, according to agreement, at 25 cents per foot, reduced amounts to $2,130.00; balance disallowed. Messrs. Baker and I disagree about the extra expense of location Fort more than one mile away from timer. I have made enquiries and do not think that any extra expense was incurred. They reserve the right to make good their claim for the balance.

(Signed)   JAMES. F. McLEOD.

—

This excerpt from 1879 sessional papers in Ottawa suggests that James Macleod's handwriting was difficult to read or that the clerk was careless. Not only has Macleod been transcribed as McLeod on five occasions, but Isaac Gilbert Baker's bill for barracks material and labour is noted incorrectly to the account of J.G. Baker & Co. Baker's Montana company became the main source of food and supplies for the NWMP in its early years.

and other supplies that had been ordered at Fort Benton was on its way. The buildings faced inwards onto a square of some 200 feet and included kitchens, storehouses, blacksmith's and other artisans' shops, a guardroom, and a magazine. But first priority was given to building a hospital and stables. Then came the men's barracks and non-commissioned officer quarters. After that, the officers' quarters would be built.

As they built, however, other thoughts rumbled through Macleod's mind. The Blackfoot had driven out Hudson's Bay Company traders when they tried to open up trading posts in their realm, and had turned back other Indian tribes and Métis hunters who came too close to their buffalo ranges. Yet they tolerated the Montana whisky traders and Fort Whoop-Up. How would they look upon the redcoats? If the Indians turned out to be hostile, the police would have no hope of help of any kind, no hope of

Fort Macleod, Alberta, was established by the NWMP in 1874 and depicted in this sketch for the Canadian Illustrated News.

reinforcement. The nearest means of communication with the outside world was at Fort Benton, 230 trail miles away. Completely cut off, the police would have little chance of overcoming any concerted, sustained attack, even once they had their fort built. None of them, other than Potts, had any experience with Indians.

Macleod's response to this nagging problem was to send Potts to the surrounding Indian camps to spread word that the Great White Mother had sent the redcoats to stop the ruinous liquor trade that was destroying them, stripping them of their wealth of ponies and buffalo robes, debauching their women, and killing off their young men in drunken brawls and fighting. Native leaders could see what whisky traders were doing to their people, but the liquor had a hold on many of them and they were powerless to resist it.

Potts did his job well, explaining to his Blood relatives that the redcoats were good men who wished them no harm. Assured by him, whom they trusted, Indians began trickling in to the redcoats' camp, first the Peigans, then the Bloods. Macleod spoke to them through Potts, elaborating on what Potts had told them. The Indians responded to the distinguished-looking Macleod. They were impressed by his respectful and courteous manner. Here was a white man who treated them as equals. They observed in the redcoats a calmness in spite of being alone in a land surrounded by potential enemies, and they quickly realized that the redcoats were very different from the whisky traders and most other white men they had encountered previously. The redcoats were not there to profit at their expense. As well, the crimson they wore reminded the

Officer Francis Dickens (second from right), a son of novelist Charles Dickens, and an unidentified officer look over the shoulder of Sub-Inspector John French, brother of the comissioner, in 1874. This early photo depicts all elements of the original NWMP uniform before the first changes were introduced in 1875.

Native people of the coats worn by honourable men their elders had met at Fort Garry years before. The scarlet tunic of British soldiers symbolized fairness, in contrast to the blue coats of the hated "long-knives" on the other side of the medicine line.

By late October the first hints of the severe winter ahead came as snow covered the ground and cold winds swept the plains. Spurred on by the weather, officers and men worked hard and the fort gradually took shape. Occasionally balmy chinook winds blew in through mountain passes, bringing with them mellow sunshine and bright blue skies, and melting all the snow in their path.

During one such respite, Macleod addressed another problem: exhausted livestock. The long trek from the Red River across the plains to the Sweetgrass Hills had decimated the animals, and now there simply wasn't enough feed on hand to restore the survivors. After Jerry Potts recommended a rancher who could tend them, Macleod decided to send 64 horses, 20 oxen, and 10 head of cattle south to the Sun River Valley in Montana, over 200 trail miles away. Macleod looked at the options, finally settling on the obvious. The best man for the job wouldn't blink at adding another 400 miles to his total in the saddle. Inspector James Walsh and a small "B" Troop detail, guided by Potts, took up the task.

Before Potts and Walsh could break camp, Macleod's offer of aid was tested when a minor chief of the Blackfoot, Three Bulls, rode into the redcoat camp on October 29. Three Bulls told Potts he had traded two good ponies for two gallons of firewater. Five men, he said, were peddling whisky at Pine Coulee, some 50 miles to the north. The firewater consumed, Three Bulls now regretted the exchange. He had come to see if the redcoats meant what they said about putting the whisky traders out of business.

Walsh's journey south was delayed. With Jerry Potts scouting, 28-year-old Inspector Lief Newry Fitzroy "Paddy" Crozier and ten men of "F" Troop rode out to investigate. They returned two days later with a half-Mexican named William Bond and four white men as prisoners, together with their trading outfit of two wagons, a quantity of alcohol, sixteen horses, 116 buffalo hides, five Henry repeating rifles, and five Colt revolvers. In his ex officio role as magistrate, Major Macleod tried the five men and found them guilty of illegally trafficking in liquor. He ordered Bond and Harry Taylor, one of the white men, as leaders of the five to pay fines of $200 each, and the other three to pay $50 each. A Fort Benton trader, Waxey Weatherwax, subsequently paid the fines of the four white men and they were released. Bond was sentenced to a term of imprisonment in the guardroom. Macleod ordered the liquor poured into the river. The two wagons, sixteen horses, and buffalo hides were confiscated, and the hides were used for bedding and winter overcoats for the police.

In later writings Colonel French described his second-in-command as "a capital fellow, a man most capable of implementing the government's instructions in the far west." Wise, tolerant, and tactful, Macleod decreed that sound judgment, firmness, and honesty would be the police standard in all dealings with both Indians and whites—and all would be treated alike. Should someone break the law in some small way, he would be spoken to, man to man, and warned. If he broke the law a second time, action would be taken against him. Fairness and impartiality were to be exercised always.

The whisky traders disposed of, Potts and Walsh led their party south. Once the animals were delivered to winter quarters, Walsh and his men returned from the Sun River immediately while Potts went on to Fort Benton to collect his family and a small horse herd. Returning to the NWMP fort, Potts was given little rest. With the scout's family barely settled, Macleod sent him to the camps of the three main tribes of the Blackfoot alliance—the Blackfoot, Bloods, and Peigans—to tell their chiefs he wanted to talk with them. The scout had told him of rumours circulating in the Native camps that hinted the redcoats were no different than the American long-knives. Some Indians were saying that the redcoats should be attacked and wiped out. Macleod wanted to put an end to this kind of talk before serious problems developed.

On December 1, *Isapwo Muksika*—Crow Big Foot, or simply Crowfoot as he would become known—chief of the Blackfoot and head of the tribal confederacy, approached the fledgling fort at the head of a retinue of chiefs and escorting warriors. Carrying an eagle feather in his left hand and wearing a blanket over his deerskin shirt, the chief, followed by his entourage, dismounted. With long black hair streaming down over his shoulders, Crowfoot strode through the gateway. Piercing black eyes swept the perimeter of the incomplete fort as he and his followers established their ground.

Officers and men stood silently—almost breathlessly—and watched as Major Macleod stepped forward to greet the visitors.

Macleod could see from the way Crowfoot carried himself, the strength of his jaw, the sweep of his eyes, that he was a man used to having his way. Yet it was also a face full of wisdom and tolerance. He judged the chief to be in his mid-40s.

Macleod extended his arm. Crowfoot responded to the redcoat's gesture, reached out and touched the open hand. Two ways of life came together. The mutual trust between Macleod and Crowfoot grew rapidly. Both were men of instinct.

Mounted on the door above Macleod's log quarters hung a buffalo head. Crowfoot named the redcoat commander *Stamix Otokan*—Bull's Head.

Shortly after their first meeting, Crowfoot said to Macleod, "You are a brave man, *Stamix Otokan*. The laws of the Great White Mother must be good when she has a son like you. We will obey those laws."

By the middle of December, the fort was practically completed. The Union Jack flew from a flagpole set up on the parade square, the two nine-pounder field guns beside it. By unanimous consent, the officers and men who had built it named the compound Fort Macleod in honour of its commanding officer.

Based on the success of the earlier foray, Macleod sent Inspector Walsh south to the Sun River country again with more horses to winter. Walsh covered another 400 miles and returned to Fort Macleod on Christmas Eve, a remarkable feat given the season and the inhospitable landscape. Walsh made one more trip to the Sun River in early spring when a "B" Troop detail reclaimed the horses plus some newly purchased remounts.

The energy of spring was in the air as Walsh and his men neared Old Man's River and led the herd to pasture. Walsh headed towards Fort Macleod's open gates, anxious to once more see his Major. They had survived their first winter and the Inspector was confident that Macleod's plans for 1875 would mean new adventures. James Walsh had now been in the field for over eight months and he knew he had earned the confidence of his immediate superior.

Chapter 5

The Road to Fort Walsh

> *Walsh was a NWMP original ... one of the most*
> *flamboyant and controversial figures ever to ride*
> *onto the Canadian plains.*
>
> B.D. Fardy, *Jerry Potts: Paladin of the Plains*, 1984

In early May, Inspector Walsh—or "Major" Walsh as he liked to be called—led "B" Troop out through the gates of Fort Macleod into the morning sun, knowing it would be some time before he saw that gate again. He glanced both ways, noting the makeshift village that was already forming. The I.G. Baker Company of Fort Benton had built a store, and other wooden structures housed a billiard hall, a shoe store, and a barber shop. A cluster of tepees stood nearby.

The Major urged his horse eastward along the trail to Fort Whoop-Up. Beside him rode Jerry Potts. Behind followed Sub-Inspectors Vernon Welch and Edwin Allen, Troop Sergeant-Major Bray, and the column of sergeants, corporals, and troopers on their saddle horses, together with eight transport wagons. Potts' family travelled with the wagons.

No one, from Walsh on down, wore a red tunic. Uniforms were packed into the wagons, preserved for parades and specific duties. On the trail they dressed in whatever they had, from brown cotton fatigues to outfits bought from Baker bull-team traders hauling supplies from Fort Benton. Walsh wore a fringed buckskin jacket and a tan slouch hat with the brim turned up at the front. It was a style popularized by a flamboyant American soldier farther south, the Civil War boy general, Colonel George Armstrong Custer of the 7th Cavalry. There was little trace of military appearance among the column except for the scattering of men who wore surplus U.S. Army clothing they had bought from the traders.

For many of the seasoned soldiers with British roots who served as Mounted Police officers, old customs were not easily broken. They preferred military titles of rank to those of the police. No doubt influenced by his Kingston Military training, James Walsh shared that preference. In his police role he rated only to be called "Captain," the equivalent military rank of inspector. Assistant Commissioner Macleod was the only officer entitled to be referred to as "Major." But as Walsh had held the rank of major in the militia, he claimed the privilege of being called "Major." By that reckoning, Major Macleod should have been called "Colonel," as his brevet rank in the militia was lieutenant-colonel, a rank he had been awarded before the Wolseley expedition of 1870. South of the border, customs were similar. Lieutenant-Colonel Custer was called "General" by most of his officers and men. He had climbed to the rank of brigadier-general at the age of 23 during the Civil War.

To the men of "B" Troop, it was just as simple to refer to their commander as "Major" as it was to call him "Captain" if that was what he wanted. Those who had left Ontario with him over eighteen months prior knew that it didn't pay to get on the wrong side of him. He wasn't an easy man by any means. Quick-tempered and often explosive, he could ream a man out better than any other officer most of them had known—with the possible exception of Colonel French—but he was always fair and they knew he'd stand up for them when they were in the right. None of them wanted a transfer to another troop, and they'd follow him anywhere. No, they didn't mind calling him "Major" if that was what he preferred.

When they reached the decrepit Fort Whoop-Up, Potts left the Fort Benton trail and led the troop east across the trackless prairie on the 160-mile ride toward the Cypress Hills. Major Walsh had a specific assignment and it was a challenge he relished. On his November trip to Fort Benton, Jerry Potts had heard talk that was also the word around the Indian camps: Whisky traders were peddling liquor into the Cypress Hills, believing they were far enough away from the Mounted Police to be free from interference. To show them they were wrong, Major Macleod directed Walsh and his troop to build a fort similar to Fort Macleod and clean out the whisky trade and any other lawlessness that came to his attention. Macleod knew how to motivate this officer "Call it Fort Walsh," he had said.

Halfway into their journey that parallelled the Chin Coulee, Walsh saw the three buttes of the Sweetgrass Hills rising out of the prairie in the south. The sight evoked memories of his stay down along the Montana border the previous fall and his first meeting with Jerry Potts.

Dr. R.B. Nevitt, the 25-year-old NWMP assistant surgeon, completed this watercolour of the growing camp outside the fort (top), which he called the "Half-breed Camp at Fort Macleod," in 1875. Before their march to the Cypress Hills it is likely that Walsh and his troop made full use of the fort's forge (bottom), shown in another work of Nevitt from May 1875.

The Forge Fort McLeod · May 12th 1875

Walsh, like Macleod, Crozier, Winder, Sub-Inspector Cecil Denny, and any other man who had witnessed Potts's trail sense, had come to hold the guide in high esteem. Potts was a man of few words, but Walsh had learned that when he spoke it was worth paying heed. His most annoying habit was saying so little. James Walsh had watched Potts translate long drawn-out speeches of tribal chiefs by uttering a single sentence. All winter the Mounties had amused themselves recalling the first cluster of Peigans and Bloods who had ridden into the fort. Major Macleod patiently listened to their lengthy greeting, occasionally looking toward Potts for some sense of their message. Finally the Métis turned to Macleod. "Dey damn glad you're here," was the only translation.

Walsh had witnessed Potts's uncanny trailblazing as they had taken livestock into Montana the previous November. In February, Potts had saved Inspector Crozier and ten of his men and three prisoners from likely death, leading them through a snowstorm back to Fort Macleod.

Major Macleod himself owed his life to Potts. In March Macleod, Denny, and two Mounties set out on a trip to Montana with Potts. Ill-prepared for bad weather, the quintet almost froze to death before a snow-blinded Potts led them to a U.S. cavalry outpost on the Marias River. Potts's reputation had grown with every deed, and Major Walsh felt fortunate to have his Métis comrade at his side.

Ahead, the Cypress Hills at first appeared as a table-like range of blue-green mounds sitting up above the plains. Walsh had seen the hills before from the east and north during the march west, but none of the troop except Jerry Potts had been into them. The new terrain was a welcome respite. They gazed in wonder at rolling jackpine-covered slopes rising on either side of them, stark contrast to the bare plains.

The Cypress Hills were a geographical oddity in the middle of the southern Canadian plains, like miniature Rocky Mountains. Parallelling the Montana border, they stretched for 200 miles before petering out to clay pan and rolling prairie to the east, and from 20 to 40 miles north and south, depending upon where you started and where you finished. Their highest point was over 4,500 feet at Head of the Mountain at the western end, and beyond was a landscape of deep ravines, sunken watercourses, grassed benches, wooded uplands, and hidden lakes. Grizzly, black bear, bison, wapiti, elk, antelope, beaver, prairie wolf, and coyote prowled through them. Evergreens of pine and spruce, and deciduous poplar, birch, and willow added to their beauty. They were also a tribal war zone around which Blackfoot, Assiniboine, Cree, and Sioux fought bitter, bloody battles. The Indians regarded the hills as the source for sudden storms, calling them the Thunder Breeding Hills. Because of the prevalence of jackpine, French-speaking Métis called them Montaigne de Cypre. This was later anglicized to Cypress Hills.

Jerry Potts led the way along a wide valley. It was a picturesque sight—the green of poplars giving way to the deeper green of pine and spruce as they swept up the hills to the heights above, spring sunshine bathing the valley and hills in an enchanting golden glow. A short distance ahead flowed clear, sparkling water, running on down the valley as far as

Walsh often rode in western buckskins. His trimmed "imperial" goatee became a trademark of many proud "B" Troop members who served under his command. Ironically, Walsh's attire was first made popular by the "boy general," George Custer. While Walsh's most popular name among Canadian Indians was "White Forehead," many Sioux, according to historian Robert Utley, called him "Long Lance."

the eye could see. Potts told them they were approximately two miles above the site of the Cypress Hills massacre of 1873, where a gang of Montana men murdered a small band of peaceful Canadian Assiniboines whom they wrongly suspected of having stolen horses from them. It was word of this massacre, which reached eastern Canada in the summer of 1873, that spurred Prime Minister Macdonald to act upon laws already passed. He finally authorized the formation of the North West Mounted Police.

It was June 7, 1875, when James Walsh ordered "B" Troop to make camp at the headwaters of Battle Creek. He nodded toward Jerry Potts. The gesture was all that was needed. It looked like a place they could call home. The next day they started building Fort Walsh.

✳ ✳ ✳

The valley's silence was shattered by the ring of steel on wood as "B" Troop axe men cut into tall spruce and pine. Now and then a shouted

Jerry Potts was born into a world of violence. When Potts was two, his father, Andrew, a Scottish employee of the American Fur Company, was murdered by an irate Peigan named One Eye. Potts grew up amid the whisky forts of the boundary country and witnessed the evils of firewater first-hand. Many years later, in 1872, Potts's mother, a Blood Indian named Namo-pisi or Crooked Back, was shot by a drunken tribe member. Two months later Jerry Potts avenged her death and vowed to destroy the whisky trade.

"Tim...ber" carried down the hill, followed by the cracking of branches and a ground-shaking crash as 60 feet of tree rolled down the slope. Each had barely ceased its downhill slide when waiting hands tossed a rope and chain around and hitched it to a team of horses that dragged it across the valley floor to a growing pile alongside a row of white canvas bell tents. Nearby Jerry Potts organized his family in their new tent home.

A few days into construction, Major Walsh sat at a table in front of one of the tents, drawing a plan of the fort on a sheet of paper. Above him a Union Jack waved from an improvised flagpole. Sub-Inspectors Welch and Allen worked a hundred yards away, pounding stakes into the ground to mark the fort's outline. Several troopers swung picks and shovels, digging a three-foot trench along the line of stakes into which fifteen-foot lengths of log would be stood upright to form a twelve-foot-high stockade, like the one at Fort Macleod.

Intent on sketching his diagram and penning notes, several minutes passed before Walsh became aware the sounds of activity had given way to a deepening silence. Looking up suddenly, he saw his men standing motionless, their attention drawn southward down the valley. He saw at once what they were looking at. Indians! A couple of hundred or more armed warriors rode toward them.

Walsh stood up. Jerry Potts ambled over to his table.

"Who are they, Jerry?" Walsh asked.

"Sioux," Potts grunted, watching them closely.

Sioux! Walsh had met some Sioux on the march west and hadn't been impressed. They hadn't met his expectations. But these men were different. Fierce, dusky faces. Glittering dark eyes darting everywhere. Big warriors, mostly bare-chested under the warm, early June sun. Long black hair parted in the centre, with braids hanging down over their shoulders. One, however, wore a white-man's hat, checkered shirt, and striped trousers. A Métis.

They reined in a few yards from where the white men had been building their fort. The Métis rode ahead to Walsh's table.

"Find out what they want, Jerry."

But the Métis spoke English. "Long-knives chase us 'cross border. Who you?"

"Redcoats of the Great White British Mother," Walsh replied, pointing up at the Union Jack behind him. "That's her flag."

But some of the Sioux spotted two of Walsh's men in U.S. Army blue. Hate danced in their eyes. "*Mela hoska!*" they shouted, pointing excitedly. "*Mela hoska!*"

The next instant Walsh and his men found themselves staring into Sioux rifle barrels.

"White man lie!" the Métis snarled. "You long-knives!"

"We're not long-knives!" Walsh hurled back at him. "We're the British Mother's redcoats!"

The Métis flung out an accusing arm, pointing at the two blue-clad men. "Long-knives!"

Walsh realized he and his men were in a dangerous position. None of them were armed. All their weapons were stacked in the tents. The Sioux were no more than a trigger-finger's squeeze from wiping them out. All he could do was try to bluff his way through.

"If any of you fire a shot," Walsh warned, not a tremor in his voice as he stared up calmly at the Métis, "more redcoats will come, more redcoats than there are buffalo on the prairie, and none of you will be left alive."

Confusion swept over the Métis's face as he stared back at Walsh. He turned to the warriors behind him, repeating what Walsh said.

Suddenly one warrior's eyes widened. He shouted, pointing at the hills above.

The others looked where he pointed. Shouts erupted from Sioux throats. The Sioux wheeled their ponies around and galloped quickly away, leaving pieces of hoof-flung grass and dirt behind as they thundered back down the valley.

Streaming through the trees covering the slopes to the northeast rode hundreds of buckskin-clad Indians. They came fast, spilling onto the valley floor.

"What the hell's happening?" Walsh demanded to know.

"Cree," grunted the taciturn Potts.

"What the hell does that mean?"

"Sioux and Cree hate each other."

The Cree galloped along the valley in pursuit of the Sioux. There were twice as many Cree as Sioux. Walsh had heard about the fighting prowess of the Sioux, but they knew when they were outnumbered. The Cree chased after them for a short distance, but seeing the Sioux were too far ahead, they abandoned the chase.

The Cree turned out to be friendly. They had long had contact with the white traders of the Hudson's Bay Company. They knew the Great White Mother's flag and the purpose of her pony soldiers. They milled around Walsh and his men, shaking hands and gesturing. Walsh invited them to join him and the troop drinking tea and smoking tobacco.

Walsh caught Troop Sergeant-Major Bray's eye. "A close one, sir," the senior NCO remarked sagely.

"Almost too damned close, Sar-Major. From now on we'll keep our guns handy. And I want double sentries tonight."

"Very good, sir."

✳ ✳ ✳

It took six weeks to build Fort Walsh. There were axe men in "B" Troop who had worked as loggers in Ontario forests before joining the Mounted Police, and others who had worked at laying foundations. When they were finished, a series of single-storey buildings backed up to the stockade and faced in on a central square. A roofless bastion stood at the northwest corner; later, a roofed bastion was erected at the southeast corner. The main gateway, in which two solid timber gates swung inwards on heavy iron hinges, faced the east. Built into one of these gates was a door just large enough to admit one person at a time. Opposite, on the west side, stood a similar pair of gates, giving

This photo shows Fort Walsh as it was in 1965. Since then the fort has been restored, with its palisades reconstructed on their original perimeter. Today it is a popular tourist destination in Cypress Hills Provincial Park.

access to Battle Creek. Post orders stipulated that the gates be opened at "Reveille" and closed at "Retreat," which was sounded at sunset. The smaller door remained open until 9 p.m. Any visitors were required to leave by sunset.

Major Walsh's quarters were on the east side of the fort, immediately north of the east gates. Next were the administration offices and officers' quarters. Along the north wall stood NCOs' quarters and an ammunition and powder magazine. The farrier's, saddler's, and carpenter's shops and stables occupied the west side. Along the south side were kitchen, bakery, and men's barracks. In the centre of the fort stood a log guardroom with three cells. Windows were freighted in by bull train from Fort Benton, 160 miles south. A tall flagpole was erected between the guardroom and the east gates. Later a quartermaster's stores were built a short distance west of the guardroom and an emergency water well was dug between the guardroom and the west gate. A latrine stood outside the stockade a short distance from the southwest corner.

All the buildings were whitewashed inside and out with clay found in a coulee a few miles south of the fort, and new coats of whitewash were added regularly. The Major believed in "spit and polish."

The Cypress Hills, photographed by geologist C.M. Dawson in 1883, show the northern uplands and more southerly foothills near Bad Buttes, Saskatchewan.

Major Walsh lost no time taking steps to establish law and order in the Cypress Hills region. Even before his men had finished building Fort Walsh, he sent out patrols to hunt down whisky traders and put a stop to the illicit traffic that in less than a generation had done as much to destroy Indian pride and end lives as a century of intertribal warfare.

In less than twelve months, however, Walsh would have more to occupy his attention than whisky traders.

Chapter 6

The Sioux Arrive in Canada

I found matters entirely different from what I expected. I never saw a command so completely stampeded as this.

Colonel Nelson A. Miles on meeting General Terry's troops on the Yellowstone River, August 1876

Like Fort Macleod, Walsh's new palisades attracted prairie life like a magnet. Cree tepees were erected in clusters, and a street of commerce rapidly took shape outside the fort's gate. I.G. Baker and a competitor named Powers, a hotel, blacksmith, and laundry were among Fort Walsh's nearby establishments.

Later that year word arrived, much to the dismay of those who respected him, that Assistant Commissioner Macleod was resigning to become a stipendiary magistrate. Walsh's independent ways and repeated disapproval of political interference likely assured that he did not get Macleod's job. That went to the Quebec-born commander of Manitoba's Provisional Battalion of Rifles, Acheson Gosford Irvine. Walsh had to be content with the freedoms he had in his own fort and his immediate accomplishments through the end of 1875. Most important, he had won the confidence of the Cree and Assiniboine.

Certainly some of that credit had to go to Jerry Potts and the new translator Walsh had hired, Louis Leveille. Both had the skill of giving their Indian brethren comfort when translating the word of Walsh or James Macleod. One Mountie who had watched Potts translate said, "His eyes gleamed as if his soul were in it and as if ... every word of it was good for the Indians."

Sioux (pictured above) and Assiniboine camps had good reason to fear white men. In 1873 a party of vengeful American wolfers slaughtered 36 children, elders and poorly armed men at one camp. This massacre on May 1 occured near the site where Fort Walsh would be built three years later.

Once Walsh had hired his new scout, Potts returned to Fort Macleod. Leveille, a Cree Métis, was more at home with the many Cree camps in the Cypress Hills.

By the autumn of 1875 it had been over two years since James Walsh had seen his wife and child. This yearning for loved ones, the constant irritation of a painful skin disease, erysipelas (also known as Saint Anthony's Fire), and possibly the wish to further his career in Ottawa prompted the inspector to take leave and return to Brockville. From Ontario he also travelled to the U.S. to seek a cure for the fever and skin inflammation that plagued him.

On May 25, 1876, 38-year old Major Irvine received a report from Ottawa advising that U.S. Army operations in Dakota and Montana would likely drive hostile Indians across the border into Canadian territory. The report further suggested that these Indians would probably use Canadian soil as a base to continue their warfare against the Americans. Ottawa military strategists concluded that escaping Indians would likely enter Canadian territory near Wood Mountain, several days' ride east of Fort Walsh.

On July 3, 1876, when the *Bozeman Times*—scooping the *Bismarck Tribune*—broke the story of the Custer massacre at the Little Bighorn River on Sunday, June 25, Major Walsh was on sick leave at Hot Springs, Arkansas, recovering from a serious attack of the skin disease.

A telegram from Ottawa told him the details of the battle 300 miles south of Fort Walsh and informed him of the likelihood of Sioux hostiles fleeing across the border into Canadian territory. The wire requested him to return to duty as soon as possible.

Walsh must have received enough relief bathing in the waters of the hot springs to offset the effects of the high temperature and skin inflammation characteristic of his disease, for he took the first available train north. In Ottawa he received a full briefing from R.W. Scott, Secretary of State. With only a brief goodbye to his family, he then returned to the United States, travelling west by rail via Chicago to Bismarck, Dakota Territory, where he boarded a Missouri River sternwheeler bound for Fort Benton. He arrived back at Fort Walsh in early August, taking over from Inspector Paddy Crozier, who had been sent there temporarily from Fort Macleod and given command.

While Walsh was returning to his isolated and relatively peaceful community north of the medicine line, another dominant influence on the future of Sitting Bull's Sioux was making his entrance to the Dakota Territory.

Colonel Nelson Miles and his 5th Infantry arrived at the Yellowstone River encampment of General Alfred Terry in the first week of August, one month after Custer's demise. Miles was part of General Philip H. Sheridan's efforts to shore up the commands of Terry and General George Crook, whose troops had been immobile since their June encounter with Crazy Horse. Terry's troops had just buried the dead at Little Bighorn and were a sorry lot, but what the army lacked in confidence at that moment was offset by sheer numbers. Terry's reinforced unit of 1,600 was ordered to consolidate with Crook's 2,100-strong column currently bivouacked south of the Rosebud Valley. Over the next two weeks Miles, who had little respect for either general, gritted his teeth as Terry and "Three Stars" Crook's forces converged along the Rosebud River. His silent disdain lasted another two weeks as the generals, neither ever spotting the enemy, prolonged their fruitless quest in eastern Montana before parting company on August 25.

Plagued by desertions, discontent in the ranks, and a restless eastern press, this combined assault found no enemy. The Indians had disappeared.

Meanwhile, in Canada, the Mounted Police viewed the forthcoming Sioux arrival with concern. They had good reason. Earlier in the year, Blackfoot Chief Crowfoot had told Sub-Inspector Cecil Denny that the Sioux had approached him with a peace offering—a twist of tobacco—asking him to smoke it as a sign of Blackfoot willingness to join their former enemies in a war against the bluecoats south of the medicine line. If the Blackfoot would join them, the Sioux would in turn cross the line and help the Blackfoot wipe out all the whites on the Canadian side. The Sioux messenger had pointed out that the redcoats were few in number and their forts could easily be taken with little loss to the attackers. But Crowfoot spurned the Sioux proposal. The redcoats were his friends, he said. The Blackfoot did not want to fight them. The Sioux angrily retorted that after killing off the American soldiers, they would cross back over the medicine line and wipe out the Blackfoot. Crowfoot promised Denny that if the Sioux crossed the border, he would send 2,000 warriors to help the redcoats fight them off.

The Mounted Police thanked Crowfoot for his friendship and his loyalty to the Great White Mother. They told him, however, that the situation would be resolved without firing a shot. Brave words, but they had no idea how they would accomplish it—if they could accomplish it.

To meet the Sioux threat, Mounted Police headquarters was moved from Swan River to Fort Macleod, and 100 men were transferred to the two southern posts at Fort Walsh and Fort Macleod, leaving only a handful in the more northerly regions. After "E" Troop joined "B" Troop at Fort Walsh, Major Walsh had 100 officers and men under his command.

As a further precaution, the Mounted Police obtained four seven-pounder field guns and ammunition from the Militia Department at Winnipeg and had them hauled to Fort Walsh. With the two nine-pounders and two brass mortars at Fort Macleod, the Mounted Police now had a small but effective artillery component available.

It was just as well. The very mention of Sitting Bull and the dreaded Sioux were enough to strike terror into the hearts of people. Although the Custer battle was an American affair, it had ramifications for Canada. The 49th parallel was only a political boundary. For generations Indians had ranged backwards and forwards between what white people called Canada and the United States. Now there was danger that the threatened Sioux presence on the Canadian plains could trigger a far-reaching Indian uprising. The entire prairies could erupt into war on both sides of the boundary.

The Canadian government was anxious to see settlement spread west. It had already promised British Columbia a nation-spanning railroad to link eastern Canada, and what financiers would be induced to spend millions of dollars on a railroad that had to be built across vast expanses of land threatened with Indian war? No settlers in their right mind would be tempted to venture out to the North-West Territories in such circumstances.

The North West Mounted Police, the only deterrent, knew the gravity of the situation. All they could do now was watch and wait.

* * *

Immaculate in gold-trimmed scarlet tunic, striped breeches, and gleaming black boots, Major Walsh paced the floor of his office. An officer had to set an example for those under him, and Walsh always made a point

It wasn't only the peaceful intentions of the NWMP, but also the leadership of chiefs like Crowfoot that helped maintain a balance of forces during tenuous times on the prairies.

of looking the part regardless of what he wore, whether it was full-dress scarlet or buckskin trail garb. He rarely had to criticize any of his men for sloppiness of appearance in uniform. Even out on the primitive frontier, the officers and men of Fort Walsh prided themselves on the belief they could stage a ceremonial parade or mount the guard with the best regiments of the British Empire. Legend had it that some of Walsh's subordinates were carried to his parade ground for inspection so that they wouldn't get dust on their polished boots.

But Walsh had other things on his mind than dress parades and ceremonials. He was worried. Not by the possibility—indeed, the overwhelming probability—of Sioux crossing the border into Canadian territory. That he accepted as part of the job. It added to the challenge of Mounted Police life. What worried him was the length of time one of his patrols had been absent.

Walsh paused in his pacing to stare out the window at the snow-swept parade ground. It was blowing so hard outside that he could hardly see the Union Jack at the top of the flagpole, flapping wildly in the

Among the non-commissioned officers at Fort Walsh, 1878, the NCO with medals sitting second from the right in the middle row is Sergeant-Major Joseph Francis. One of James Walsh's most trusted men, Francis rode in the charge of the Light Brigade at Balaclava some twenty-odd years earlier.

An 1878 Fort Walsh patrol shows the scarlet tunics that would always distinguish the northern policemen from the bluecoats farther south. It was the pennoned lances carried by Walsh's patrols that reputedly earned him the name "Long Lance" among some Sioux lodges.

driving wind. It was already close to the middle of December. Winter had swooped down on the Cypress Hills with a vengeance. In November he'd received word from his scouts watching the border south of Wood Mountain that a large band of Indians was approaching. He had sent Sub-Inspector Edmund Frechette to investigate, and now he was wondering if the patrol had run into trouble, something the men couldn't handle. Had the Indians—almost undoubtedly Sioux—turned out to be hostile?

Walsh wished he had gone down there himself, but he couldn't administer his command and patrol the border country south of Wood Mountain at the same time. That was why he had subordinate officers—to carry out such duties, to help take the load off his shoulders. Besides, he had already ridden south, both before he had gone on sick leave and since he'd returned. The Indians, he decided, were probably the same ones who had been camped along Rocky Creek since early October. About a thousand of them, hunting buffalo just north of the Milk River. He had satisfied himself they weren't an immediate threat, and he had left two Métis scouts behind to keep a discreet watch on them. In November, when the Indian encampment moved north, his scouts high-tailed it back to Fort Walsh to report the change. That was when he sent Frechette and a patrol south. Frechette had only arrived at Fort Walsh with "E" Troop in October, and this was an opportunity for him to get acquainted with the country. But now Walsh had second thoughts.

Of course, bad weather could be a factor, he realized, staring out the window and eyeing the mounds of snow piling up around the buildings. He focussed on the flakes packed hard into the corners of the windows. The blizzard could have blocked the trails, he decided. Lord alone knew what the country east of the Cypress Hills was like. It was pretty open down there; Frechette could be having a hard time of it.

Walsh fought his own impatience. He would give Frechette one more day.

* * *

Walsh let out a bellow. "Sar-Major!"

Even through the whitewashed log wall separating Walsh's office from the orderly room next door, Sergeant-Major Joseph Francis, decorated veteran of the 13th Light Dragoons, who rode with the Light

Brigade in its immortal charge into Russian cannon at Balaclava 22 years earlier, heard the Major's shout and hurried to answer it.

"Sah!" he barked, standing to attention in front of Walsh's desk and snapping a regimental salute.

"I want a patrol, Sar-Major—a sergeant and eleven men. Full service order, field rations for ten days." Walsh inclined his head toward the window. "That blizzard's dying down now, but it's still damned cold out there and there'll be a lot of snow on the trails. I'm taking them down to the Wood Mountain country. It'll be a hard ride, so tell them to dress warmly. We're going looking for Mr. Frechette's patrol. They're overdue. They could've run into trouble from the Sioux. Sub-Inspector McIllree is next senior officer. He'll be in command here while I'm away."

"Very good, sir."

"And tell Leveille I want to see him right away."

"Yes, sir."

"All right, Sar-Major. That will be all. Carry on."

Sergeant-Major Francis gave another parade ground salute and marched out of the office. Shortly after, a knock sounded on the door.

"Come in," Walsh called.

The door opened and Louis Leveille, a six-foot Métis who, with his brother Pierre, had been a scout on the march west, stepped in—a blast of frigid air rushing into the room with him. Leveille quickly shut the door behind him.

"You want to see me, my Major?" Leveille asked in his usual polite, smiling manner, tipping his fur cap with his hand as he stopped in front of Walsh's desk.

"Yes, Louis," Walsh replied, smiling up at the older man. He liked Leveille, regarding him as the best scout in the Mounted Police, certainly one of the two best he had seen. His only peer was Jerry Potts at Fort Macleod. "Mr. Frechette's patrol is still out. They should have been back by now. He could have run into trouble with those Sioux who were heading north toward the line. I'm taking a patrol down toward Wood Mountain to find out what's happened."

Walsh paused for a moment, allowing the man to make his own choice. Leveille was his chief scout, but he was in his 60s. The trip could be a hard one and Leveille had already done more than his share, especially since the Little Bighorn. Perhaps he needed a rest.

But Walsh needn't have concerned himself. "I go with you, my Major," Leveille promptly volunteered, taking advantage of Walsh's pause. "You, me ... we go together."

Walsh grinned, not bothering to hide his pleasure. "Good man, Louis. I could use you on this trip." The fact that Leveille knew the Sioux and their language might save lives.

* * *

Walsh led his patrol through the fort's east gateway. Louis Leveille rode beside him, the butt of a Henry repeater protruding from his saddle scabbard. Just outside the gates, three trails branched off, barely visible after the wind and snow of the last few days. One led south to the U.S. border 45 miles away, one north to the sprawling village of log cabins that had sprung up a few hundred yards from the fort, the third leading up into the hills. It was the third trail they took, which would eventually lead them out of the Cypress Hills at the eastern slopes and on to Wood Mountain, several days' ride away. They huddled into their buffalo coats, bracing themselves against the biting December cold as their horses climbed into the snow-covered hills.

It was the 13th, twelve days until Christmas. They'd be lucky if they were back by then. Despite the isolation of Fort Walsh, their troopmates would celebrate the festive season in fine style—at least as fine a style as any place on the frontier.

It was a good 45 miles to the southeastern slopes of the Cypress Hills. The trail was covered with snow, hard going for the horses plunging and heaving their way through heavy drifts. It took them more than two days to get there.

From there on, the country levelled out somewhat. It was more open, but the weather worsened as another blizzard swept down from the north. There were few trees, and men and horses bore the full brunt of snow and wind. The men pulled their fur caps as far down over their ears as they could get them, but even then the unprotected portions of their faces turned red from the icy wind-driven cold. Instead of riding boots and spurs, which all too readily froze to the steel stirrups of their Imperial cavalry saddles, they wore moccasins and long black woollen stockings.

Snow drifted in heavily across the trail as they pushed southeast along the south bank of the frozen White Mud River. The world was shades of white and grey. They could not distinguish horizon from sky, the two blending into one another. It was country easy to get lost in. They searched for landmarks but could find none other than the river.

At night they pulled into a hollow or a coulee or a clump of trees where they built themselves a fire if they could find wood or dried buffalo

At one point in its early history, Fort Walsh had to be "de-liced" while its police force lived in tents on the flatlands outside the palisades. A second tent camp existed in 1876 when "E" Troop, recently transferred to reinforce the detachment, required shelter until the fort was enlarged.

dung to burn, huddling together to keep warm while they cooked their dinner. In the morning they climbed out of their blankets, rebuilt their fire, ate a hasty breakfast, then resumed riding.

They were more than halfway to Wood Mountain—it was the fifth day out of Fort Walsh—when they saw a party of horsemen struggling through the deep snow toward them.

As the two parties drew closer, Walsh could see it was Sub-Inspector Frechette's overdue patrol, its horses almost played out.

"Mr. Frechette!" Walsh greeted the sub-inspector as he reined in. "I've been damned worried about you."

Frechette's dark, bearded face peered out from the upturned collar of his buffalo coat. His normally round, cheerful face was gaunt, hollow cheeked. The men behind him didn't look any better.

"What happened?" Walsh asked.

"We had a bad time travelling, sir," Frechette rasped. "Weather's been terrible. Deep snow covering the trails, not much wood or buffalo chips to burn, food gave out. We couldn't travel half the time. Bad weather kept us in camp four days on one occasion, three days on another."

"Any sign of the Sioux?"

Frechette nodded. "We found 52 lodges camped about ten miles north of the line. They were heading toward Wood Mountain."

The antithesis of the whisky traders who had preceded him, Jean Louis Legare was a merchant who showed great sympathy for the plight of the Plains Indians. Later (as pictured here), he was a successful retailer in Moose Jaw, Saskatchewan.

Although it was only early afternoon, Walsh ordered camp made. They had passed a stand of pine trees a mile back and they withdrew to it. Gathering windfall and brush, the men got some fires burning and melted snow to make hot tea. While Frechette's weary men settled gratefully around the campfires, Walsh's men attended to their horses and gave them a good rubbing down, then fed men and horses from their own supplies.

Tin cups of steaming hot tea in their hands, Walsh and Frechette sat at one of the campfires talking.

"These Sioux didn't admit to taking part in the fight against General Custer, sir, but my scouts saw some of them with U.S. Army Springfields, and they had a number of mules with army brands. Probably taken at the Little Bighorn. They told me American soldiers were driving them out of their country and that there are more Sioux coming. We went back down along the boundary line looking for more of them, but we didn't find any. One of my scouts went below the line for twenty miles or so but didn't see any more Sioux. I decided, in view of our supplies running low and the condition of the horses, that we couldn't stay away any longer."

They remained camped together until the next morning, when Walsh ordered Frechette and his men to return to Fort Walsh in easy stages. He gave them what rations his patrol could spare, together with forage for the horses, knowing he could reprovision his patrol at Wood Mountain settlement.

The weather had moderated and the second blizzard that had swept out of the north had died down, although the temperature remained cold.

It took Walsh's patrol another two days to reach Wood Mountain, arriving four days before Christmas. They rode into the settlement—a scattering of Métis log cabins, two trading posts, and a disused boundary commission depot the Mounted Police used whenever they visited the settlement. Walsh reined to in front of Jean Louis Legare's trading store.

Swinging down from their saddles, Walsh and Louis Leveille stepped into the log building. "Hello, Mr. Legare," Walsh said to the tall, black-bearded Quebec trader standing behind the counter.

The 35-year-old Legare smiled. "Ah, my good Major. So nice to see you." He reached for Walsh's hand and they shook. Then Legare shook hands with Leveille. "How are you, Louis?"

"Well, thank you, Jean Louis, well," Leveille replied with his usual good-natured smile.

Louis Leveille and his brother were fixtures in the west. Louis would become a strong supporter of the Sioux during their stay in the Cypress Hills.

After a few opening comments about the bad weather they'd had, Walsh got to the point of his visit. "My scouts tell me American Sioux are headed this way. Have you heard anything about them?" If anyone at Wood Mountain knew of the coming of the Sioux, it would be Jean Louis Legare. Indians for miles around were his friends. The Sioux would come to him to trade. His reputation for honesty and fairness had spread far and wide.

Legare nodded. "Yes, Major. A dozen Sioux turned up here four days ago. I think they were … how you say … feeling their way to see if it would be all right for others to follow? They got some provisions, then left. The next day a lot more turned up. Then two days ago, Black Moon and even more Sioux arrived at White Eagle's camp. I hear this from some of White Eagle's Sissetons who came in yesterday to trade. They tell me there are among these new arrivals some who fought against General Custer at the Little Bighorn."

Walsh asked Legare a few more questions, then he and Leveille left the trading store, remounted their horses, and the patrol rode out of the settlement, heading for White Eagle's camp. White Eagle's Sisseton Sioux had fled north across the border in 1862 following what became known as the Minnesota Massacre. This ugly event had started when a few Sioux randomly attacked settlers in August. All Sioux became the hunted, and of the 2,000 who surrendered, 38 were eventually hung simultaneously on December 26, 1862, as the main perpetrators. It was in this climate of revenge that the Sissetons had first crossed the medicine line seeking asylum from the Americans. Grateful for the sanctuary they found, they had lived peacefully throughout their fourteen years north of the line.

It took Walsh and his patrol over an hour to reach the Sisseton camp, a scattering of cone-shaped buffalo-hide tepees squatting in deep snow among brushland four miles east of Wood Mountain settlement, countless smoke columns drifting skywards in the unusually still prairie air. Walsh could see that it had doubled in size since the last time he visited it.

They rode into the camp and stopped in front of White Eagle's lodge. Walsh and Leveille swung down from their saddles and shook hands with the Sisseton chief. "It is good to see you, White Eagle," Walsh said, Leveille interpreting. Walsh glanced around. "I see your camp has grown much larger since the last time I was here."

"Yes," White Eagle replied. "We have been joined by other Lakota who have just crossed into the White Mother's land. Black Moon, chief of all the Lakota, brought them. I have told them the country of the White Mother is different from the White Father's land. Here people live at peace."

Indians gathered around. Among them were a number of younger warriors, strangers who eyed Walsh and his men with a mixture of caution and curiosity.

"I would like to talk to them," Walsh said, "and tell them about the White Mother's laws. If they want to stay here, there must be no doubt in their minds as to how they're to behave."

White Eagle called a meeting. They assembled in the council lodge— Walsh and most of his redcoats, Leveille, White Eagle, Black Moon, the other Sioux chiefs and headmen, and as many others as could fit inside the big buffalo-hide lodge. Walsh and Leveille stood before them, the Sioux sitting cross-legged on buffalo robes spread in a circle on the ground around them.

White Eagle introduced Walsh. "This is White Forehead, soldier chief of the *Shagalasha*—the British Mother's redcoat pony soldiers. He is the law on this side of the medicine line. He speaks straight, not like the Americans. You can trust him."

Walsh eyed the brown faces and black eyes staring back at him. He began speaking to them, taking the time to allow Leveille to translate his words into the Lakota dialect. "Now that you have crossed into the Great White Mother's country, you must learn to obey her laws, as your brothers the Sissetons did. I will tell you what those laws are, but first I will ask you some questions, and I will take your answers to the White Mother's big chief at Fort Macleod, who will pass them on to the Great White Mother across the big water." Walsh pointed to the east. "Now, tell me, why did you come to her country?"

Black Moon stood up, proud and dignified, as befitted the hereditary chief of all the Lakota, his black eyes meeting the intense brown eyes of the redcoat chief. His voice was deep and clear. Even though the council lodge was full, there was no sound except the occasional crackling of the fire in the centre of the lodge. "We were driven from our homes by the Americans. We have come here seeking peace, peace we have not been able to find in the land of the White Father. We hope we can find it here in the *Shaganosh* [British] Mother's country. A long time ago, our grandfathers fought beside redcoat soldiers of the *Shaganosh* Mother's grandfather in the war against the Americans. Our grandfathers told us we would find peace in her land if we ever needed it." Black Moon glanced down at White Eagle, seated beside him, and put his hand on the Sisseton chief's head for a moment, then continued. "Our brothers the Sissetons realized the truth of this many long suns ago. That is why we come to the *Shaganosh* Mother's country. For years we have not slept soundly. Now we look for a place where we can live peacefully. We are tired of war. We are tired of being pushed from our land, tired of being chased from one place to another. We are tired of being hunted. We are tired of being shot down like dogs."

When Black Moon finished, he sat down.

Walsh asked, "Do you intend to remain in the White Mother's country during the winter, renewing your strength, then in the spring return to your own country to resume your war against the Americans?"

"No! No!" Black Moon and several others shouted in unison. "We want to stay here on this side of the big road," Black Moon said. "We beg you to ask the *Shaganosh* Mother to have pity on us."

All eyes were on Walsh, on his bright red coat with its rich gold trim down the front and on the collars and sleeves. The heat from the fire and the bodies seated in the council lodge had warmed the place up, and he had taken off his buffalo coat and fur cap. The white of his forehead, where it was protected by his hat from the sun, stood out pale against the weathered colouring of his face in the late afternoon light, and the newly arrived Sioux could see why he was called the White Forehead Chief.

In front of Walsh sat the chiefs of some of the best fighting men in North America, described as the finest light cavalry in the world: Spotted Eagle, war chief of the Sans Arcs, a striking young man with incredibly light eyes; Long Dog, war chief of the Hunkpapas, a ferocious-looking warrior covered with bullet and knife wounds, yet with a twinkle of humour in his eyes; Little Knife, older than most of the other warriors, but with a drawn face that had an innate kindness to it. War chiefs who commanded the respect of their fellow tribesmen, war chiefs who had the power to wipe Walsh and his few redcoats off the face of the earth, were asking him to beg the Great White Mother to have pity on them. But Walsh did not fear them. He believed in Colonel Macleod's way— that honesty, justice, and fair play would win the peace.

"Do you know," he asked them, "that all people living in the White Mother's country—white man and red man—must obey her laws?"

"We are strangers to the laws here," Black Moon replied. "We ask you to tell us what they are."

Walsh nodded. "All right. First of all, it is against the law for anyone to take the life of another—to kill any man, woman, or child. You must not injure any person, nor steal from—nor give false testimony against—another. You must not take another person's horses, guns, robes, lodges, wagons, or anything else. You must not damage, injure, destroy, burn, or remove anything from anyone else without their permission. No woman or female child shall be violated, and it is the duty of every man to protect them. You must not cross the international boundary line—what the Indian people call the medicine line, or some of you call 'the big road'—to run off horses from other Indian tribes or to raid them or anyone else, or to make war on American soldiers or the American people. The Great White Mother lives at peace with the Americans."

After Walsh finished, Black Moon stood up and made a speech, again imploring the White Mother to have pity on his people, saying they would obey her laws. Several of the others rose after Black Moon and made similar speeches.

Walsh promised to convey their words to the White Mother's big redcoat chief at Fort Macleod. He was emphatic, however, about driving home the point that they must not go back across the border to make war on the Americans, then return to Canadian territory seeking protection. "If you have any such intentions, you had better pull down your lodges and go back to your own country and stay there."

"No," Black Moon insisted, shaking his head vigorously. "We do not want to go back. We have left there for good."

White Eagle invited Walsh and his men to eat with his people and spend the night in his camp. Walsh promptly accepted, realizing he had made a good impression on the Sioux for White Eagle to extend such an invitation. With the right kind of treatment, he just might be able to control the Sioux, even the notorious Sitting Bull. The U.S. government hadn't treated them fairly. They might respond to justice. If by treating them honourably he could handle them—if he could tame them where Custer and the 7th Cavalry failed—he would go down in history.

He already had a fort named after him. Apart from Colonel Macleod (who, to the applause of constables, NCOs, and officers across the prairies, had succeeded Colonel French as commissioner upon French's resignation earlier in the year), Walsh was the only Mounted Police officer to earn this distinction. Inspector Brisebois had tried it, naming the fort on the Bow River after himself, but Colonel Macleod and later Major Irvine had overruled him and renamed it Fort Calgary (according to Sub-Inspector Denny, Calgary was Gaelic for "clear, running water"). Brisebois had resigned not long after. Even Custer hadn't had a fort named after him—not while he was still alive.

✳ ✳ ✳

The next morning, as Walsh and his patrol were about to mount their horses and leave White Eagle's camp, the Sisseton chief, accompanied by Black Moon and the other Sioux chiefs, approached him.

"Black Moon wants me to ask you something before you go," White Eagle said to Walsh, Leveille interpreting.

Walsh looked over White Eagle's shoulder at Black Moon, Spotted Eagle, Long Dog, and the other Sioux chiefs standing impassively behind him on that cold, still, December morning. Snow was piled up around the conical-shaped lodges, and smoke drifted up from the vented tops, leaving the smell of wood smoke hanging heavily in the air. "Go ahead, White Eagle."

"Black Moon and the others beg the Great White Mother to let them have a few bullets each so they can hunt the buffalo. Their women and children need food. The men used up their bullets fighting off the bluecoats and now have none left. All they have are bows and arrows or lances. Some have only knives lashed to long poles. Others have only lassos, and the only way they can hunt is by chasing the buffalo on their ponies, roping them and dragging them off their feet, then stabbing them with knives until they're dead. Many of their best ponies are used up from the long ride here. Without bullets they have no other way to hunt and their families will starve. We help them, but we use up our food quicker and we don't know how long it will take us to hunt more buffalo and build up our supply again."

Walsh looked past White Eagle again, seeing the drawn faces of Black Moon and the others. Not a smile among them. He noted the scraggly buffalo robes over their shoulders as they stood shivering in the cold. There were buffalo between Wood Mountain and the east end of the Cypress Hills. His patrol had sighted fresh buffalo dung on the way. The refugees and White Eagle's Sissetons would have to hunt them while the herds were still in the region. They couldn't wait while he wrote to Fort Macleod for instructions as to government policy with regard to the refugee Sioux. He had to make a decision now, on the spot. But then, that was one of the things Walsh liked about being a Mounted Police officer out on the frontier. He could make up his own policies and procedures as the need arose. Out on the frontier there was no Secretary of State or bureaucratic official too far removed from the scene to know what was really going on. He—Major James Walsh— was the government out here.

"The Great White Mother doesn't want anyone in her country to starve," he told White Eagle and the others. "If she can be satisfied that none of you will use any bullets she allows you to fight the Americans— that you'll use them for hunting food only—she will let you have enough for hunting. But she doesn't want you sending any bullets to friends and relatives across the line."

"No," White Eagle replied, shaking his head emphatically. "They will be used for hunting only."

"All right," Walsh replied, nodding his head. "I'll speak to the trader at the settlement, Jean Louis Legare, and tell him to allow each head of a family enough bullets so they can hunt the buffalo."

Tension disappeared from Sioux faces. Black Moon, Spotted Eagle, the other Sioux chiefs, and their people could breathe easy, at least for the time being. The Great White Mother had taken them in. They would be free from harassment by the long-knives. They could ride the plains and hunt the buffalo the way the Great Spirit, *Wainga Tanka*, meant them to, the way they always had, as far back as any of them could remember.

Black Moon had brought 2,900 Sioux—men, women, and children—with him. They were a mixture of Hunkpapas, Ogalalas, Minniconjous, Sans Arcs, Blackfeet (not to be confused with the Canadian Blackfoot), and Two Kettles. They were the first of the Sioux refugees from the Little Bighorn to cross the medicine line. They were not the last.

Chapter 7

Under A Flag of Truce

*The Buffalo like the Indian stood in the way of
civilization and in the path of progress and the
decree had gone forth that they must both give way.*

General Nelson Miles

The year 1877 had started with another storm. James Walsh stared south
from his fort in Cypress Hills at the fresh blanket of snow. His thoughts
narrowed from the entire Sioux nation down to the one man he knew he
must soon face—Sitting Bull. It had been six months since Walsh had
first heard of the Little Bighorn and Custer's demise, and it was hard to
deny the tension that came with the Sioux. Through the fall, Sitting Bull
had continued to elude the U.S. Cavalry. Other Sioux were not so lucky.

Generals Terry and Crook had continued their search for the missing
Sioux in the United States. Acclaimed Indian fighter Crook's sole
"success" had been at Slim Buttes, South Dakota, where he massacred
37 lodges of Sioux. He had also almost starved his own army to death
applying some misguided strategies. Terry had even less luck. Critics in
the U.S. Congress pointed out that the three-month campaign was costing
about $1 million per dead Indian, and the Yellowstone River Expedition
was finally abandoned.

A new campaign was launched with Colonel Miles and the tenacious
"Three Stars" Crook heading north. Beyond the medicine line, NWMP
Inspector James Walsh received word regarding Crook's destruction of
the Slim Buttes village. But both Walsh and Crook's more immediate
concern was the whereabouts of Sitting Bull.

The last reported sighting of Bull was in late October, when 37-
year-old Colonel Nelson A. Miles, at the head of ten companies of the
5th United States Infantry—15 officers, 434 NCOs and men, and 10

scouts—caught up with him and a formidable gathering of warriors, including Gall, Pretty Bear, and several other chiefs, just north of the Yellowstone River near the mouth of the Powder. Sioux raiders had attacked two of the wagon trains carrying supplies to Miles's encampment at the mouth of the Tongue River.

Miles and Sitting Bull faced each other under a flag of truce and parleyed. Miles was wearing a long bearskin coat to ward off the October chill, earning him the nickname "Bear Coat." He demanded Sitting Bull surrender. Sitting Bull refused, saying he wanted to hunt buffalo, and he accused the soldiers of frightening off the herds. He wanted the soldiers to leave him and his people alone so they could hunt buffalo and elk in peace. He also asked to be left alone so he could go to the Fort Peck Indian agency, farther north along the Missouri River, and trade for rifle ammunition to enable them to hunt for their winter supply of meat. Miles refused Sitting Bull's request, telling him that nothing short of complete surrender would be acceptable. Sitting Bull said he would not surrender and be put on a reserve. He told Miles the Yellowstone was Indian country and the soldiers had no right to be there.

Negotiations broke off and fighting followed. To give the women, children, and old ones a chance to escape, Sitting Bull's warriors set fire to the prairie grass and, under cover of the smoke, attacked the soldiers. Fearing that he would be surrounded, Colonel Miles ordered his accompanying artillery piece to open fire, breaking up the Sioux attack and forcing them to retreat. During the fighting, more than half the Sioux—hungry, tired, and running out of bullets— surrendered, but Sitting Bull escaped with the remainder, although they were forced to abandon much of their camp equipment. The soldiers chased them for 40 miles before Sitting Bull and his followers disappeared into hilly country.

* * *

Major Walsh knew as much about Sitting Bull as anyone in Canada. And that wasn't all that much. Many rumours and a few newspapers had reached Fort Walsh. During the long evenings, Walsh reread everything written on the Sioux. As early as a year before the Little Bighorn, the *Fort Benton Record* described Sitting Bull as a bloodthirsty villain who had committed more murders than any other Indian since the days of the Wyoming massacre. He was a treacherous scoundrel, reports said, who had made threats against white men all his life and vowed to kill every soldier who crossed his path.

In the days before the formation of the NWMP, Hudson's Bay Company traders frequently warned of the dangers of a Sioux invasion of the Canadian plains. Only the opposition of the Crees, Saulteaux, and the Blackfoot alliance had prevented it. During the Red River insurrection in 1869-70, the ghost of a rumour had travelled all the way to Ottawa: Sitting Bull—known for his fierce opposition to white advancement along the Missouri, the Yellowstone, and the Bighorn rivers—had let it be known that if Louis Riel's Métis wanted help, he and the Sioux would give it. A year or two later, the Sioux approached the Cree and Saulteaux, suggesting they form a mighty alliance to rise against the encroaching white man and throw him back off the buffalo plains. But the two Canadian tribes rejected the suggestion. They did not trust the Sioux and particularly resented any moves by them to hunt buffalo north of the medicine line.

* * *

Hunkeshnee—or Sitting Bull as he became known to the white man—was reputedly born on the bank of the Grand River, a tributary of the Missouri, in Dakota Territory, between 1831 and 1834. Most sources say he was the only son of Returns Again, a Hunkpapa warrior who was something of a mystic. There were many stories about Sitting Bull's early years. One told how he became a hunter of renown while still a boy. It was claimed he had a fight with an Indian older than himself, whom he killed after sustaining an injury that gave him a permanent limp, from which he got his name, Lame—or Sitting—Bull. Another story had it that he was attacked by a young buffalo bull while still a boy, that he grabbed it by the horns and wrestled it to the ground, flipping it so that it landed backwards on its rump. Yet another story claims that the name Sitting Bull was chosen by Returns Again after he heard strange sounds from a buffalo bull that he interpreted to be four names the bull was communicating to him: Sitting Bull, Jumping Bull, Standing with Cow, and Lone Bull.

Early in his childhood, Sitting Bull became a medicine man—a priest, mystic, and politician. By the time of Canadian Confederation, he was prominent in the Council of the Strong Hearts, an elite soldier society of the Hunkpapa Sioux, and chief of the Hunkpapas. He was known across the frontier as a warrior to be reckoned with—not only among the Lakota but for the white man and other Indian tribes as well.

Sitting Bull rose to become right-hand man of the great Sioux chieftain Red Cloud, the only western Indian to win a war against the

This drawing, done later in Sitting Bull's life, recalls Sitting Bull's first coup in a Hunkpapa fight with the Crow. Sitting Bull was said to have received his name as a result of this victory at age fourteen.

white invaders. During several years of conflict with the United States government over Indian rights, both Sioux chiefs developed an implacable opposition to white men, and soldiers in particular. In 1868, Red Cloud signed a treaty that restored the Bozeman Trail hunting lands to the Sioux and made Bighorn River country an Indian territory, restricting access to white wolfers and buffalo hunters. The onslaught continued, however, and Red Cloud, sensing the inevitable, refused to renew the struggle. Sitting Bull held out against the white invaders and refused to cede any Indian land. The U.S. government had granted the Sioux their sacred Indian land of the Black Hills of Dakota for life, but when gold was discovered there the government gave in to white demands for protection against the Indians, and sent troops onto Indian land. The government tried to buy the land back, but Sitting Bull refused.

He saw no end to the conflict between Whites and his people other than defeat of one side or the other, and in an attempt to make a concerted stand for what he considered his people's rights, he proceeded to unite the Sioux and Cheyenne to stand against the government. Many warriors from the agencies and the buffalo plains joined him, determined not to die peaceably but to fight for their rights. This led to a series of clashes between the U.S. military and the Indians, culminating in the Sioux and Cheyenne victory over Custer and the 7th Cavalry at the Little Bighorn.

Now all Sitting Bull and his followers could do was keep on the move through deep snow and hills, hunting for food wherever possible, watching for pursuing soldiers, moving on the instant they appeared. But it drove home an overwhelmingly important conclusion—the old cherished days of the "red man" had gone. The tide of white invasion rushed on over the buffalo ranges. There seemed only one escape—north to the land of the *Shaganosh*.

Chapter 8
The White Forehead Chief

*No Indian that ever lived loved the white man and
no white man that ever lived loved the Indian.*
Sitting Bull to Colonel Miles, October 1876

Louis Leveille knocked on Major Walsh's office door.

"Come in." Walsh watched as Leveille stepped inside and stopped in front of the desk.

"My Major," he said, his tone polite as usual, a half smile creasing his dark, lined face. "Scouts just ride in from the White Mud. Say big band of Sioux heading north along Rocky Creek toward border."

Walsh's brow furrowed. It was March, nine months since the Little Bighorn. A hint of spring was in the air, the sun higher in the sky each day. The snow would soon be gone from the Cypress Hills and the border country along the White Mud and Wood Mountain. It promised to be a long summer.

"Is Sitting Bull with them?" Walsh asked.

Uncertainty marked Leveille's face as he shook his head slightly. "The scouts, they could not be sure, my Major."

That left Walsh little alternative but to ride down there on the assumption Sitting Bull was with them. Although the hereditary chief of all the Lakota, Black Moon, was already on Canadian soil, it was Sitting Bull who wielded the real power among the Sioux. It was Sitting Bull above all others with whom Walsh would have to deal. A sense of destiny was upon him.

Turning over command to the next senior officer, 28-year-old Sub-Inspector John Henry McIllree, a graduate of Britain's Royal Military College at Sandhurst, Major Walsh rode out of Fort Walsh at the head of a patrol of several men and three Métis scouts. It would have been easy

This re-creation of an original Sitting Bull pictograph shows him wearing his Strong Heart war bonnet and striking a coup against an Assiniboine boy he would adopt as a "brother." The boy was given the name Jumping Bull and attended to Sitting Bull at the Sun Dance days before Little Bighorn. Sitting Bull did the original work about 1870, and his follower, Four Horns, copied the drawings of the sitting buffalo bull as a signature of his chief.

for an unknowing observer to take Walsh for a scout rather than a policeman. He wore his fringed buckskin coat and slouch hat instead of the gold-trimmed scarlet patrol jacket and gold-banded blue pill-box forage cap prescribed in NWMP dress regulations. But Walsh recognized the importance of the British scarlet. He carried his patrol jacket and pill-box carefully packed in his saddle-bags, ready to be donned prior to meeting Sitting Bull. He intended to ascertain Sitting Bull's plans, explain Canada's laws, and tell him he and his followers would have to obey them if they wanted to remain in Canada, just as he'd told Black Moon, Spotted Eagle, and the others before Christmas. He may not have considered the irony of himself at the head of a few men facing the notorious leader of the feared Sioux and laying down the law. On the other hand, if he had thought about it, it might well have appealed to his sense of history.

Three days later, Walsh and his patrol camped halfway between the Pinto Horse Butte and Indian Cliff, the westernmost point of Wood Mountain, about 120 miles east of Fort Walsh and 30 miles north of the border. The trail was still splotched here and there by winter snows, and in the ravines and river bottoms where the spring sun hadn't yet penetrated, snow still lay deep.

"We should find them somewhere between here and the boundary line," Walsh said to Leveille as they sat drinking tea in front of the campfire that night. "If they kept north along Rocky Creek, they'd have reached the White Mud and followed it across the line, presumably."

His back propped against his saddle, Leveille sipped the steaming sugar-laced tea, looking across the top of his tin mug at Walsh.

"Tomorrow we'll ride down as far as the line, Louis," Walsh said, "and try to pick up their trail if they've crossed over. If they haven't, we'll sit there and wait until they do, or perhaps we'll cross over and try to find out just where the hell they are."

The next morning, Walsh and Leveille, with the other two Métis scouts, Joseph "Cajou" Morin and Louis Daniels, headed south, leaving the others of the patrol in camp, standing by for orders. They rode toward the White Mud River, across prairie littered with ravines and low buttes, sudden ridges, and table-top plateaus, country covered with new spring grass pushing its way through old blackened grass burnt over by prairie fires the previous autumn. They reached the White Mud by late afternoon, at a place known as the Mud House—a hole dug in the river bank, the front lined with tree trunks and other pieces of timber, that was used as a shelter in bad weather by Métis buffalo hunters and traders. The area was known as the Mauvaises Terres—the Bad Lands.

"Still no sign of those Sioux," Walsh said, standing in his stirrups and gazing southwards along the river. He looked around at the valley, at high, almost perpendicular cliffs reaching up some 300 feet toward a cloud-flecked blue sky, alive with flights of birds soaring high above them, seeking trees to nest in. He scanned the small round hills and hummocks littering the mile-wide valley, then pointed to a stretch of plain on the far side of the river, about half a mile away. "We'll make camp over there. Tomorrow morning we'll split up and search both sides of the river for a ways and see if we can find any sign of them."

Next morning they struck camp and saddled up, guiding their horses along the river flats, following the river as it swung south. They hadn't been riding long when Walsh sighted a rock cairn a few hundred yards away. The Indians called it a "stone heap." Upon reaching it, he reined his horse to a stop and sat looking down. The cairn stood in long spring grass, rising above the toe of his stirruped boot. The rocks had been cemented together. Two wooden plaques had been built into it, one facing north, the other south. Carved words on the north side stared mutely up at him: British Possession. On the south side the words read U.S. Territory.

Walsh's eyes remained on the cairn for a moment, then peered into the distance beyond. Over there stretched Montana for as far as the eye could see and then some. The river flowed on, its whitish water sparkling in the morning sunlight.

But still there were no signs of Indians. For all Walsh and his scouts could see, they were alone in these vast spaces.

No one said anything until Walsh broke the silence. "Louis, take Daniels and head east across the river. Circle out for about fifteen miles. See if you can pick up any sign of the Sioux trail. Cajou and I'll head west. We'll meet back here later on."

Leveille's face showed concern. Walsh caught the look, saw the older man open his mouth to say something, pause, then shrug, and close it again. Walsh knew what Leveille had been about to say: that he feared for Walsh's safety and wanted to ride with him, but there were times when Leveille, as chief scout, had to take charge of others, and this was one of them.

The two parties split up, Leveille and Daniels splashing their horses into the river, crossing to the east side, then circling out. Walsh and Morin headed west.

Morin's eyes seldom left the ground in front of him. After riding for about seven miles he suddenly stiffened in his saddle, then pointed triumphantly. "T'ere, Major! No more'n a couple hours old."

Hundreds of unshod pony tracks and furrow marks made by countless travois cut across in front of them from their left, leading up from Montana Territory, little more than an arrow flight to the south.

They followed the trail northward until it reached the White Mud, then swung in and followed the river's course as it flowed from the west, then northwest. From the sharpness of the trail it was clear the Indians had passed by only a short time before.

Walsh and Morin had been riding alongside the hills and hummocks bordering the river for a mile or two when they spotted an Indian sitting motionless on his pony, watching them from the top of a hill ahead. A moment later another Indian appeared on top of another hill. "Two In'ian, Major … up on them hills."

"I see them," Walsh replied. "Keep on riding."

They rode on, keeping the same pace. Soon more Indians appeared on the hilltops and hummocks until it seemed as though every hill and hummock had an Indian on top of it, sitting motionless on their ponies, rifle butts propped against their thighs.

"They must be setting up camp just ahead," Walsh said.

The Indians watched the two riders for a moment longer, then began hand-signalling to one another.

"T'ose In'ian, Major … tryin' to figure out who we are."

"Just keep on riding, Cajou. Don't give them any idea they might have us worried."

Morin shook his head. "I ain't worried if you ain't, Major. I'm part-Sioux anyway."

Soon they rounded a hill at a bend in the river. Across on the other side in front of them, Indians were busy putting up a good-sized camp. Suddenly shouts in Lakota sounded the alarm. Panic erupted. Women throwing buffalo-skin coverings over crossed-pole lodge frames shrieked in fear, then began pulling them down again. Children cried. Indians grabbed their ponies for a quick escape. Snatching up rifles, warriors rushed to the river bank to hold off the two riders.

"Tell them to put down their rifles!" Walsh rasped. "They're in the Queen's country now!"

The river was no more than 50 yards wide at this point. Morin shouted in the Lakota dialect at the Indians on the far bank. They shouted back.

"T'ey think we advance party of American cavalry, Major!"

"Tell 'em who we are!" Walsh ordered, reaching into his saddle-bag to pull out his red patrol jacket. He'd intended to put it on before they reached the Sioux camp, but they'd come across it so suddenly he hadn't had time. Then two horsemen appeared unexpectedly from behind hills on the other side of the river, galloping toward them, one shouting at him.

"My Major—be careful!"

Walsh twisted in his saddle, looking over his right shoulder. "God damn it!" he exclaimed, recognizing Leveille and Daniels, wishing they hadn't caught up with him yet.

Renewed panic broke out among the Indians at the sight of the two scouts. Screaming women and children ran from the camp. Warriors at the river's edge threw rifles up to their shoulders and prepared to fire.

Walsh saw what was happening. If the Sioux had mistaken him and Morin for the vanguard of a pursuing force of U.S. Cavalry about to attack them, they would have been even more convinced of it now, with Leveille and Daniels galloping toward them on the far bank. Walsh felt instant sympathy for the Sioux, especially the women and children fleeing the camp. They had suffered so much already from attacks on their camps. Reaching the medicine line, they must have thought themselves safe at last. Now this! If he and Cajou could just get across to them and explain who they were …

Waving his red jacket at the Sioux, Walsh kicked his horse into the shallow river, Morin at his side. They hardly got any distance at all before the Sioux shouted a final warning to stay back.

At that moment, Leveille and Daniels swung their horses into the river, splashing their way across to join them.

While Morin shouted again to the Sioux that they weren't Americans, Walsh peeled off his buckskin coat and slouch hat and pulled on his scarlet jacket and pill-box.

As soon as Leveille drew level with Walsh, he slid his rifle out of its saddle scabbard, levered a bullet into the breach, and pulled the rifle to his shoulder, ready to fire. The Métis were used to fighting the Sioux. He wasn't scared of them.

But Walsh had other ideas. "Don't, Louis!" he ordered, thrusting up his arm and pushing Leveille's gun barrel in the air.

At the sight of the bright red coat, a mixture of emotions showed on Sioux faces—confusion, wonder, enlightenment, relief. None of them had seen a redcoat before, though they had all heard about the red-coated pony soldiers of the *Shaganosh* Mother who ruled the land beyond the stone heaps. But some of the Sioux feared the white man had donned the red coat to deceive them.

Holding a tight rein on his excited horse, Walsh shouted at them, Leveille interpreting, "My name is Walsh. I am chief of the British Mother's redcoats in this region. Your people—White Eagle and the Sissetons, and Black Moon, Spotted Eagle, Long Dog—call me the White Forehead Chief."

"How do we know there are not long-knives following?" a warrior called across the river.

"Send out scouts," Walsh called back as soon as Leveille repeated the warrior's words in English. "If the scouts see American soldiers coming, you will know I am lying. But if they do not see American soldiers, you will know I speak the truth. Why would I want to enter your camp with just three mixed-bloods with me if what I say is not true? I would be at your mercy then, and you would surely kill me."

The Sioux talked among themselves for a moment, then signalled Walsh and his Métis scouts to cross the river.

When he reached their side of the river, Walsh ran his eyes over them, looking for one who might be the notorious Sioux leader. "Is Sitting Bull with you?"

"No," they answered.

"Continue putting up your lodges," Walsh said, glancing at the partially completed camp. "You are safe here. You are in the White Mother's country now. American soldiers will not follow you here."

Reassured, most of the Sioux resumed putting up their lodges. But some warriors held their rifles ready, looking at the red-coated figure of Walsh, while others stared apprehensively back along the river.

Walsh stepped down from his saddle. Leveille and the other two scouts did the same.

"If Sitting Bull is not with you," Walsh said to the Sioux, "who is your chief?"

A tall, imposing-looking man of about 70 stepped forward. "I am Four Horns," he said. "I am chief of these people."

Walsh shook hands with him. "Which tribe are you?"

"We are Teton Lakota ... Hunkpapa people, followers of my adopted son, Sitting Bull."

"Where is Sitting Bull? I have heard he is on his way here."

Four Horns' eyes flitted from Walsh to Leveille as the Métis translated Walsh's question. Then he replied, "He is still on the other side of the Missouri, but he is looking this way."

Walsh's ears pricked up. So Sitting Bull is looking this way.

"Is it really true," Four Horns asked, "that the bluecoats will not follow us here? Is it really true they will not follow us beyond the stone heaps?"

"Yes. You are in the White Mother's country. American soldiers will not follow you. You are safe here. But there are laws here, laws all people who live on this side of the stone heaps must obey. I would like to talk to you, your headmen and councillors, and your people about those laws. When you have finished putting up your camp, I would be pleased if you would call your people together so I can talk to them."

While the Sioux finished putting up their lodges, Walsh and his scouts wandered around the camp, watching. Hands clasped behind his back, Walsh eyed one lodge in particular, almost completed, buffalo robes dividing its interior into several curtained sections for its occupants. Its owner, a warrior of about 50, noticing the redcoat watching, stopped what he was doing and smiled at Walsh. Walsh returned the smile.

"I am Little Saulteaux," the warrior said, stepping over to Walsh and offering his hand.

Walsh took his hand and shook it, then looked around for one of his scouts to interpret. Louis Daniels, hovering a few yards away, ambled over. Speaking through Daniels, Walsh and Little Saulteaux talked. Little

Saulteaux took Walsh and showed him the lodge's interior. He introduced Walsh to his two wives, who were helping him with the lodge, then to his two daughters, aged about fifteen and eighteen, and to his niece, a beautiful young woman with dark, mild eyes. Named White Tooth, she was tall and slender, graceful in her movements. Walsh would remember her as the finest-looking young woman of any race he had ever seen. She was from the Red Cloud agency and had been visiting her relatives when United States troops attacked Four Horns' camp, putting the band to flight and preventing her return home. Little Saulteaux and his family were all clean and well dressed, indicating him to be a man of some affluence.

As they talked, Walsh raised his hand to stifle a yawn.

"Would White Forehead like to rest in my lodge?" Little Saulteaux asked, his eyes darting from Walsh to Daniels.

Walsh sensed it would put the Sioux at ease if he did drop off to sleep in their camp. It would also show he wasn't afraid of them. He turned to Daniels. "Tell Little Saulteaux yes, I would like that."

Little Saulteaux spoke to his wives, who spread buffalo robes on the ground inside the lodge.

"Thank you, Little Saulteaux," Walsh said, taking off his pill-box and loosening his scarlet jacket. "This is very kind of you."

Walsh lay down on the buffalo robes, settling himself into a relaxed position, and Little Saulteaux padded out of the lodge. Walsh was soon asleep.

It seemed only minutes later when he felt himself being shaken awake by Daniels. "Major ... Four Horns and the Sioux ... they all outside waitin'. They'd like to hear what you got to tell 'em."

Walsh climbed to his feet, put on his pill-box, and stepped out of the lodge into bright sunlight. Daniels pointed to the front of the camp along the river, where Indians were packed along the banks—men, women, children, old people—some sitting cross-legged on the ground, others standing. Walsh and Daniels strode toward them. Four Horns stepped forward. Louis Leveille joined Walsh to act as his interpreter, while Cajou Morin strolled over to stand beside Daniels, just behind Walsh.

Walsh scanned the brown faces in front of him. All appeared anxious to hear what he had to say.

After a few words with Four Horns, Walsh addressed the Hunkpapas. "By now you all know who I am. There are laws here that everyone—red man and white man—must obey." He then went on to outline the laws, as he had done with Black Moon and the first of the Sioux refugees from the Little Bighorn three months earlier.

"If you obey these laws, you may remain in the White Mother's country. The redcoats will protect you. You will be safe, as safe as if you were surrounded by ten thousand friendly warriors. You and your families can sleep soundly. But if you will not obey the White Mother's laws, you must go back where you come from."

Four Horns rose from the buffalo robe he had been sitting on. "We are glad to hear what you have to say, White Forehead. We are tired of fighting and running. Our women and children need a place to lay down their heads and sleep peacefully. We want peace. We ask only that we be allowed to hunt the buffalo as *Wainga Tanka* meant us to. We will take your words into our hearts. We will do as you say."

Four Horns had just finished speaking when a lone warrior rode into camp. He leaped off his pony at the edge of the grouped Indians, then, seeing Four Horns, made his way toward the Hunkpapa chief. He smiled at some in the assembly whom he seemed to know, waving at others. He eyed Walsh once as he threaded his way to Four Horns. Reaching the older man, he greeted him and they shook hands. They exchanged words, during which the new arrival eyed Walsh again.

"That wouldn't be Sitting Bull, would it?" Daniels said into Cajou Morin's ear.

"Don' know," Morin replied.

Four Horns said something else to the warrior, who then lowered himself, sitting cross-legged at the front of the group of Indians. Walsh was about to speak again when the warrior suddenly jumped to his feet and stared belligerently at him. Walsh looked back at the newcomer, also wondering whether he was Sitting Bull. Then the warrior flung out an accusing arm, pointing at Walsh, a tirade of Lakota words rattling from his mouth.

Walsh glanced sideways at Leveille. "What's he saying, Louis?"

Leveille waited until the warrior had finished, then scowled as he answered Walsh's question. "He say the first time he met you was on the Missouri at Fort Buford. The last time was on the Yellowstone at Bear Coat's camp. He say you are American long-knife."

Walsh was struck momentarily speechless by the accusation. The warrior continued. "This *wasichu* [white man] wears a red coat, but he is a long-knife spy, one who would kill Indian people while they sleep. You should make him your prisoner. He should not be allowed to leave this camp."

"You lie!" Louis Leveille shouted, reaching for his revolver.

Walsh clapped a hand on Leveille's arm. "Easy, Louis. That's not the way."

Consternation clouded Sioux faces as they stared from the warrior to Walsh. Four Horns seemed as bewildered as any of them.

While Leveille told Walsh what the warrior had said, Walsh—staring at his accuser—realized he couldn't be Sitting Bull, who was in his 40s. This warrior was younger.

Walsh held up his hands, appealing to the assembly to stop the muttering and occasional shouting that had broken out among them. "You have heard what I said," he told them, Leveille barely managing to restrain his anger long enough to interpret. "If this man tells the truth, then I have deceived you. But who is he? Is he one of you? Do you know him well? Is he a friend of yours and not an enemy?" Walsh turned to face the warrior. "What is your purpose? Are you trying to stir these poor people up? Look at them. They're your blood. Have pity for them. I've never seen them before, but I can see what they've been through. As long as they're here in the White Mother's country, I'll do what I can to protect them. You've never seen me before, not unless you've been here on this side of the stone heaps. Maybe you've seen someone down on the Yellowstone who looks like me, but it wasn't me. I've never been to the Yellowstone, and I've never been in Bear Coat's camp."

The warrior still glared at Walsh. "I have seen you. I know you know me."

Now it was Walsh's turn to point an accusing finger at the warrior. "You're a god-damned liar! I've never seen you before and you've never seen me." He looked at Four Horns. "I don't know who this fellow is, but there's little doubt in my mind that he's no friend of yours. I advise you to keep a close watch on him."

Leveille was getting just as angry as Walsh, and he clearly itched to throw himself at the warrior who had shown his good Major such disrespect, but Daniels and Morin held him back.

Distress showed on Four Horns' lined face. Many of his people turned anxious eyes southward again.

"The hearts of my people beat with fear once more," Four Horns said. "We thought we could sleep peacefully tonight, now that we are in the White Mother's country, but I fear my people will not be able to do so."

"None of you need fear, Four Horns," Walsh replied. "The White Mother will protect you."

Four Horns' face was tight. Walsh's remark, meant to allay his fears, had not done so.

"Would it put the hearts of your people at rest if I remain in your camp tonight?" Walsh asked.

"Yes."

"Then I will stay with you tonight. But there is one thing I ask."

"What is it, White Forehead?"

"This man"—Walsh pointed at the visiting warrior—"I ask that you also hold him in camp tonight. There is one more thing I ask. I will hire two or three of your best young men to ride south, back on the other side of the stone heaps, to a place called the Burnt Timber. They will find a large band of agency Indians there, Yankton Sioux under Chief Medicine Bear and his war chief, Black Horn. Tell them you are holding White Forehead a prisoner in your camp."

Four Horns shook his head. "You are not a prisoner, White Forehead."

"If I attempted to leave your camp, your warriors would stop me. Send your young men, Four Horns. Have them tell Medicine Bear and Black Horn what I said." Walsh glanced at the visiting warrior standing scowling back at him a few feet away. "Then we'll see who is the liar."

✳ ✳ ✳

The next morning Walsh stood in front of Little Saulteaux's lodge with Louis Leveille, both rested after a good night's sleep. Above, a warm spring sun shone out of the sweeping blue sky, with only a few scattered clouds far off to the northwest. Thousands of ponies grazed on new spring grass on the hills back of the camp. On the other side of the camp, the White Mud flowed southeast to cross the border into Montana before emptying out into the Milk farther on. Here and there along the banks, scattered clumps of budding willows fringed the river, and rose bushes dotted the higher ground. Robins, meadowlarks, sparrows, hawks, and blackbirds darted here and there.

The mellow spring sunshine had brought the people out of their lodges to enjoy the idyllic surroundings, and everywhere Walsh looked he saw men, women, and children engaged in a variety of activities: women rearranging their family lodges and possessions, children playing around the tepees, and men in twos and threes or small groups sitting on hilltops talking and smoking. Women walked around the camp carrying blackened pots of water for boiling or meat for cooking, or bearing skins for tanning or robes for mending. Here and there old men sat in front of their lodges, sunning themselves and smoking their pipes. Despite what the warrior from the south had told them the previous afternoon, the fact that Walsh had remained in their camp overnight, seemingly unconcerned, had reassured many, perhaps even most of them, for there was an atmosphere of relaxation and lightheartedness around the camp.

After awhile, Walsh heard a noise from along the valley and looked in the direction from which it came. At first he could see nothing, but a moment or two later, a mighty procession of horsemen swept around the bend in the river. Two hundred warriors in war paint, feathers bobbing up and down with the movements of their ponies as they trotted forward, were riding toward the camp. As they drew closer, Walsh recognized Chief Medicine Bear and his war chief, Black Horn, in the lead.

They rode proudly, as fine a procession of fighting warriors as Walsh had ever seen. He smiled. It was good to see them, and he felt touched that these Yankton Sioux, whom he had come to know from his patrols along the border, had answered the call of a *Shaganosh* redcoat.

Then Black Horn spotted Walsh and cantered ahead toward him. Reaching the redcoat officer, the Yankton war chief jumped down from his pony and threw his arms around Walsh, embracing him as a close friend.

"Ahh, White Forehead! I knew it was you from the description the Tetons gave me."

"Hello, Black Horn," Walsh replied through Leveille. "It is good to see you."

Black Horn looked around as Four Horns and the Hunkpapas approached. "Where is the man who said White Forehead is a long-knife? Let him come forward."

Four Horns sent some of his braves to bring forth the warrior from the south. They returned several minutes later, faces sombre. "He is gone. He must have left during the night."

Four Horns' brows drew together in a heavy frown, his black eyes glittering in sudden anger. "How could such a thing happen? I gave strict orders he was to be guarded!"

"It is just as well he is gone," Black Horn said. "If he had still been here, I would have demanded you bring him to me."

Black Horn put a hand on Walsh's shoulder. "My friends," he said in a deep, booming voice. "This man is White Forehead, chief of the redcoats. What he says is law this side of the big road. I came here prepared for war." He pointed to his painted and feathered warriors sitting with their ponies nearby. "Now I am glad to find it is not necessary. But I tell you— had one hair of White Forehead's head been harmed, your camp would not now be standing. The White Forehead's tongue is not crooked."

Four Horns stepped forward, his eyes meeting those of Walsh. Both men waited as the interpreter said, "I am sorry the White Forehead's words were doubted. On behalf of myself and my people, I pledge to obey your laws."

"Think no more of it, Four Horns," Walsh replied, Leveille repeating his words in the Lakota tongue. "But I am disappointed that you allowed that man to leave your camp. You must do better. The young men must obey the White Mother's laws and not commit any acts of war against her people or the Americans."

Four Horns nodded. "It will be done, White Forehead."

Chapter 9

Fearing No Evil

The Scout never forgot Walsh's bravery. Word of this feat travelled from camp to camp and was told over and over again by eyewitnesses. White Sioux [James Walsh] ... had won their highest respect.

Iris Allen in *White Sioux*, 1969

Walsh returned to his fort, but his stay there was short. Then he was in the saddle again, heading back to the border country of the lower White Mud with Sergeant Robert McCutcheon, three constables, Louis Leveille, and another scout, Gabriel Solomon. Scouts had reported more Sioux heading north from the Milk River. This time they were sure it was Sitting Bull.

Four Horns had told him Sitting Bull was still below the Missouri, but he'd had enough time to cover the distance from the Missouri by now. And with the possibility—indeed, the probability—that Colonel Miles was on his trail, Sitting Bull would have every reason to get across the line as soon as he could. The moccasin telegraph would have told him the redcoats were allowing the Sioux to cross, that the Sioux would find peace in the White Mother's land, that they could even get bullets to hunt the buffalo. That was far more inviting than what the Americans were giving their agency Indians.

This time Walsh wore his uniform as he left the fort. Even though the red coat dirtied all too readily on the trail, he wasn't going to wear buckskin and slouch hat and be taken for American cavalry again. Not with Sitting Bull. Walsh wanted the Sioux chief to know right away who he was dealing with.

The May weather was ideal for travelling, and in two days they reached the lower White Mud. After some time looking around, they

After the spirit had been allowed ample time to exit the body, the corpse would be taken from this perch and buried by the Sioux.

found signs where a large Indian camp had stood—fire pits, lodge rings, an abandoned blackened cooking pot, grass cropped by a large herd of ponies—and a fresh trail leading north. Near the campsite was a scaffolding—a wooden platform about six feet high supported by four willow saplings—and on the platform was the body of a dead Indian wrapped in a blanket. The platform stank of death in the warmth, and Leveille urged his reluctant cayuse alongside it, stood in his stirrups, and peered at the body. Reaching out, he pulled the blanket aside, studied the body for a moment, then covered it again before sitting back down on his saddle and allowing the horse to trot quickly away from it.

"Dead Sioux," he said. "Died a few days ago, look like. Died from bullet wounds."

They followed the trail until darkness forced them to stop and make camp for the night.

Next morning they were on the trail again, and after three hours of riding they found themselves among a maze of hills. A little farther on they spotted Indian lookouts on the hilltops ahead and they knew they were approaching a camp. The lookouts sat motionless on their ponies, watching them. This time there was no hand-signalling from one to another. This time there would be no mistaking them for U.S. Cavalry. The bright red coats of Walsh and his men left no doubt who they were.

They emerged onto a grassy flat with a wooded stream angling in from the northeast on their right, the Pinto Horse Butte just beyond. Ahead, no more than a half mile away, stood a large, semi-circular camp of buffalo-hide tepees spread across the grass, their conical shapes and crossed-pole frames outlined against the dun-coloured buttes in the background.

Reaching the edge of the camp, they reined in and swung down from their saddles. They had barely done so when several warriors appeared from among the tepees and strode toward them. Leading them was a magnificent looking Indian, bare-chested and muscular. Walsh recognized him instantly as Spotted Eagle, war chief of the Sans Arcs, who had crossed into Canadian territory with Black Moon and the first of the refugee Sioux last December.

Spotted Eagle stopped in front of Walsh and reached out to shake his hand. Walsh gripped the war chief's hand firmly. Spotted Eagle's eyes flickered to Leveille. "Tell the White Forehead it is good to see him again. Tell him this is the camp of *Tatanka Yotanki* [Sitting Bull]." The warrior made a gesture of respect. "This is the first time only a handful of *wasichu* soldiers have dared approach *Tatanka Yotanki*'s camp."

"Tell Spotted Eagle I am glad to see him again, Louis," Walsh replied. "Tell him I would like to meet Sitting Bull, that I have been sent by the Great White Mother's soldier chief to pass on her greetings and to talk about her laws."

Spotted Eagle introduced the warriors. Then he said, "Wait here, White Forehead. I will tell *Tatanka Yotanki* you are here. He will be pleased to meet you."

While Spotted Eagle left to carry Walsh's message to Sitting Bull, the warriors mixed with Walsh and his redcoats. Leveille and Solomon asked about the numbers of warriors, women, and children in the camp, how long they had been on the trail, the numbers and whereabouts of any more Sioux following. Indians appeared among the tepees and scores of brown faces—men, women, and children—stared at them and their red coats. All, however, kept their distance.

Soon Spotted Eagle reappeared from the centre of the camp, accompanied by an older Indian in his early to middle 40s, with several minor chiefs following behind. As they drew closer, Walsh's attention was drawn to the limp of the man beside Spotted Eagle. He was about five feet ten inches tall, bow-legged, with a muscular build, glittering black eyes, broad pock-marked face, prominent hooked nose, firm mouth. His black hair was parted in the middle in typical Sioux fashion, with two long braids hanging forward over his shoulders.

At the same time, Sitting Bull eyed the bright red tunics of the Mounties. Sergeant McCutcheon was standing a little apart from the others, and Sitting Bull, perhaps drawn by the three gold stripes and crown on his sleeve, veered toward him and shook hands with the surprised sergeant. Then Spotted Eagle pointed at Walsh, and Sitting Bull padded toward the officer. Spotted Eagle introduced them and they shook hands.

Sitting Bull's grip matched Walsh's in strength. The two men eyed each other for several seconds, Walsh looking into piercing black eyes that seemed to penetrate to the very depths of his soul.

"Tell Sitting Bull he and his people are welcome in the Great White Mother's country," Walsh said to Leveille, "but there are things they must know about living here."

Sitting Bull stared at Walsh's scarlet coat with its rich gold braid, the likes of which he had never seen before. When Leveille finished interpreting, Sitting Bull answered in a deep voice. "*Tatanka Yotanki* is happy to hear the Lakota are welcome in the White Mother's country. We want to know about living here."

"Perhaps we could all get together," Walsh replied, "and I can tell your chiefs and headmen about the Great White Mother's laws as well. Then they can tell your people."

"Yes," Sitting Bull agreed. "That is good, let us sit in the council lodge and you can talk to us."

They walked toward the centre of the camp and filed into a lodge much larger than any of the others. Buffalo robes were spread across the grass floor of the lodge, and Sitting Bull and his minor chiefs and headmen sat on the robes in a semi-circle, with Walsh and Leveille standing in front of them. Walsh began his speech, the same one he had given to Black Moon and Four Horns earlier. "There are laws in the White Mother's country that everyone must obey. Everyone is equal before the law, but anyone who breaks it—Indian or white man—will be punished."

As Walsh talked, the Sioux listened, with all eyes on the redcoat officer and his mixed-blood interpreter. Occasional murmurs of "*Washtay, washtay*" (it is good), greeted his words.

"You must obey the White Mother's laws if you want to stay in her country. You are safe here. The American soldiers will not cross the medicine line unless the White Mother's soldier chief invites them. But there is one thing you must understand. You cannot use the White Mother's country to go back and forth across the medicine line fighting the bluecoats. If you want to keep fighting, you must go back where you came from."

Sitting Bull stood up. "I buried my weapons before I crossed the medicine line. I will do no wrong in the land of the White Mother. If we do anything bad on the other side of the line, we will stay there. We will not come back here asking for protection. My heart is good except when I see a long-knife."

Sitting Bull reached into the front of his buckskin shirt and pulled out a gold medal suspended from a rawhide thong around his neck, holding it in front of him so Walsh could see the effigy of King George III. "Once the Lakota were *Shaganosh* Indians," Bull said. "A long time ago, our grandfathers fought for the White Mother's grandfather against the Americans. Our grandfathers fought beside *Shaganosh* soldiers who wore red coats." He pointed at Walsh's scarlet patrol jacket. "Coats red like yours. They were good men. They shared their food and tobacco with the Lakota. They treated the Lakota as brothers. When the fighting was over, the *Shaganosh* gave our country to the Americans. They did not tell the Lakota why they did this, but they said to our grandfathers that if we should ever want to find peace, to come north to the land of the redcoats. That is why we came. We are tired of fighting. We seek peace.

"For years the Americans pushed us around, from one place to another. They made treaties with us, but they broke the treaties whenever it suited them. They took away our sacred ancestral land in the Black Hills. They forgot that the land they pushed us from belonged to us. *Wainga Tanka* gave it to us. The White Father sent soldiers to force us onto reservations, but we did not want to go on reservations. The land was no good. The White Father had no right to do that. He sent *Pahuska* [Custer] against us, but we rubbed him out, and the long-knives who rode with him against us in the valley of the Greasy Grass [Little Bighorn]. But we knew that this was only one battle. The long-knives would never rest until they punished us for what happened, even though *Pahuska* carried the fight to us. If he had left us alone, there would have been no dead. *Pahuska* would be alive today."

Sitting Bull paused to collect his thoughts, then continued. "Yesterday I was fleeing from *wasichus*, cursing them as I went. Today they erect their lodges beside mine and defy me." He waved his arm at Walsh. "The White Forehead Chief walks to my lodge alone and unarmed. He gives me the hand of peace. This is a good thing. A new hope enters my heart. I am in another land, among *wasichus* different from any I have ever known—men of the White Mother who speak with honour. Have I fallen? Am I at the end?"

When Sitting Bull finished, other chiefs got up and spoke. Spotted Eagle told of the blue-coated soldiers who had harassed his people, never giving them time to rest or hunt. He sought only food and peace after being forced to seek safety in the land of the White Mother for the sake of the tribe's women and children. Others said they liked the idea of justice for all but found it difficult to understand why they should not be allowed to strike back at their American enemies across the line. What difference, they asked, should it make to the White Mother if they attacked the Americans? They would not be doing any harm to her or her people.

Walsh, however, was adamant—as he had been earlier with Black Moon and Four Horns—that they must never do this. As long as they remained in the White Mother's country, under her protection, there could never be any attempt to seek revenge south of the stone cairns.

The Sioux asked Walsh if they could be allowed bullets to hunt the buffalo. They had used their ammunition fighting off the long-knives, they said. Walsh knew he would have to allow them ammunition for hunting. He couldn't let Black Moon and Four Horns have ammunition and not allow Sitting Bull and his people the same privilege. He realized, though, after hearing Sitting Bull speak, that the Sioux chieftain held a deep and bitter hatred for the American soldiers, and that he might well be tempted to recross the line and strike back at them if he could obtain enough ammunition.

"Yes," Walsh replied, "but none of it is to go back across the medicine line. It will be allowed for hunting only. I must be assured that you will only use the bullets to hunt food. Only then will I let you have enough for hunting."

Sitting Bull repeated what he had already said, that he would do no wrong in the White Mother's country and that if he or any of his people crossed back to their own country and did wrong, they would not return to the White Mother's country seeking sanctuary.

After the speech-making had concluded, Sitting Bull said to Walsh, "You and your redcoats, you will eat with us ... yes?"

"We would be pleased to eat with you, Sitting Bull."

"And you will stay the night with us?"

"It will be an honour."

Sitting Bull smiled, seemingly touched that here were white men prepared to eat and sleep among his people.

The next morning, Walsh and his men were preparing to leave Sitting Bull's camp when three Indians from south of the border rode into the camp herding five horses.

"South Assiniboines from down along the Missouri, near Fort Buford," Leveille said, watching them. "The one in front, he is White Dog, the Assiniboine war chief. Sitting Bull offer him a hundred horses if he join the Sioux in the big fight with the soldiers last year."

Walsh watched the three South Assiniboines, who were quickly surrounded by Sioux. From the laughing and gesticulating going on, it was clear they were all friends. The Assiniboines seemed to be telling the Sioux about their journey across the prairie.

"T'ree of those horses they got," Gabriel Solomon said, inclining his head at the gathering a short distance away, "they stolen. They belong to that black-robe." Solomon glanced at Leveille. "You know the one, Louis ... Father de Corby. He been roaming around in the Cypress Hills. T'ree of those horse, they belong to him."

"Are you sure about that, Gabriel?" Walsh asked.

"Sure. I know those horses."

"You and Louis wander over there and take a good look."

The two scouts strolled over and joined the Sioux gathered around the three South Assiniboines to take a close look at the horses. They returned ten minutes later. Solomon nodded at Walsh. "T'ey the same ones ... the black-robe's."

"That right, my Major," Leveille added. "They bragging about how they run them off."

"Oh, they are, are they?" Walsh replied. He glanced at Sergeant McCutcheon. "Sergeant, take two of the men and go over and arrest White Dog. He's got to learn he can't cross into this country and break the law any damned time he feels like it."

Sergeant McCutcheon and two constables, accompanied by Solomon, walked over to where the three Assiniboines, surrounded by over 60 Sioux warriors, were still boasting about their exploits. Major Walsh continued saddling his horse.

"White Dog," Sergeant McCutcheon said through Solomon, interrupting the Assiniboine war chief, "you're under arrest for stealing horses."

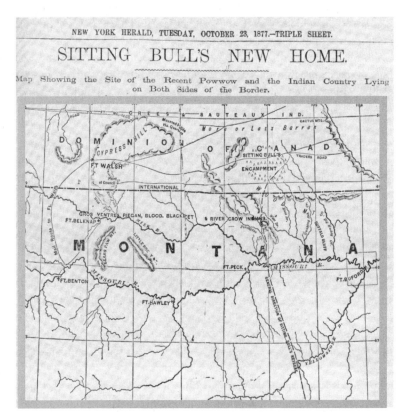

SITTING BULL'S NEW HOME.

The RCMP Museum in Regina retains this New York Herald *headline that "put Fort Walsh on the map" in 1877.*

White Dog looked astounded when the Métis scout translated the sergeant's words. Incredulous, he demanded to know why he was being arrested. He looked quickly around, obviously encouraged by the presence of the Sioux warriors around him, confident they wouldn't let these three *wasichus* in red coats take him.

By this time, Walsh had his horse saddled. Looking over at the gathering, he sensed that White Dog was not taking his arrest quietly. "What's going on over there, Louis?" he asked.

Leveille told him what he could hear of the conversation.

"Come on," Walsh said to Leveille and the remaining constable. "Bring the leg irons," he ordered the constable as he and Leveille started toward the gathered Indians. The constable reached into one of the saddle-bags, pulled out two pairs of leg irons, and ran after Walsh and Leveille.

Walsh pushed his way through the circle of Indians, Leveille and the constable behind him. White Dog was arguing with the sergeant.

Walsh clapped a hand on White Dog's shoulder. "You say you won't be arrested, nor will you give up the horses. White Dog, I arrest you for theft. Sergeant! Disarm these three Indians. They're all under arrest."

Sergeant McCutcheon and his two constables quickly disarmed the three South Assiniboines.

"Hand me a pair of those leg irons, Constable," Walsh said over his shoulder to the man behind him. The constable passed the leg irons to him. Walsh dangled them in front of White Dog's eyes. "Now tell me where you got those horses, how you got them, and what you intend doing with them, or I'll lock these on you and haul you back to Fort Walsh."

Silence descended over the entire camp as Leveille interpreted Walsh's words into language that everyone there understood clearly. All eyes were on the red-coated officer and the Assiniboine war chief. While Solomon and one of the constables separated the three stolen horses from the others, the Sioux warriors stood dumbfounded by the redcoats' cool courage. Some were ready to fight for their Assiniboine brothers, some stood undecided what to do, and others were prepared to see if the redcoats would carry out their threat to arrest the Assiniboines and take them away as prisoners.

White Dog looked around at the Sioux faces, seeking support, but all he saw was hesitation. Feeling defeat, he lost his cockiness and mumbled that he did not know it was wrong to take the horses. When travelling across the prairie it was the custom in the Milk and Missouri rivers country to take any horses found wandering loose and only return them if called upon by the owner to do so.

Walsh didn't believe him, but he decided to give him the benefit of the doubt. He was well aware of the plains tribes' fondness for running off other owners' horses, which was theft under the Queen's law, but the Mounted Police showed leniency to Indians, letting them off with stern warnings until they had learned that running off horses was against the law. He decided to warn White Dog and release him, although he would seize the horses and take them with him, returning them to the priest on the way back to Fort Walsh. He then lectured White Dog on obeying the law in the White Mother's country.

But defiance danced in White Dog's eyes. He had been deeply humiliated in front of the Sioux. Glaring at Walsh, he muttered, "I will meet you again."

Walsh caught the implication of White Dog's words. "What did he say, Louis?"

"He say he meet you again, my Major."

"Tell him to repeat those words, Louis."

When Leveille translated Walsh's demand, White Dog refused. But his bluff had been called again, and he was further humiliated before the Sioux.

"Withdraw what you said," Walsh ordered, holding the leg irons up in front of White Dog's face again, "or I'll clap these irons on you and take you back to Fort Walsh."

White Dog replied that he had not meant to make a threat. Again Walsh didn't believe him, but he decided to take no further action, and he let him go.

Walsh's purpose had been achieved. Sitting Bull and the Sioux had witnessed an example of British law. The Great White Mother's redcoats had not backed down. It would give Sitting Bull something to think about, Walsh believed.

Fifteen minutes later, Walsh and his men mounted up and rode out of Sitting Bull's camp. The string of stolen horses trotted with them. Walsh never looked back, but he sensed that hundreds of eyes were still on him.

Chapter 10

Teaching the Assiniboines a Lesson

> *Convey the government's appreciation to Inspector*
> *Walsh and those under his command for their*
> *courage and determination.*
> Secretary of State R.W. Scott to Major Irvine, June 1877

Chief Little Child stood in front of his lodge, one of fifteen Saulteaux tepees perched in a clearing beside a stand of fragrant birch and poplar on the rolling, grass-covered prairie at the foot of the northeastern slopes of the Cypress Hills. It was a warm, sunny day in late May 1877, and the small camp occupied a peaceful stretch of buffalo range. The only thing disturbing the tranquil morning was the approach of a noisy bunch of South Assiniboines. Little Child watched them uneasily.

Others of his band were equally concerned as they stood outside their lodges while the Assiniboines drew closer. Little Child glanced at his braves. Several were on the verge of fleeing for the temporary safety of the nearby trees.

Shaking rifles and war clubs, the shouting horsemen rode as though they were on the prowl for trouble, jogging up and down on their ponies as they trotted closer. There were 200 of them or more, seven times the number of Saulteaux braves.

Little Child looked like a leader. He was tall, muscular, handsome, and self-confident, not easily intimidated, but even he felt apprehension at the ominous appearance of the strangers in full war regalia.

Little Child knew several large bands of Sioux had crossed into the White Mother's country since the beginning of the last big cold. He had often felt that his small band might experience trouble if the Sioux proved belligerent. He had visited Fort Walsh to express his concern, but the redcoats had assured him they were in control of the country, that they would protect him and his people.

The Assiniboines looked as though they would ride right through the Saulteaux camp until the last moment, when their leader yanked on his reins and the whole band followed, skidding their ponies to a stop at the edge of the camp. Little Child recognized Crow's Dance, even under his war paint. For two days, Crow's Dance and his band had camped beyond a rise half a mile away. The prior afternoon he had come to Little Child with five or six others, haughtily proclaiming that he was forming a buffalo hunting camp and that all smaller camps in the area would have to hunt under his rules. "We are brothers of the mighty Lakota of Sitting Bull," Crow's Dance had boasted. Despite this clear attempt to intimidate the Saulteaux, Little Child hadn't shown any enthusiasm for the proposition. Now Crow's Dance had returned with his warriors to change the Saulteaux chief's attitude.

Crow's Dance legged his pony forward until its nose pushed past Little Child's head, its shoulder nudging his chest. The Assiniboine chief stared at Little Child.

"What answer does the little tribe chief give now?" Crow's Dance demanded.

"I am a British Indian standing on British soil," Little Child replied, looking back up at Crow's Dance unwaveringly. "The only chief I obey is the redcoat chief at the log fort in the Thunder Breeding Hills."

Crow's Dance sneered. "Hah! Redcoat chief? I care nothing for your redcoat chief! If I see him, I will cut out his heart and eat it."

Jeering and laughing, the Assiniboines edged their ponies closer. One warrior uttered a blood-chilling war cry, causing some of the Saulteaux to cower.

"So, you will not submit to my rules, hah?" Crow's Dance raised his arm, shaking his rifle. "Aiiiyeee!" he yelled, jabbing his heels hard against his pony's flanks. The startled animal jumped forward, knocking Little Child backwards. Leaning forward, Crow's Dance swung his rifle and struck Little Child in the face with the barrel.

Whooping wildly, the Assiniboines followed Crow's Dance's lead, kicking their ponies in among the Saulteaux lodges, pulling them down, scattering kettles, pots, and travois, and scooping up buffalo robes. Barking dogs snapped at the ponies' hoofs. The Assiniboines shot the dogs, killing nineteen.

The frightened Saulteaux scattered, running for the trees. Some of the Assiniboines fired rifle shots over their heads. Others stampeded the Saulteaux ponies.

By the late 1870s, camps of the Assiniboine, Sioux, or other plains tribes had the same look, and all were full of sombre, hungry faces dreading the forthcoming winter.

When they finished wreaking havoc and destruction, with not a Saulteaux lodge left standing, the Assiniboines—laughing and whooping—galloped back to their own camp.

* * *

Anger clouded Major Walsh's face as he sat in his office listening to Little Child tell his story. Also in the office were Sub-Inspectors McIllree and Allen, Sergeant-Major Francis, and Louis Leveille, who was interpreting Little Child's words. After retrieving his horses, Little Child had ridden 30 miles to Fort Walsh to protest the South Assiniboines' outright defiance of the White Mother's law.

In the Major's office, when Little Child came to the part where Crow's Dance had said he would cut out the redcoat chief's heart and eat it, Walsh leaned forward and said, "We'll see about that!"

Little Child didn't have to remind Walsh what the redcoats had told him when he visited the fort: that they would not tolerate behaviour of this sort. Walsh knew very well what the Mounted Police position was, what it had to be. Even though no one had been seriously injured, he couldn't afford to ignore this incident. The very foundation of the law the NWMP was responsible for enforcing throughout the North-West Territories was at stake. If he did not act, word would spread across the prairies like a grass fire. Outnumbered as they were, the Mounted Police routinely performed dangerous tasks with a mere handful of men, riding into Indian camps and arresting armed lawbreakers in the face of hundreds of volatile warriors. If any Mountie backed down even once, none of them would be able to carry out any of these duties again.

Walsh had another compelling reason not to ignore Little Child's complaint. Barely two weeks had passed since his visit to Sitting Bull's camp. Although the Sioux had promised to abide by Canada's laws, Walsh could not be sure they would keep their word. Crow's Dance and his followers were troublesome agency Indians from Montana's Bear Paw Mountains region, 100 miles south of Fort Walsh. If they were allowed to defy Canadian law, it would make a mockery of his words to Sitting Bull that the White Mother's law must be obeyed. News of swift and effective action against Crow's Dance would get back to the Sioux just as quickly and verify to them that the law was sacrosanct.

When Leveille finished interpreting Little Child's story, Walsh spoke to Sergeant-Major Francis. "Assemble a patrol, Sergeant-Major. Two NCOs and twelve men. Full service order, field rations for four days. I want to lead them out of here in 30 minutes."

"Very good, sir." Sergeant-Major Francis saluted and left the office.

Walsh glanced at Leveille. "Louis, take Little Child over to the "B" Troop kitchen and have the cook rustle him up some food. Then find him a fresh horse. I'll want him along to identify Crow's Dance."

Leveille led Little Child from the office.

Eyebrows raised, Sub-Inspector McIllree looked at Walsh. "Only fourteen men, sir? Will that be enough? The South Assiniboines won't have the respect for the scarlet tunic that our tribes have. They'll likely put up a fight."

"I mustn't strip the post if I can avoid it, John," Walsh said, meeting the Sandhurst graduate's questioning eyes. "I have to keep a full troop here in reserve in case the Sioux cause any trouble. If we get into anything we can't handle, I'll send a man back here posthaste and you can follow up with reinforcements."

Walsh turned to Sub-Inspector Allen. "Edwin, I want you to accompany me as second-in-command. And my compliments to Surgeon Kittson. I want him along as well. There could be casualties."

"Very good, sir."

* * *

A sergeant, a corporal, and twelve men filed out of the "B" Troop stables as a trumpeter in front of the orderly room raised his shiny instrument to his lips and sounded "Boot and Saddle." The trumpet's brassy notes blasted across the barrack square, conveying an air of urgency. The sergeant threw a hurried glance over his shoulder.

"On the double, men," he shouted, breaking into a run.

They lined up quickly in two ranks on the parade ground in front of the flagpole. Swinging up onto his saddle, the sergeant watched them dress ranks.

"Stand to your horses!"

Men drifted out of their log barracks and lined the edges of the parade ground, curious to know what was happening. No one had been told—not even the NCOs and men making up the patrol—and rumours caught hold even faster at Fort Walsh than they did at Fort Macleod. The one on most lips had Sitting Bull breaking his promise to Major Walsh and going on the warpath. Runners-up had the Cheyennes smashing through the lines of U.S. troops and fighting their way north to the Canadian border, or the unpredictable Cree chief Big Bear going on a rampage along the North Saskatchewan.

The sergeant bellowed the command: "Patrol! Prepare to mount ... Mount!"

With military precision, two lines of red-coated men pulled themselves up onto their saddles, gathered their reins, then rammed their carbines into leather buckets strapped to their saddles behind their right legs.

"Form ... patrol!"

The rear rank moved ahead to merge with the front rank, forming a single line facing the front.

"Patrol, right ... dress! Eyes ... front!"

The sergeant reined his horse around to face his front, waiting for the officers. He didn't have long to wait. Sub-Inspector Allen, followed by Surgeon John G. Kittson a horse's length behind, rode onto the parade ground. The sergeant and Allen exchanged salutes and the sergeant turned the patrol over to him, taking his place at the right of the patrol. They sat to attention, tall and straight, like proud scarlet centurions. Off to the left flank, poker-faced Louis Leveille slouched forward on his saddle beside Little Child. The two officers sat their saddles in front of the patrol, waiting for Major Walsh.

Walsh's orderly waited with the Major's horse in front of his office. The presence of the post surgeon on the patrol fuelled the rumours that were going around. Why the inclusion of a medical officer unless there was likely to be shooting and the possibility of wounded men?

A moment later Major Walsh appeared, pulling on his white gloves as he exchanged a few words with Sub-Inspector McIllree. Behind McIllree, Sergeant-Major Francis stood to attention, awaiting any last-minute orders. Someone spread word among the men watching from the edge of the parade ground that half of "E" Troop had been warned to stand-to on a moment's notice to ride out to assist Major Walsh's patrol should they be required.

Having finished his brief conversation with Sub-Inspector McIllree, Major Walsh stepped forward, took the reins from his orderly, and swung up onto his saddle. He trotted his horse over to the patrol and exchanged salutes with Sub-Inspector Allen. After running his eyes quickly over the patrol, he tersely told them what had happened, where they were going, and what he intended they would do.

Then Walsh shouted the command: "Patrol! From the right, form half-sections ... walk-march!"

He led them out through the front gates in a column of twos. The sentry saluted as Walsh rode by. Once they were beyond the stockade, the command to trot rang out.

Silence hung over the men inside the fort as they watched the patrol ride away. Some had been close enough to hear the Major's words, and only now were they realizing the seriousness of the situation.

The patrol trotted its horses past the scattering of log cabins, shanties, and tents that made up Fort Walsh village, 500 yards north of the fort. In the village, heads turned and tongues wagged as the patrol drummed by. The comings and goings of Mounted Police patrols were an everyday event, but a patrol of that size moving at a fast trot was cause for concern, especially when Major Walsh himself was leading it. The villagers saw that the Indian who had galloped into the fort an hour earlier was riding with them. These things added up to a sure sign of trouble somewhere, and it could only be Indian trouble!

A feeling of apprehension gripped the traders, storekeepers, billiard hall keeper, gamblers, laundresses, wolfers, and other occupants of the village. Most of them had drifted in from Fort Benton. They lived within the shadow of Fort Walsh, where they were afforded some degree of protection, but they knew there were already enough Sioux between the Cypress Hills and Wood Mountain to wipe out the relatively small force of Mounted Police. If there was one thing they didn't want, it was more Indians from below the line.

The patrol rode north along the valley for a short distance, then swung up into the hills and headed northeast. The only sounds were the

Senior Surgeon John Kittson (inset) nursed the men marching west across the burnt prairie in 1873, and within his first year had countered outbreaks of typhoid, "prairie cholera" accompanied by unrelenting diarrhoea and syphilis. Dr. Kittson (right) poses with Miss Graham, the first white woman to visit Fort Walsh, and his groom (left).

jingle of bits, the creak of saddle leather, and the drumming of horses' hoofs on the ground. Walsh sensed a growing exhilaration as the wind in the men's faces and the co-ordinated power of the horses took their effect. The animals smoothly carried their riders at a canter over the green-grassed hills dotted with groves of spruce and jackpine, interspersed with clumps of aspen and poplar.

Near sundown, as they rode onto a sweep of gently sloping ground, they came upon a herd of 60 buffalo grazing their way slowly northward. Hearing the approaching horses, the wary bulls formed a protective circle around the cows and calves, lowering their massive heads, horns jutting menacingly forward. As the patrol detoured around them, Walsh's mind flashed back to that great march when the Mounted Police rode into the west. He remembered the first mighty herd of buffalo. Colonel Macleod was so impressed by them that he recommended the buffalo head be featured on the NWMP badge.

By eleven o'clock that night, May 25, they reached the Saulteaux camp. Riding down from the hills, they saw by moonlight the paler smudge of tepee shadows against the trees in a shallow basin below.

Hearing approaching hoofbeats, figures slipped out of the tepees, fearing the possibility of another visit from the South Assiniboines, ready to run for the trees. Little Child called out to them. Walsh could hear the relief in their voices as they replied.

Little Child pulled his horse to a stop beside the tepees and jumped to the ground. The Saulteaux crowded around him, relieved to see him with the redcoats. Excited babble broke out among them. After several minutes, Little Child pushed through them and spoke to Leveille. The scout turned to Walsh.

"They say Assiniboine camp move, my Major."

"Let's have a look where they were camped," Walsh replied, glancing up at the moon. There was enough light for them to pick up the Assiniboine trail.

They rode over the rise and Little Child showed them where the Assiniboine camp had been. Walsh and the patrol waited on their horses while Leveille and Little Child studied the ground in the moonlight. After several minutes, eyes glued to the ground as he circled out from the abandoned campsite, Leveille found what he was looking for.

"There it is," he said, pointing. Furrows made by tepee poles dragged by ponies, together with countless pony tracks, left a trail readily seen by moonlight.

With Leveille and Little Child out in front, the patrol pushed its tiring horses northward. They rode for an hour, then Walsh called a halt. Unsaddling their horses and giving them a rub-down and a feed, they rested for the next hour before saddling up again and resuming their pursuit of the Assiniboines. Long fingers of grey and crimson began streaking the eastern sky when Leveille and Little Child, scouting ahead, sighted the camp. They cantered back to the oncoming patrol and reported to Walsh.

Leaving Sub-Inspector Allen in charge of the patrol, Walsh rode ahead with Leveille and Little Child to a lone hill on the broken prairie. Walsh and Leveille dismounted and climbed to the crest, leaving Little Child with their horses. Fringed by young cottonwoods, the Assiniboine camp was spread across a wide plateau, with a quiet stream flowing gently along one side. In the emerging dawn, some 250 lodges stood silent as a graveyard. Nothing moved other than grazing ponies and a hazy column of smoke spiralling up from the smouldering remains of a large fire.

"Judging by the number of lodges down there," Walsh said, studying the camp through his binoculars, "I'd say there's a hell of a lot more warriors than the 200 Little Child estimated. More like 300, perhaps even 400, wouldn't you say, Louis?"

Leveille nodded. "I would say so, my Major."

"No guards or lookouts from what I can see," Walsh went on, sweeping the binoculars around the camp. "Pretty damned sure of themselves. It's about time they learned that there's law and order on this side of the line." He handed the binoculars to Leveille.

"That smoke coming from the middle of the camp," Leveille said after a moment, "look like been big ceremonial fire. Prob'ly had big war dance. Fire hasn't been out long. Must've danced all night. Now they sleep. That big lodge closest to smoke ... the purple and yellow one ... that's the sacred war lodge. Crow's Dance ... he be inside. Him and the headmen and their favourite bucks."

"Good. That'll make it easier. At least the ones we want—or most of them—will be together. If they're still asleep when we ride into that camp, we might be able to take them by surprise."

Leveille passed the binoculars back to Walsh. Turning his attention away from the camp, Walsh glassed the surrounding prairie. He soon found what he was looking for. "See that butte over there?" he said, pointing.

Looking where Walsh pointed, Leveille saw the butte off to the right, about 100 feet high, jutting up out of the prairie half a mile from the Assiniboine camp. A small silvery blue lake lay beside it. "Yes, my Major, I see it."

"We'll use that as a place to fall back on after we've made the arrests." He slipped the binoculars into the pouch on his shoulder belt. "Let's return to the patrol."

Bellying back from the brow of the hill, they rose and quickly climbed down to the prairie below, where Little Child waited with their horses. They cantered back to the patrol. Walsh called them to gather around.

"The Assiniboine camp is about 2½ miles ahead," he said. "It's bigger than we were led to believe. Probably contains about 400 potentially hostile warriors, not 200 as I was first told."

The men glanced uneasily at one another.

"There's no denying the possibility of danger," Walsh continued. "But we're going into that camp to make the necessary arrests. It's still early and it looks as though they're all asleep. We'll try to surprise them. We'll make the arrests, then get out of there as fast as we can. It's essential you all pay strict attention to orders and carry them out promptly." His eyes swept the faces in front of him. "Any questions?"

There were none.

Walsh's eyes moved to Surgeon Kittson, standing beside Sub-Inspector Allen. "Doctor, there's a butte half a mile from the camp. We'll use it as a rallying point. I want you to set up a position there. Take two men. There's loose rock around the base. Get them busy building a defensive breastwork for us to fall back on when we leave the camp. Prepare to attend to any wounded."

Walsh glanced at Leveille. "Go with the doctor, Louis."

Leveille opened his mouth to protest. He didn't want to be separated from Walsh, but one look at Walsh's face told him the Major's mind was made up.

Walsh handed him his binoculars. "From up on top of that butte, you should be able to see what's happening in the camp. I want you to stand by to ride back to Fort Walsh for help as fast as you can if it looks as though we're going to be in any trouble we can't handle."

Then he ordered, "All right, men. Mount up."

They covered the distance quickly, while Surgeon Kittson, Leveille, and two men detoured to the butte.

The only sound in the camp was the barking of a dog and the drumming hoofs as the police horses cantered in among the buffalo-hide tepees. Straight to the war lodge they rode, scarlet tunics vivid in the early morning sunlight. Bridle bits jingled as Walsh signalled them to halt in front of the big purple-and-yellow war lodge.

When he gave the signal to dismount, leather creaked as riders swung down from their saddles. "Horse holders, take the horses," Walsh commanded quietly. "Corporal, you and two men stand by in front of the war lodge to secure whatever prisoners we pass out. Sergeant, take three men and surround the lodge. Pull up the pegs and go in under the sides. Remainder, follow me."

With quick, energetic steps, Walsh reached the war lodge entrance, Sub-Inspector Allen and Little Child immediately behind him. While Walsh pulled back the covering flap and peered inside, the sergeant took his three men and ran to encircle the lodge, bending down to work the tepee pegs loose, then lifting the sides and crawling under. As they did, Walsh and the others filed in through the entrance. In less than a minute, redcoats lined the inside of the war lodge.

More than two dozen copper-hued bodies, still in their war paint, lay sleeping on buffalo robes spread across the grass floor. The sounds of snoring assailed the policemen's ears. Stench from foul emissions and dried sweat filled the lodge. None of the sleeping Assiniboines stirred.

Recognizing Crow's Dance, Little Child pointed. Walsh stepped across sprawled bodies, leaned over the snoring Assiniboine chief, and hauled him to his feet, hustling him out through the entrance into the arms of the waiting corporal. At the same time, Sub-Inspector Allen and a constable gathered all the weapons they could find.

Little Child pointed to another Assiniboine, Crooked Arm. The sergeant pulled the startled Crooked Arm to his feet, pushing him toward the entrance. Little Child pointed to others. Quickly the redcoats dragged them to their feet and trundled them over to the entrance. Everything was happening very quickly, and a series of vivid images remained in their minds long after it was all over—brown bodies slashed with red or yellow or black war paint, red coats and yellow-striped blue breeches, shining brass cartridges in polished leather belts, buffalo robes kicked around the lodge, startled bloodshot eyes staring up at them, a trooper cursing as he stooped to pick up a pair of handcuffs he'd dropped, a buffalo-hide war shield and tasselled lance hanging from a lodgepole, painted symbols on the war lodge walls. They heard the urgency in Major Walsh's voice. "Any others?"

Sudden hate flared in Little Child's eyes as he glanced around the now largely empty war lodge once more. He pointed to another Assiniboine warrior.

"Take him too," Walsh ordered.

It was over within minutes. Crow's Dance and 21 astonished Assiniboines stood handcuffed together outside the war lodge. But now pandemonium swept the camp as the rest of the Assiniboines realized there were intruders in their midst. Warriors' shouts mixed with the shrill screeching of Indian women. Camp dogs scampered backwards and forwards, yapping noisily, snapping at the heels of the police.

Walsh shouted above the din. "Mount up!"

The men needed no encouragement, grabbing their horses and swinging up onto their saddles. Scarlet figures on prancing horses swung around in half-sections. Dust swirled up from beneath iron-shod hoofs as horses wheeled and turned. The patrol marched out of the camp as quietly as it had entered, only this time herding Crow's Dance and 21 handcuffed prisoners.

* * *

From the top of Kittson's butte, Leveille could see the Assiniboine camp through Walsh's binoculars. He could see the patrol exiting the camp and heading towards the butte, the prisoners shuffling along behind. Two more redcoats trailed, making sure none got loose. He could see Walsh riding alongside the patrol, ensuring they all got safely out of the camp, that there were no stragglers. The Assiniboines in the camp seemed frozen by anger or confusion.

Leveille's face relaxed. His Major was unhurt, safe—at least for the moment. He scrambled down to the foot of the butte to rejoin Surgeon Kittson and the two men as they worked, dragging rocks into place to complete a breastwork around the butte's base. The lake, rippled by a prairie breeze, protected it from the rear.

As the patrol reached the butte minutes later, Surgeon Kittson looked up from what he was doing, ran his eyes over them quickly, and said, "All back unscathed, I see."

"We're not finished yet, Doctor," Walsh replied. Reining his horse around to face his men, he ordered, "Patrol—dismount! Get the horses under cover behind the butte. Mr. Allen, detail the men to help complete that breastwork. The prisoners, too—they can help. Then position the men behind the breastwork ready for action."

Under the direction of Sub-Inspector Allen, men and prisoners carried rocks from where they lay scattered on the ground and placed them on the growing improvised defensive wall. Every so often a trooper looked across the half mile of grassed prairie between the butte and a low rise that hid the Assiniboine camp just below. The sounds of warriors yelling war whoops and women screeching encouragement at them carried across the morning air. Occasionally a rifle shot cracked out from the camp, the first shot startling one or two of the men working on the breastwork. Then the beating of a rawhide war drum started. The climbing sun shone down on the men as they worked.

Standing behind the breastwork, Walsh watched the approach from the camp. Beside him, Leveille listened intently, trying to catch anything he could of what the Assiniboines were shouting in the camp. Surgeon Kittson knelt on the ground, laying out his shining surgical instruments on a white towel spread on top of a medical saddle-bag. Beside them he placed a bottle of antiseptic, field dressings, and rolls of bandages.

"They're working themselves into an attacking mood," Leveille said.

A short time later, the noise from the camp died down. Having moved all the loose rocks they could get their hands on to build up the breastwork, the men stared expectantly in the direction of the camp. Sub-Inspector Allen positioned them along the defensive wall, standing behind the rocks where they could, kneeling where the rocks weren't as high, their single-shot .577 calibre Snider-Enfield carbines pointing in the direction of the camp. Tension building, they waited.

Not long after, a sudden outbreak of war whoops rose into the air, and a few minutes later hundreds of Assiniboine warriors surged over the rise and poured toward the butte, some on ponies, others on foot.

The handful of Mounties facing them wrestled with their individual emotions as the yelling Assiniboines streamed forward. They were vastly outnumbered—25 to 1—and even behind their rock wall it would be a long time to hold off the Assiniboines before any sort of help could get to them. They would be lucky if reinforcements reached them before nightfall—if their ammunition lasted that long, which was doubtful. And Leveille hadn't even left for Fort Walsh yet.

"Hold your fire, men," Sub-Inspector Allen ordered. "Wait for the command."

When the Assiniboines were no more than 200 yards away, Walsh said to Leveille, "Tell them that's far enough, Louis. If they come any closer, I'll give the order to open fire."

Upon hearing Leveille's shouted warning, the Assiniboines stopped. The whooping and yelling died down, then one of them called out to the redcoats.

"They want to talk, my Major," Leveille said.

"Good," Walsh replied. "Let's go talk to them. Take command while I'm gone, Mr. Allen." Then he climbed over the breastwork, Leveille's tall, spare frame beside him.

Without hesitation, Walsh strode toward the Assiniboines. At the same time, three of the Assiniboines advanced to meet him. Both parties stopped within 30 yards of each other, and one of the Assiniboines, who identified himself as a chief, called out to Walsh.

"He want to know why you come to their camp and take Crow's Dance and the others," Leveille said.

"The Lakota call me the White Forehead," Walsh had Leveille call back. "I am chief of the Great White Mother's redcoats at the log fort at Cypress Mountain. We enforce the law on this side of the medicine line. You have crossed the medicine line into the White Mother's country. Crow's Dance and the others broke the law by tearing down the Saulteaux camp, striking the Saulteaux chief, and killing their dogs. That is why we took them from your camp. We are taking them back to the log fort, where they will be judged for breaking the law."

"We tried to stop them," the Assiniboine chief said, "but we couldn't. They would not listen to us."

"They should have listened," Walsh said. "What they did was bad."

"What will happen to them?"

"Those found guilty will be punished. They will be locked up in the log fort."

There was an angry outburst from one of the Assiniboines when Leveille interpreted Walsh's words.

Walsh shouted for silence. "In the White Mother's country, everyone must obey her laws. No one is above the law. If white men had done this, the same would happen to them. Worse—they would be dealt with more severely because there would be no doubt that they knew very well how wrong it is to behave like that. No man will be punished for something he did not do. If any of your people are found innocent, they will be released."

"If you let Crow's Dance and the others go," the Assiniboine chief pleaded, "we promise to obey the White Mother's laws."

Walsh shook his head. "It's too late for that. The law has already been broken. Our Indians who obey the law have suffered because of the actions of Crow's Dance and those who followed him. Now Crow's Dance and the others must be taken to the redcoats' fort to answer for what they did."

There was another angry outburst, this time from two of the Assiniboines. "There are only a few of you. We can attack you and easily kill every one of you."

"That would only result in a lot of blood being spilled," Walsh told them. "A lot of you will be killed. You might kill me, but Crow's Dance and the others will be killed. More redcoats will come, and any of you left alive will be punished for your foolish talk and foolish actions. The White Mother's laws will still be enforced. The wisest thing for all of you is to return to your lodges and behave yourselves. Crow's Dance and the others will be treated fairly. I've already told you that. Any of those judged not guilty will be released."

The three Assiniboines discussed these words of White Forehead. One angrily urged an immediate attack on the redcoats, but the chief and the other Assiniboine argued for restraint, clearly fearing the ultimate consequences of their actions.

"If you will not let Crow's Dance go, will you let our young men go?" the Assiniboine chief asked. "If they did wrong, it was because they acted foolishly and only did what they saw the older ones doing."

* * *

Carbines still pointing across the top of the breastwork, the Mounties watched the Assiniboines gathered on the prairie 200 yards away. Some of the Assiniboines sat on their ponies, others stood bunched in small groups, yet others sat on the ground, rifles resting across their knees as they watched and waited.

Alongside the butte, Major Walsh sat on a saddle on the stony ground within the protective wall of rocks. Beside him sat Sub-Inspector Allen, writing on a notepad the answers Little Child gave Leveille in reply to Major Walsh's questions. In front of the Major, guarded by the corporal and a constable, stood several of the younger Assiniboine prisoners, handcuffed to one another.

Adhering to a rule of law, Major Walsh had made a concession to the Assiniboine chief. He was holding a preliminary hearing into the actions of the younger braves who had followed their war chief's example in intimidating the Saulteaux, tearing down their camp, and stampeding their ponies. If he found there was not enough evidence to convict any one of them in a court of law, he would release them. It was a procedure he would have had to follow at Fort Walsh anyway. The concession was to hold the preliminary hearing then and there. It was a wise move on Walsh's part, demonstrating to the Assiniboines the fairness of redcoat justice.

Less than an hour later, Walsh again met the Assiniboine chief out in front of the butte. This time he and Leveille took nine of the younger prisoners with them.

"Here are your young men," Walsh said to the Assiniboine chief. "I have questioned Little Child and I'm satisfied they were led on by Crow's Dance and the older warriors. So I'm letting them off, as you asked, with a warning to behave themselves in future. But I'm taking Crow's Dance, Crooked Arm, Bear's Down, and ten of the older ones—who should have known better—to the log fort at Cypress Mountain. They broke the law and must answer for it. I warn you: if any of you try to stop us or to interfere in any way, Crow's Dance and the others will be shot. It'll be a long journey to the fort. You can make it easier for them by bringing their horses for them to ride, or you can let them walk. I don't care which, but they'll have to keep up with us one way or the other. Are you going to bring their horses?"

The Assiniboine chief sent some braves back to the camp to bring the prisoners' horses.

"Now go back to your camp," Walsh said in parting. "Don't try to follow us. I don't want to hear of anything like this happening again. If I do, I'll be back. I'll come after you, wherever you go. If I have to come back, I'll bring more redcoats with me next time."

To the relief of all back at Fort Walsh, the gates were swung open at eleven o'clock that night to allow Major Walsh and his tired but triumphant patrol, with their Assiniboine prisoners, to ride through.

Chapter 11

Emissaries from America

*I was particularly struck with Sitting Bull ... short
stature but with a pleasant face, a mouth showing
great determination and a fine high forehead.
When he smiled, as he often did, his face brightened
up wonderfully.*

A.G. Irvine in correspondence, 1877

The day after Major Walsh and his patrol returned to Fort Walsh, Major
A.G. Irvine, the force's new assistant commissioner—who had arrived
from Fort Macleod during Walsh's absence—sat in his ex officio role as
a magistrate and tried Crow's Dance, Crooked Arm, and the other eleven
Assiniboine prisoners.

After considering the evidence, Irvine dismissed the charges against
nine of the Assiniboines, but convicted Crow's Dance, Crooked Arm, and
two others. He sentenced Crow's Dance to six months' imprisonment with
hard labour in the Fort Walsh guardroom, Crooked Arm to two months,
and two of the headmen to three months and one month respectively.

Afterwards, Irvine wrote a report to Secretary of State R.W. Scott in
Ottawa, commending Inspector Walsh for his prompt conduct in the arrests
of Crow's Dance and the others, and adding that the actions of the patrol
would have a great effect on all the Indians in the west. Irvine pointed out
that it was a matter worthy of congratulations that such a small number of
Mounted Police could ride into a large Indian camp and take thirteen of its
leading warriors as prisoners. The Secretary of State duly replied, asking
Irvine to convey the government's appreciation to Walsh and those under
his command for their courage and determination in carrying out the arrests.

It was more than coincidence that Major Irvine happened to be at
Fort Walsh at that particular time. Colonel Macleod had sent him to the
Cypress Hills to talk to the Blackfoot, who had moved down that way in

search of buffalo. The Blackfoot and the Sioux were hereditary enemies, despite Sitting Bull's earlier overtures asking for their help in his war against the Americans. The buffalo had been none too plentiful in 1877 in the country in which the Blackfoot, Bloods, and Peigans hunted, and these tribes were moving eastwards in search of the herds. None of the Canadian tribes—the Blackfoot alliance, the Cree, Saulteaux, or the North Assiniboines—would welcome the Sioux intrusion onto their hunting grounds. Nor would the Métis, who also depended upon the buffalo for food and other necessities. Colonel Macleod was anxious that none of these warlike groups should get too close to the Sioux. The last thing he or the government wanted was tribal clashes. He had, therefore, instructed Irvine to impress upon the Blackfoot alliance tribes the Great White Mother's concern that there be no fighting among her children.

Although indiscriminate slaughter by Indians and whites (whites because of the trade in buffalo hides, which were in demand in the east for overcoats, blankets, floor rugs, and other cold-weather items) on both sides of the international boundary was drastically reducing the size of the once plentiful herds, the Canadian government in 1876 had estimated there were enough buffalo to feed its western Indians for another five years. Now, however, with some 5,000 additional buffalo-eating Indians on Canadian soil, that estimate had been revised. It was unlikely the buffalo would last any longer than half that time. The Canadian Indians would quickly notice the growing shortage—if they hadn't already noticed it—and they would just as quickly blame the Sioux. This would add to the long-standing enmity between them, which could lead to intertribal battles. Such warfare could spill over onto the American frontier as well. The sparsely staffed Mounted Police would be hard pressed to stop it. Little wonder Colonel Macleod was concerned.

In a report dated May 30, 1877, to Prime Minister Alexander Mackenzie, Macleod stated what he thought the government's stance on the Sioux question should be. Macleod was a compassionate but practical man. He believed the Sioux should be persuaded to return to their own country and that the United States government would be glad to secure their return. For one thing, the presence of so many Sioux just north of the border would be a source of continual anxiety for the Americans, who would fear the Indians might take it into their heads to strike back, especially as the Mounted Police didn't have the manpower to stop them. He also believed the Sioux would become a burden on the Canadian government because of the growing shortage of buffalo and the trouble of various kinds this would cause. Macleod firmly believed that it was the growing concentration of various tribes from the Cypress Hills to Wood Mountain that could prove to be his Achilles heel.

Discussing these matters with Walsh, Major Irvine passed on Macleod's instructions that the police outpost that had been established under Sergeant Alexander R. Macdonell at Wood Mountain after the arrival of Black Moon and the first of the Sioux refugees in December 1876 be increased to a strength of 20, and that Walsh personally move down there to take charge while the Sioux question remained unsettled. This would allow him to keep a closer watch over the Sioux and to influence their conduct to a greater degree than he could from Fort Walsh. During Walsh's absence, Inspector Crozier, commanding "F" Troop at Fort Calgary, would return to Fort Walsh and take his place.

Major Irvine also mentioned that he would talk to the Blackfoot and also visit Sitting Bull while he was in that part of the country. He would tell the Sioux leader to keep his people clear of the Blackfoot during buffalo hunts. He also intended to talk with him about matters generally and ascertain how long he planned on remaining in Canada.

Walsh might have wondered why Major Irvine would go to the trouble of interviewing Sitting Bull, going over the same ground he himself went over less than a month before. What did Irvine hope to prove? Too much contact with different senior Mounted Police officers might confuse Sitting Bull. It might also weaken Walsh's influence over him. Walsh felt he had done a good job of handling Sitting Bull, and all the Sioux for that matter, but he sensed that Irvine was meddling with his command and he resented it. There was irony in the situation. James Walsh had just returned from an Assiniboine camp of 400 warriors with thirteen headmen in tow. This superhuman result and his apparent ability to overcome staggering odds made him the logical choice to personally try and maintain peace in Sioux country against even greater odds. But he might also have seen his temporary transfer as a demotion to isolation with a command less than a quarter the size of Fort Walsh. The surprise imposition of his new posting no doubt increased Walsh's suspicions about the politics of his job. Now both he and Sitting Bull shared a common distrust—both had been run off "their land."

✳ ✳ ✳

Although Major A.G. Irvine was an efficient officer of unquestioned courage, he and James Walsh were cut from different cloth. Irvine had been promoted to assistant commissioner from the rank of inspector

An unidentified groom, Dr. John G. Kittson, Colonel James F. Macleod, and Sub-Inspector Edmund Dalrymple Clark are pictured here in regular duty uniforms, probably taken at Fort Walsh in 1877. Word of Sitting Bull's pending arrival led Macleod to redeploy many of his men from Fort Macleod to the Cypress Hills.

almost a year and a half earlier, in January 1876, at a time when he was junior to Walsh by almost a year. Both his lineage and his recent history may have had something to do with the rapid ascent.

Born at Quebec City on December 7, 1837, Acheson Gosford Irvine's grandfather was the Honourable James Irvine, long a member of the executive and legislative councils of Lower Canada. His father was a distinguished soldier, who was assigned to accompany the Prince of Wales (later King Edward VII) on his visit to Canada in 1860. After young Irvine studied civil engineering, he briefly went into the lumber business before attending military school at Kingston and joining the militia, where he held the rank of lieutenant. Unlike his fellow officer Major Walsh, who had opted out of the Wolseley expedition to the Red River, Irvine had gone west as major of the Quebec Battalion of Rifles. Following the end of the Métis insurrection, Irvine was given command of the military garrison at Fort Garry, twenty miles upriver from where the first NWMP assembled and trained at Lower Fort Garry. In his charge was a battalion of infantry and a regimental staff consisting of 20 officers and 244 NCOs and men. After disbandment of the garrison, he was called to Ottawa, commissioned an inspector in the North West Mounted Police on May 7, 1875, and assigned responsibility for bringing to justice the perpetrators of the Cypress Hills massacre of 1873. He was successful in this, arresting the men at Fort

Major A.G. Irvine became James Walsh's immediate superior in 1875 and was in regular contact with Walsh during the Sitting Bull years. Over time he came to share much of Walsh's perspective, but written documents suggest he fuelled the negative impression Ottawa developed towards Walsh.

Benton, but they were subsequently discharged by an American extradition hearing, which found there was insufficient evidence against them.

A slight man with keen grey eyes and a quiet, earnest manner, Irvine had a reddish spade beard that made him look older than his 39 years. He was a diplomat, a conciliator, a man who could contain himself when such was politically smart. He was nicknamed "Irvine the good," possibly a double-entendre and surely a testament to his character. Corporal John George Donkin, a former British soldier who served in the North West Mounted Police from 1884 to 1888—eighteen months of that service while Irvine was commissioner—described him in his book *Trooper and Redskin in the Far North-West* as "one of the most thorough gentlemen who I have ever had the honour to serve under."

Walsh had first met him in 1875, when Irvine passed through Fort Walsh while escorting two more of the Cypress Hills killers, who had been arrested on Canadian soil, to Winnipeg for trial. The next time Walsh saw him, he had to salute him as his superior officer.

✳ ✳ ✳

On the eve of Major Irvine's departure from Fort Walsh to carry out Colonel Macleod's orders, six Sioux warriors rode in with word that three Americans had turned up in Sitting Bull's camp. The three claimed to be acting on behalf of the United States government and were trying to persuade the Sioux to return to their own country and surrender to the army. One of the three was a "black-robe"—a priest; one said he was Colonel Miles's chief scout; and the third was a Métis interpreter. Sitting Bull had sent his warriors to tell Major Walsh, adding that his young men all wanted to kill the three, but he had given his word to refrain from killing and was holding the three for the Mounted Police.

Edmund Dalrymple Clark, seated in front of A.G. Irvine and James Macleod (center row), had a short, tragic career. The nephew of Sir John A. Macdonald, Clark earned the wrath of Commissioner French less than three weeks into the march west. He was blamed for an imbalance in provisions and dismissed as quartermaster. After French's departure, Clark thrived as the popular adjutant at Fort Macleod. In 1879, the year he achieved the rank of superintendent, Clark picked up a fatal fever at Fort Walsh and died in 1880.

The next morning, Major Irvine and Sub-Inspector Edmund Dalrymple Clark, the adjutant recently arrived from Fort Macleod, started for Sitting Bull's camp at the Pinto Horse Butte, accompanying Major Walsh, Sub-Inspector Allen, and a small escort as well as the six Sioux warriors. They reached the Sioux camp at noon the next day.

As they rode into the camp, Indians emerged from their lodges. They gave the redcoats a warm welcome, the men shaking hands with the Mounties as they rode by. Irvine later recalled some shaking his hand so heartily they almost pulled him off his horse. He was struck by the size of the warriors, whom he described as "tremendously big men." Men, women, and children surrounded them. The children were frightened of the *wasichus* at first, but after Irvine smilingly chucked one or two under the chin, they lost their fear and became quite friendly.

Walsh introduced Irvine to Sitting Bull, who invited the redcoats to eat with him. After the meal, Indians and redcoats entered the big red-and-black council lodge, where buffalo robes were again spread on the grass floor, the redcoats sitting in front of Sitting Bull. Behind the Sioux chieftain were his lesser chiefs and his bodyguard, muscular warriors who stood naked except for breechclouts and moccasins. Many carried scalps at their belts, taken from soldiers at the Little Bighorn. Each was armed with a U.S. Army carbine. Indians packed the lodge. Hundreds more gathered outside. The sides of the lodge were rolled up to allow air to circulate and so the people outside could hear what was being said.

The proceedings opened with due ceremony. One of the chiefs said a prayer to *Wainga Tanka*, than a redstone peace pipe with an elaborately carved stem was lit and passed around among Sitting Bull and his chiefs and the redcoat officers.

In speeches Sioux emphasized that they were originally British Indians who had fought for the White Mother's grandfather, and they produced more medals awarded to their grandfathers as proof of this. The Americans had given them little peace, they said, and had driven them from one place to another, breaking treaties, attacking their camps, and killing their women and children. They had come to the White Mother's country seeking peace. They hoped she would give them sanctuary in her land and protect them from the Americans.

They spoke bitterly of the three Americans who had come to their camp. The foremost of these, the Right Reverend Father Martin Marty, an abbot of the Benedictine Order who had instituted schools on the Indian agencies in Dakota, spoke the Lakota tongue fluently. The other two were Colonel Nelson Miles's scout John Howard and William Halsey, an agency interpreter. They carried letters from the Catholic Church and the U.S. Commission of Indian Affairs and had been sent to talk to the Sioux and try to persuade them to return to their own country. Walsh had foreseen something such as this happening and had spoken to Sitting Bull about it, gaining his promise that if any Americans came to his camp to talk to him about returning, he would not kill them but would hold them for the redcoats. Given the fact that Miles's forces had attacked Sitting Bull's people at the end of his last powwow with the bluecoats, the Sioux chief had displayed significant restraint. The scout and the interpreter would have surely been put to death had it not been for Sitting Bull's pledge to Walsh, and the same fate would likely have befallen Father Marty, whose claim that he didn't know he was in Canada cast suspicion on his integrity.

Now Sitting Bull said to Father Marty, "You knew that the long-knives were trying to kill us. Why did you wait until half my people were killed before you came? Why should I return to the White Father's country only to give up my weapons and my horses?"

Irvine addressed Sitting Bull and his people, saying much that Walsh had already told them. "Now that you are in the White Mother's country, you must not cross over the boundary line to fight the Americans, then come back here. We will allow you bullets so you can hunt the buffalo for food, but none of these bullets are to be used against white men or other Indians. You see only a few of us, but the White Mother has a mighty army that she can send out here if she has to, and if her children do wrong she will punish them. You were wise in telling us that the three Americans had come to your camp. We started out at once, as soon as your messengers told us. I will take them out of your camp. We will protect you from anyone who comes here. The Americans cannot cross the line after you. You and your families are safe in the Queen's country. You can sleep soundly and not be afraid."

The redcoats pitched their tents among the Sioux lodges after the meeting was over, and the officers ate their evening meal in Major Irvine's tent with Father Marty as guest. Afterwards the redcoats mixed with the Indians, and Irvine's adjutant, Sub-Inspector Clark, strolled alone through the camp. He wrote: "I never saw such a happy people. Sounds of rejoicing were heard on every side ... The tom-tom was in full swing, coupled with weird chants and dancing. I saw many horses and mules bearing the brand of Custer's regiment and many carbines and ammunition pouches taken in the battle of the Little Bighorn. In the midst of all this rejoicing one Indian alone seemed unable to shake off a feeling of sadness—Sitting Bull. He wandered here and there as though deep in thought over all he had gone through. I went to him, offered him my pipe, which he took and smoked. Two lodges were offered to us, and by eleven o'clock I turned in to my blanket. How singular it seemed! Here we were, a few white men, sleeping calmly in the dreaded camp of Sitting Bull."

In his book *The North-West Mounted Police 1873-1893*, John P. Turner wrote: "Late that night someone tapped gently at the front of Irvine's tent, and the next minute Sitting Bull, accompanied by another Indian, entered quietly and sat down. Through the interpreter, the assistant commissioner entered into a long conversation during which he questioned Sitting Bull about the Custer fight and received a lot of intimate information that the chief urged him not to make public. Sitting Bull said, among other things, that he knew 12 days before Custer arrived at the Little Bighorn that he was coming; that most of the 7th Cavalry fought with their revolvers and the butts of their carbines, as the latter seemed to clog after the first shot; that the Indians pulled them off their horses and killed them with knives and coup-sticks.

"As the chief prepared to leave, he proffered his beaded moccasins to Irvine as a memento and shook his hand."

The next day, Irvine and his party left Sitting Bull's camp with Father Marty, John Howard, and the interpreter and headed back toward Fort Walsh. Major Walsh, after informing Sitting Bull of his new proximity, rode off in the opposite direction to take up his posting at nearby Wood Mountain.

Irvine told Ottawa that he accepted Abbot Marty's posturing at face value. He downplayed the affront to British sovereignty and wrote Secretary Scott, "It would have been embarrassing for U.S. authorities to explain an official emissary operating in the North-West Territories."

After the Americans were returned to the border and Irvine concluded matters at Fort Walsh, he returned to Fort Macleod, where he wrote a comprehensive report on his discussions with Sitting Bull and the other chiefs. Even the Catholic priest had concluded that, given the options, Sitting Bull was "better off on British soil." Irvine expressed his belief that the Sioux under Sitting Bull were not likely to cause much trouble.

Ottawa did not share Irvine's views. The federal government was anxious to see the Sioux return to their own country, fearing that Sitting Bull's presence would attract more hostile American Indians to cross over into Canadian territory. Food sources were disappearing too quickly as it was, and besides, the Sioux presence among the Canadian tribes was potentially explosive, given the history of intertribal warfare.

The Americans also wanted the Sioux back. They did not want large numbers of their troops tied down by the threat of attacks across the border. Their first attempt to persuade the Sioux to return had been unsuccessful, but now diplomatic negotiations between Ottawa and Washington were stepped up.

Ottawa encouraged Macleod to discourage Sioux plans to stay in Canada. Naively implying that they had the power to force the warriors out of the country, the government told their head Mountie, "Our action should be persuasive, not compulsory."

Persuasion would have little affect on Sitting Bull—or on his boss, James Walsh.

Chapter 12

The Nez Percé
Cross the Medicine Line

*I think that in his long career, Joseph cannot accuse
the government of the United States of one single
act of justice.*

Anonymous officer quoted in
The Long Death by R.K. Andrist

Sixteen hundred miles west and south of Sitting Bull's camp, in the lush
green lands of the Wallowa Valley, Oregon Territory, over 3,000 Chopunnish
Indians made their home. Called the Nez Percé by early French explorers
because of their bone nose ornaments, they had lived peacefully on land
occupied by their ancestors for the past 200 years. Many of the Nez Percé
spoke English and had become fine farmers. They lived in permanent houses;
grew grain and vegetables; raised horses—including the famous Appaloosa,
a breed they had developed—cattle, sheep, and pigs; embraced Christianity;
and not only lived in harmony with their white neighbours, but had welcomed
them. They even made way for a continuing flow of immigrants, until the
inevitable happened. More and more whites wanted their land.

Predictably, covetous and influential white men pressured the
government in Washington to move the Nez Percé from their homeland,
and Washington duly ordered the Native peoples to move eastward over
the mountains to reservations located on poorer land. The Nez Percé felt
great consternation at the prospect of having to give up their ancestral
lands. Their chief, Echoing Thunder—known to the whites as Joseph—
was an intelligent, peaceful, law-abiding man. He made a special journey
to Washington to plead for his people to be allowed to remain where they
were. His pleas, however, were ignored. When he asked the white chiefs

why his people could not stay, they couldn't—or wouldn't— answer him. Even General Oliver Otis Howard, the area military commander, spoke on the Nez Percé's behalf, arguing that it was a mistake to move them and suggesting that Congress be induced to allow them to remain in their beloved Wallowa Valley. But Washington responded by giving the Nez Percé as much consideration as it had given the Sioux. They had 30 days to move their stock and possessions.

It was the spring of 1877. Nez Percé stock was scattered far and wide and the rivers were in flood. Joseph asked for more time. General Howard was given the task of conveying

Chief Joseph's monumental march to freedom ended 30 miles from the Medicine Line, when a snowstorm and the troops of General Miles made escape impossible.

Washington's decision. He had no choice but to tell the Nez Percé that if they took one day longer than the 30 Washington had stipulated, their horses and cattle would be seized. The long-suffering Indians tried to comply with the order, but they couldn't drive their cattle across the Snake River. They began moving what they could, leaving some of their people to look after the cattle until the river went down, but greedy whites overwhelmed them and ran off the cattle.

This was too much. White Bird, the war chief, called on the warriors to fight. Joseph protested, urging his people to comply peacefully with Washington's order, but the young men were in no mood to listen. They struck back at the white man with a ferocity few would have believed them capable of. From June 1877, the Nez Percé were destined to go down on the pages of history alongside the Sioux, fighting the United States Army in one of the most bitter and protracted campaigns in the annals of Indian warfare.

Joseph reluctantly accepted the will of his warriors and devoted himself to what his war chief saw as the only course open to them. Taking their women and children and all the possessions they could carry, and driving their horses ahead of them, Joseph and White Bird struck out over the mountains and plains for the country of the redcoats.

Pursued by General Howard's cavalry and a column under Colonel John Gibbon, the Nez Percé warriors fought off attempts to overtake them, to head them off, to block them in, to surround them, to cold-bloodedly wipe them out. They trekked over mountain passes, skirted the headwaters of the Yellowstone, and crossed the Missouri, all the while inflicting heavy casualties on the pursuing soldiers. They defied all odds by travelling 1,400 miles and reaching the Bear Paw Mountains by the end of September. They were less than 50 miles from redcoat country, less than 100 miles south of Fort Walsh.

In August, as part of the ongoing effort to intercept the Nez Percés, Brigadier-General Nelson "Bear Coat" Miles had been ordered north from Fort Keogh, at the confluence of the Yellowstone and Tongue rivers. With four companies of the 5th Infantry, three troops of the 7th Cavalry, a large contingent of white and Crow scouts, a twelve-pounder Napoleon gun, a breech-loading Hotchkiss, and a long pack train, he set out.

✳ ✳ ✳

In a land where modern telegraph lines had been only partly strung and the white man's means of communication were still tenuous, Sitting Bull's camp was kept abreast of the latest developments. The messenger who rode into Sitting Bull's camp was a Nez Percé warrior on an exhausted pony. Long-knives had surprised Joseph and White Bird in the Bear Paws, he told the Sioux. The Nez Percés had fought them off, inflicting many casualties, but the long-knives had them surrounded. With Sioux help, however, they could break out and escape north across the medicine line.

Excited Sioux braves clamoured to go help their Nez Percé brothers—and to strike back at the hated long-knives!

Sitting Bull's camp had grown with the arrival of warriors from other Sioux camps nearby, all well aware of the Nez Percé's flight, all eager to fight the long-knives. Sitting Bull called a council. Together with war chiefs Spotted Eagle of the Sans Arcs and Broad Trail of the Ogalalas, the Hunkpapas and Sitting Bull sat around the council fire and talked. Joseph's running fight with the long-knives reminded the Sioux of their own flight to freedom. Joseph had paused in the Bear Paws long enough to hunt much-needed buffalo before pushing on to the medicine line. But he had been surprised by Bear Coat, who had come up from the Yellowstone in a series of forced marches and surrounded them. Surely the Great Spirit—or the Almighty—would not abandon them now, with less than 50 miles to go.

We must help them, was the overwhelming sentiment of the warriors. They need us. Let us go back across the medicine line and show the long-knives how to die! Our brothers need us. We cannot turn our back on them.

But we promised to obey the law in the White Mother's country, others counselled. It is against her law to make war.

Word of the unrest reached Wood Mountain. In the midst of an unseasonable snow squall, Major Walsh and a party of his men arrived at Sitting Bull's camp and pitched tents south of the hundreds of clustered lodges—right in the path of anyone who left the camp to go to the medicine line.

Walsh rode into the Sioux village and sought out Sitting Bull and his council. "If any of you go to help the Nez Percés," Walsh bluntly warned Sitting Bull and the assembled Sioux chiefs, "the peace and security you now enjoy in the White Mother's country will cease. Anyone who crosses the medicine line with hostile intent will sacrifice forever a shelter that you have all boasted of and cherished."

Having warned them, Walsh made his way to his tent south of the Sioux camp and waited. While some of his men slept, others sat huddled in their blue greatcoats around their campfire, watching the Sioux camp.

The discussion in the council lodge continued after Walsh left. Outside, the young warriors were growing impatient. Hundreds painted themselves for war. War drums started, war dances around ceremonial fires followed.

The council deliberations carried on all night, but could not come to any agreement. Walsh's warning had given them food for thought. They still needed a sanctuary.

The war drums beat their chilling message. Eerie shadows danced against the lodges.

Just before sunrise, a wounded Nez Percé warrior rode into Sitting Bull's camp. White Bird had broken through the soldiers with 98 warriors, 100 women and children, and 300 horses! They were heading for the medicine line.

There was no more time for discussion. All eyes were on Sitting Bull, eagerly waiting for his signal.

"Send for White Forehead," Sitting Bull ordered.

His cavalry cloak flapping in the cold, blustery wind, Walsh waded through deep snowdrifts to the council lodge with Louis Leveille—narrow-brimmed hat pulled down over his forehead—beside him.

In 1885 Chief Joseph was exiled with 150 followers to Washington State's Colville reservation, where he spent his last ten years, denied the right to return to Idaho. "My home is in the Wallowa Valley," he said. "My father and mother are buried there ... a small piece of land for my people with a teacher, that is all I would ask." Joseph died at Colville in 1904, some said "of a broken heart."

"White Bird has broken out of the long-knives' encirclement with almost a hundred warriors and a hundred women and children," Sitting Bull said. "Many of the warriors are wounded and the women and children are sick and hungry and tired. We ask how will they be received if they reach the medicine line and cross over? What will the redcoats do if the long-knives follow them across the medicine line?"

"The long-knives won't follow them across the line," Walsh said. "We will treat the Nez Percés the same way we treated the Lakota when they came to the White Mother's country."

"Would the White Mother object to us riding to the medicine line to help them once they cross over ... to bring them here to our camp?"

"No ... as long as none of you cross the line. As long as none of you fire at American soldiers on the other side."

Sitting Bull turned to face his war chiefs. "You heard *Wahonkeza*. We go to the medicine line to help the Nez Percés. Prepare the camp to take them in."

Walsh decided to go with them to make sure the Sioux warriors didn't forget their promise. Before they left the camp, however, Sioux scouts rode in to say a large number of white men were approaching the camp from the medicine line. Instant panic broke out. It must be long-knives coming to attack them!

Walsh held up his hands to quell the panic. "They're not American soldiers. They will not cross the medicine line."

The Sioux were not convinced.

"Then I'll ride down there and find out who they are," Walsh said.

He took his patrol and, accompanied by the Sioux scouts, rode toward the border. Some 200 armed warriors followed.

The approaching "white men" turned out to be White Bird and the remnants of Joseph's Nez Percés, who had already crossed the border. According to John P. Turner, "They were in pitiable condition; women suffering from grievous wounds, children with broken arms and legs, warriors in ghastly condition, practically all without exception suffering enough to wring the heart of the most seasoned policeman. One woman particularly attracted sympathetic eyes. She had been shot in the breast and the ball had turned upward passing through the side of her head. Despite her condition, she valiantly rode a small pony with a child strapped upon her back. All were fearful that the troops might be following, but it was subsequently learned that Miles had not crossed the Milk River. Soon White Bird and 98 Nez Percés men, 50 women including Chief Joseph's daughter, about as many children and 300 horses were being cared for by the Sioux."

If the condition of the Nez Percés sickened Major Walsh and his men, its impact on Sitting Bull was even greater. He had just witnessed what the Great Father's promises meant—death and heartbreak for his people.

Chapter 13

'A Land Where Men Tell Us No Lies'

> *The President has instructed us to say that he*
> *desires to make a lasting peace ...*
> General Terry at Fort Walsh, October 17, 1877

"I would do much for you, *Wahonkeza*," Sitting Bull said to Major Walsh. The two men sat with Louis Leveille, smoking pipes and drinking the sugar-laced tea Walsh had brought with him. Walsh rested his tin cup beside the small fire in the middle of Sitting Bull's lodge. He said nothing, knowing the Sioux chief was wrestling with his request. Finally the response came. "Do not ask me to do this!"

"At least come to Fort Walsh and listen to what the Americans have to say," Walsh said. "You won't have to go back if you don't want to."

Sitting Bull was silent for a moment. Then he asked, "Who heads the peace commission that wants to meet with us and ask us to return to the country we left?"

"General Terry," Walsh replied, then braced himself as Leveille repeated the name in the Lakota dialect. He knew what to expect.

Sitting Bull scowled. "One Star Terry?" his deep voice exploded. "Terry! I cannot believe this! You want me to meet One Star Terry? The Americans are stupid enough to send him at the head of a peace commission to try to persuade me to take my people back across the medicine line and give myself up? Terry is the soldier chief who led the battle against us last year. The one whose soldiers shot down our women and children. The one who sent *Pahuska* to kill us at the Greasy Grass."

Sitting Bull spoke so forcefully, so angrily, so fast, that Leveille had trouble keeping up with the translation. His anger was intensified by his awareness that Bear Coat Miles was still hovering just below the border, having forced the surrender of the Nez Percés at the Bear Paw Mountains a fortnight earlier.

"You saw what the long-knives did to the Nez Percés," Sitting Bull said. "They drove White Bird out of the country and sent Joseph to prison. They deliberately shot down old men, women, and children. Now they come here to offer us homes, after taking from the Nez Percés the homes they had occupied for 200 years. What had Joseph and his people done to deserve that sort of treatment? They were always friendly with the whites. Many of them lived in homes like the white man. They had schools and churches and believed in the white man's God. If that is how the Americans treat people who befriended them, how would they treat the Lakota, people they call hostiles, people who fight back? We had to fight back. They forced us to, because they lied to us and broke their word and took away our land, as they took away Joseph's land. Now they want to lure us back across the line. Hah! Never."

Iron determination was part of James Walsh's nature. Colonel Macleod had instructed him to get Sitting Bull to Fort Walsh to meet with the United States peace commission, and Walsh resolved to carry out his orders. After hours of friendly persuasion spread over three days, Sitting Bull finally agreed to go to Fort Walsh to meet the commission in spite of his animosity toward General Terry, but only with the assurance that Walsh would accompany him and a delegation of Lakota chiefs, and that the delegation would be under the protection of the Mounted Police.

✳ ✳ ✳

A full moon shone down on the Fort Walsh stockade on the evening of October 16. Although he stood far from the fire and the bluecoat guests of Major Macleod, Sitting Bull was there, delivered as promised by a possibly smug Major Walsh.

Perhaps more than any other event, Sitting Bull's entrance into the meeting with General Terry demonstrated "the remarkable influence of 'Long Lance' Walsh," as historian Robert Utley would later describe it.

Bull no doubt took some joy from the lone tribal dancer painted in black and white who waved his scalp-clad coup stick before the crowd. Sir Cecil Denny remembered how Rain-in-the-Face "recounted his deeds ... pointed to these grisly trophies and told how he had used this stick on American soldiers at [Little Bighorn]. Major Walsh knew of the dancer's

Likely based on original sketches by NWMP Assistant Surgeon R.B. Nevitt, this painting and a second sketch of Sitting Bull (right) attributed to New York Herald correspondent Jerome Stillson, appeared in eastern periodicals after the October 17 council at Fort Walsh (above).

claim to be the slayer of Custer himself. He watched the coup stick as it waved closer and closer to General Terry and his tight-lipped entourage."

✳ ✳ ✳

At three o'clock in the afternoon of October 17, 1877, less than three weeks after the wounded and starving Nez Percé refugees had entered his camp, Sitting Bull limped into the officers' mess at Fort Walsh, the largest room in the fort, where the meeting with the United States peace commission was to be held.

Sitting Bull wore a wolf-skin headdress and a blackened elk-skin shirt with large white dots, a blanket draped around his body, and a pair of richly beaded moccasins. Spotted Eagle followed, naked to the waist except for a cartridge belt over one shoulder. White paint was daubed on his chest and arms and he carried a heavy piece of wood, several feet long, from which three long knife blades protruded at right angles near one end.

The U.S. peace commissioners were already in the mess room, waiting by the stone fireplace. Brigadier-General Alfred H. Terry, six feet six inches tall, a distinguished-looking man with keen blue eyes, a dark beard, and a weathered complexion, headed the commission that consisted of himself, the Honourable A.G. Lawrence as his fellow commissioner, and two army captains as their staff.

SITTING BULL.

Behind Sitting Bull and Spotted Eagle followed Bear-That-Scatters and the other Sioux chiefs of the delegation. General Terry and the other members of the peace commission watched them with interest as they entered, General Terry particularly as he came face to face with his old adversary.

The last person of the Sioux delegation to enter the mess was, to everyone's surprise, a woman—Bear-That-Scatters' wife. It was almost without precedent for a woman to attend such a conference. James Walsh and the few present who knew Sioux protocol were aware that her presence had been designed by Sitting Bull and the Sioux to be a supreme affront to the U.S. commissioners.

After the Indians had entered the mess room, Colonel Macleod, Major Walsh, and several other Mounted Police officers followed. Sitting Bull went over to Major Walsh and shook hands, then shook hands with Colonel Macleod. General Terry stepped forward to shake hands with Sitting Bull, but the Sioux leader gave him a disdainful glance and then ignored him, shuffling the Sioux chiefs to the other end of the room.

Momentarily discomfited by the deliberate snub, General Terry moved back to the other three commission members.

The officers' mess was only large enough to accommodate the Sioux, the Mounted Police officers, the U.S. peace commission, and three or four others, including General Miles's chief scout John Howard and two American newspapermen, Jerome Stillson of the *New York Herald* and Charles Dehill of the *Chicago Times*. Buffalo robes were spread across the floor and the Indians sat down on them while the commissioners, their staff, and the newspapermen sat at two tables facing them. As soon as the two commissioners sat down, Sitting Bull objected to the presence of their table and would not consent to the meeting beginning until it was removed, allowing him an uninterrupted view of Terry and Lawrence.

Colonel Macleod, Major Walsh, and the other Mounted Police officers took their seats at the other side of the room and the meeting began.

This sketch of Fort Walsh (probably by R.B. Nevitt) during the 1877 commission shows Sitting Bull's travelling tepee and supply wagons.

The interpreter stood in the centre of the room, ready to translate what was said.

After a few introductory words by Colonel Macleod, General Terry rose to his feet and faced Sitting Bull. "We are sent to you as a commission by the President of the United States at the request of the Government of the Dominion of Canada to meet you here today. The President has instructed us to say to you that he desires to make a lasting peace with you and your people. He desires that all hostilities shall cease and that all shall live together in harmony. He wishes this not only for the sake of the whites, but for your sakes too. He has instructed us to say that if you return to your country and refrain from further hostilities, a full pardon will be granted you and your people for all acts committed in the past, and that no matter what those acts have been, no attempt will be made to punish you or any of your people. What is past shall be forgotten, and you will be received on as friendly terms as other Indians have been received.

"We will explain to you what the President means when he says you will be treated the same as other Indians who have surrendered. Of all the bands that were hostile to the United States, yours are the only ones not surrendered. All other bands have come into their agencies. Of these bands, not a single one has been punished. Every man, woman, and child has been received as a friend and all have received food and clothing. Every one of you will be treated in the same manner. It's true that these

"A cold wind blew across the prairie when the last buffalo fell," said Sitting Bull after returning to the United States. "[It was] a death wind for my people."

Indians have been required to give up their horses and arms, but part of these have been sold, and whatever money was received for them will be expended for their owners' benefit. Already 650 cows have been purchased for the use of the Indians along the Missouri River. If you abandon your present mode of life, the same terms will be offered to you.

"The President cannot, nor will he, consent to your returning to your country prepared for war. He cannot consent to your returning prepared to inflict injuries as you have done in the past. He invited you to come to the boundary of this country and give up your arms and ammunition and go to the agencies assigned to you, and give up your horses except those required for peaceful purposes."

The Indians watched General Terry and listened to the interpreter translate his words into Lakota. Most faces showed no expression. Sitting Bull sat smoking his pipe. His black eyes measured those present, ignoring the bluecoat who now towered over him. When Terry paused and the interpreter spoke, Sitting Bull's lip curled contemptuously from time to time, and Spotted Eagle winked when he glanced over at Major Walsh.

"Your arms and horses will be sold," General Terry went on, "and cows bought with which you can raise herds to supply you and your children long after game has disappeared. In the meantime, you'll receive clothes and provisions the same as the other Indians. We've come hundreds of miles to bring you this message. We've told you before that it's our desire that all live in peace. Too much white and Indian blood has flowed on the battlefield, and it's time that bloodshed should cease. Of one thing, however, it's our duty to inform you: that you cannot return to your country or your people with arms and ammunition in your possession, and should you attempt to do so, you will be treated as enemies of the United States. We ask you to consider carefully what we have told you, and take your time and weigh your answer."

General Terry resumed his seat. All eyes now shifted to Sitting Bull, awaiting his response. Sitting Bull leaned over to Spotted Eagle for a moment and listened as the Sans Arcs war chief spoke quietly. Then Sitting Bull rose to his feet, threw one end of his blanket over his shoulder, and stepped forward.

"For 64 years you have persecuted my people," he said in his deep voice, looking at Terry and making a sweeping movement with his arm. "What have we done that we should have to leave our country? We had no place to go, so we took refuge here. On this side of the line I first learned to shoot and be a man. For that reason I have come back here. I was raised here, and today I shake hands with these people." He raised a hand, pointing at Colonel Macleod and Major Walsh, then stepped over to them and shook hands with them again.

Suddenly he whirled and this time glared at General Terry. "That is the way I came to know these people. We did not give you our country. You took it from us. See how we live with these people?" He pointed at the red-coated officers again, but his eyes remained on Terry. "Look at me. You think I am a fool, but you are a greater fool than I am. This house, the home of the English, is a medicine house—a place of truth— and you come to tell us lies. We do not want to hear them. Now I have said enough. You can go back where you came from. Take your lies with you. I will stay here."

Turning his back on General Terry, Sitting Bull stalked back to his place among the Sioux and sat down on the buffalo robe again. Another chief rose in his place, stepped forward, and launched a tirade of verbal abuse at the general, followed by two more after him.

Then, prodded by Sitting Bull, Bear-That-Scatters' wife rose and began to speak. She spoke so softly that the interpreter had to listen carefully.

"Speak up, woman," he said. "I can't hear you."

She raised her voice in compliance. When she finished, the interpreter stood in the middle of the room, frowning. He looked from the Indian woman to General Terry, then back to the woman again, the frown still creasing his forehead. After a moment he turned back to face Terry, stepped forward several paces, then, in a lowered voice, said, "She says, General, that you won't give her time to breed."

A hushed silence descended over the room and Bear-That-Scatters' wife resumed her seat. Another Sioux chief took her place and said a few words, then returned to his seat.

Then there was another silence. This time none of the Indians moved. When the silence persisted, General Terry spoke to the interpreter. "Ask them if I am to tell the President of the United States that they refuse the offer made to them."

When the interpreter repeated General Terry's question, Sitting Bull, without bothering to rise, replied, "I could tell you more, but I am through. If we told you more, you would not believe us. That is all I have to say. This country does not belong to you. You belong on the other side of the line. This is a land where men tell us no lies."

Sitting Bull had barely finished when The Crow, a middle-aged Hunkpapa, got to his feet, stepped over to Colonel Macleod and Major Walsh, and embraced them. Then he turned to General Terry. "You see how we like the Grandmother's redcoats? How dare you come here to talk to us! This country is not yours. The Great Spirit does not want us to do bad things. The redcoats hide nothing from us. We will live with them. You want to hear more from us? For 64 years you shook hands with our people, but you always betrayed us and brought us new hardships. You can go back where you came from and stay there. We will stay here."

General Terry said, "Do you refuse the President's offer?"

"I have said what I believe," Sitting Bull snapped back. "That should be enough!"

The meeting broke up and Sitting Bull returned to his lodge outside the fort's gates. Shortly after, Colonel Macleod and Louis Leveille followed Sitting Bull to his lodge. Sub-Inspector Dalrymple Clark, accomplished in shorthand and the official recorder of formal talks, accompanied the commissioner and his interpreter. Colonel Macleod wanted to talk to the Sioux leader in case there was any hope of persuading him to accept General Terry's offer. He wanted to impress on him that although he and his people claimed to be British Indians, they were really American Indians who had found refuge on British soil.

"Your only hope of livelihood," he told Sitting Bull through Leveille, "is the buffalo, but in another two or three years there will be very few of them left. Hunters in your country are killing them off so quickly that there won't be enough of them left to migrate north of the border. When that happens, you can't expect anything from the White Mother except protection as long as you behave yourselves. She will have enough of her own Indians to look after. Your decision to reject the offer of a pardon by your White Father will affect not only your own lives, but those of your children. It is well to think about this before it's too late. I urge you to carry my words to your people and to think about them fully. It is particularly important that you tell your young men what I have said, that you warn them against doing anything wrong in case they become disobedient and act rashly and involve the rest of you and get you all into trouble." He told Sitting Bull that he had just come from signing a treaty with the Blackfoot, who had shaken hands with him and said they were happy with it. "The same thing will happen if you return to your own country," he said.

In reply, Sitting Bull repeated his grievances against the Americans, expressing his bitterness toward them for having pushed him and his people out of their sacred tribal lands, particularly the Black Hills of Dakota. Sub-Inspector Clark recorded the substance of Sitting Bull's response as interpreted: "We did not give them our land any more than you would have done had it belonged to you ... We want to live in this country and be strong and happy ... You will see more of our tribe crossing the line. The Great Spirit gives us plenty of buffalo ... I know you will not let the long-knives harm us. The Americans gave us sweet words; they promised us flour and cattle, but if we go back, they will kill us ... I could never live there again ... We did not wish to fight; they started it ... Here there is nothing but good. If they liked me, as they say, why did they drive me away ... ? Today you heard one of our women speak to the Americans—she spoke the truth. We want to raise our children and be friends with all people here. We will live in peace with the red children of the Great White Mother ... We are friends with you and the other officers; it was on that account that we came to meet the Americans today."

Colonel Macleod was sympathetic toward the Sioux, despite the views he expressed in his recommendations to Ottawa. He knew much of what they said was true. He also knew that the Sioux and the Nez Percé exiles they now cared for were in bad shape. The chill of winter was in the air. Sitting Bull had accommodated both Walsh and himself by coming to the meeting with General Terry. The chief deserved something in return. Before they left the fort, Macleod ordered that an issue of ammunition for hunting, some provisions and tobacco, and a blanket be given to Sitting Bull and each member of his delegation.

General Terry, his staff, and their military escort left Fort Walsh the next day. Major Walsh and an escort of Mounted Police rode with them to the Montana border. The Mounties were sorry to see them go. The plains remained an empty place and new faces were rare. Friendships had been made and many tales swapped. The Americans expressed their pleasure at the hospitality given them and then continued on their way. Walsh returned to Fort Walsh and arranged supplies for the 150-mile trek back to Wood Mountain.

* * *

A rousing roar of welcome echoed around the Pinto Horse Butte when Major Walsh rode into the Sioux camp with Sitting Bull, Spotted Eagle, and the Sioux delegation a few days later. Rumour had swept the camp that Sitting Bull had been lured to Fort Walsh to be turned over to the Americans as soon as they arrived. The people were delighted to see this was not so. White Forehead had again been true to his word.

When the people were told about the meeting with General Terry and what Sitting Bull had told the Americans, they shouted their approval. As Walsh's small company made their way through the camp, everyone wanted to talk about the news. Celebrations followed, with singing and dancing and the beating of rawhide drums. Those who had spread the rumours were berated for having doubted the word of the *Shaganosh* Mother.

The next day, as Walsh made his way out of camp, he turned to wave his goodbye. "*Wainga Tanka* is looking over us!" said Spotted Eagle. Walsh sensed an early winter in the air. "*Wainga Tanka* and a few red-coated friends," he muttered.

Chapter 14

Walsh Goes East

Wainga Tanka. *Look down on your son. If what I have done is not good, then strike me at the feet of* Wahonkeza.

Chief Long Dog

Major Walsh was probably the first white man Sitting Bull found he could trust. For his part, Walsh liked and admired the resolve of the Sioux chief. A strong bond grew between them. Walsh also developed a deep sympathy for the Sioux people. He found them to be straightforward, moral, and normally good-natured, with a strong sense of family and community, and compassion for their older people. They seemed eager to give their hand in friendship to anyone who was genuinely friendly toward them. But their experiences with white men, especially American solders, had made them cautious. Walsh was critical of U.S. policies toward the Sioux and Indians in general, and he knew the Sioux had much to complain about. At least one American newspaper, the *Fort Benton Record,* normally anti-Indian in sentiment, condemned its own government's treatment of the Nez Percé.

Although Sitting Bull claimed he was tired of fighting and had buried his weapons on the other side of the medicine line before crossing into the White Mother's country, he hadn't lost the old desire for a great Indian alliance against the bluecoats. Five thousand Sioux concentrated in the Wood Mountain region were a start. Walsh's presence had prevented the Sioux leader from taking his warriors and riding to help the embattled Nez Percés in their fight with General Miles, but if the Nez Percés had eluded the U.S. military and reached the safety of Canada intact, the addition of Joseph and White Bird and their warriors would have given Sitting Bull a greater feeling of power. The joining of the Sioux and the Nez Percé in a common front would have been the beginning. Then if the Cheyenne broke clear of the long-knives and escaped to the White Mother's country …

But his people needed a rest. Before reaching Canadian soil they had been constantly on the move—running from soldiers, fighting when they had to, then running again—for a long time. They had used up most of their ammunition and they needed to recover their strength. Their reception upon crossing the line had been cordial. The redcoats allowed them ammunition for hunting, and the buffalo were plentiful, at least for the time being. No one bothered them and they were happy enough, although some of the younger warriors, listening to the older ones boasting around the campfires of their prowess in battle and the glories of the warpath, often thirsted for excitement and a chance to relive the old days of stealing horses and other plunder in war party raids. Tribal instincts were hard to suppress.

Sitting Bull had told Walsh about the approach of the Nez Percés before the Major was aware of it. And he later told him the warlike Cheyenne were on their way to Canada, although the U.S. Army stopped them before they got far. Who knew what would have happened if the Nez Percé and the Cheyenne had reached the Canadian border in force? The possibilities provided the press on both sides of the line with material for speculation.

Sitting Bull was a hot topic of news. The *Fort Benton Record*, the *Manitoba Daily Free Press* of Winnipeg, the *Saskatchewan Herald* of Battleford, the *Globe* of Toronto, the *Montreal Witness*, the *New York Herald*, the *New York Tribune*, and the *Chicago Times* kept readers across North America on the edges of their chairs. The newspapers could all report on the politics of Washington and Ottawa, but most comment on the Sioux and Sitting Bull in particular was pure speculation. Only a few white men could see inside Sitting Bull's camp, and they lived in isolation at the Wood Mountain NWMP detachment.

Before the U.S. peace commission meeting at Fort Walsh, one newspaper warned its readers that Sitting Bull had approached the Blackfoot to join him in a war against the Americans. Another's headlines declared that Sitting Bull was preparing for a spring campaign against the whites, adding that the Assiniboines, Gros Ventres, Peigans, and even the Crows (who invariably aligned themselves with the U.S. Army, serving as scouts in the army's campaigns against the Sioux) would join him. The *Toronto Globe* warned that the Sioux camps in the Wood Mountain region were likely to "erupt at any time," adding that a report from Helena, Montana, claimed Sitting Bull, who had a plentiful supply of ammunition stashed near the medicine line, was on the verge of leading all the tribes on the northern plains against the U.S. Army.

The stories increased after news of the peace commission's failure. The *Fort Benton Record* reported that Sitting Bull had approached most of the Canadian tribes and the Gros Ventres of northern Montana in an effort to form an alliance and "clean out all the whites and have the country" to themselves. A white trader at Fort Belknap on the Milk River near the Bear Paw Mountains considered the situation "critical." Two weeks later, the *Fort Benton Record* reported that residents of Battleford on the North Saskatchewan River were worried by a rumour that Sitting Bull had formed an alliance of Sioux, Blackfoot, and Stonies and had made overtures to the Cree with the intention of carrying out widespread raiding. Rumours held that a big Indian camp had formed east of the Cypress Hills and was growing hourly with new arrivals; the Blackfoot had formed an alliance with Sitting Bull and the remnants of the Nez Percé, and the Blackfoot along the Belly River were rushing to the warpath; attacks on Fort Macleod and Fort Walsh were imminent; Canada's vast North-West Territories and the small contingent of Mounted Police who had served so well were now under siege.

By this time Canada's politicians in the east and far west were growing restless with the Indian problem. Ottawa did not want the trouble of dealing with them, while western settlers' fears were constantly fuelled by the rumours that always seemed to be circulating.

Early in 1878, Major Walsh had an opportunity to lay some of these rumours to rest and also learned the truth behind some of the news stories when he travelled to Montana and points east on his way to Ottawa. He had been ordered to report to the Canadian capital to confer with Secretary of State Scott on the Sioux question, and to perform recruiting duties for his undermanned force in eastern Canada. He travelled to Fort Benton and Helena in Montana, caught a stagecoach in Helena to Corinne, Utah, where he boarded a Union Pacific train eastward for Chicago and Detroit.

While at Helena and Chicago, Walsh found himself sought after by newspaper correspondents eager to interview him about Sitting Bull. Glad to be away from his enforced isolation at Wood Mountain, the dapper Mountie enjoyed the attention. He answered at length questions put to him by the journalists and was quick to refute stories appearing in the newspapers predicting a confederation of all the Indian tribes in opposition to the whites. He denied emphatically any suggestion that Sitting Bull was part of such a scheme.

"Where do you think these stories come from, Major?" asked one journalist.

"In my opinion," Walsh stated, looking the journalist in the eye, "army scouts."

"Army scouts, Major?"

Walsh nodded. "Yes. And perhaps from some traders—even the occasional half-breed—who pass on these yarns to scouts anxious to curry favour with their superiors. It's nothing for scouts to magnify an ordinary Indian buffalo hunt, for instance, into a sweeping raid against the whites. Some of General Miles's expeditions have been founded entirely on the reports of scouts who've been had by some plains joker or by some rag-tag Indians."

In Fort Benton and Helena, Walsh became aware of some of the exaggerations given life by Miles himself. Walsh was amused to hear that he had supposedly misplaced some of his 5,000 Sioux the previous summer. Miles claimed that 1,300 Sioux had been seen south of the boundary. Walsh dismissed this as impossible. Likewise, he was bemused on learning of Miles's letter to headquarters saying Walsh had ordered Sitting Bull out of his territory after a falling out. Finally he learned that Miles had arrested the Nez Percé leader, Joseph, while under a flag of truce. The more he heard about Miles, the more Walsh believed the general based a large part of his campaign on misinformation and desperation.

Walsh also learned more about the ill-advised choice of General Terry to head the previous October's unsuccessful peace commission. Unquashable rumours of a roaming band of 5,000 Sioux had left the U.S. Secretary of State uneasy and uncertain about supporting the commission's agenda. Finally Terry and his entourage were sent towards Fort Walsh with two sets of orders. If Sitting Bull was north of the boundary, he should be offered terms of peace. If he was in U.S territory, Terry was to personally lead military operations and arrest Sitting Bull.

Walsh was no diplomat. Encouraged by reporters from the *Helena Herald* or the *Chicago Times*, he freely commented on U.S. frontier problems, past and present. "In my opinion, any Indian troubles in the future will probably grow out of agency frauds. Oh, a few war parties might attack wagon trains or raid an occasional ranch, but the big problems will be dissatisfaction with life on the reservations, with Indian agents holding out on food they're supposed to be giving the Indians."

The journalist scribbled shorthand notes on a pad, then looked up at Walsh again. "There was a report, Major, that General Sheridan had been informed that the Sioux on British soil are being allowed to make generous purchases of rifle ammunition from traders."

Walsh's face tightened. "Yes. General Sheridan wired Colonel Macleod about that. Mounted Police officers are most careful to issue permits to traders authorizing them to supply each male Sioux head of family with ten rounds of rifle ammunition for hunting purposes only. The issuance of these permits is at the option of the post commanders at Fort Walsh and Wood Mountain only, and permits are issued only to certain traders known to us to be thoroughly reliable. At all times, great caution is exercised to ensure that this allotment is not exceeded. And, I might add, we're continually watching all the trails in the west. My men at Wood Mountain are always on the alert to prevent any attempts to smuggle arms or ammunition to Sitting Bull's camp or any other Sioux camp."

When Walsh reported to Ottawa, Secretary of State R.W. Scott impressed upon him the need to have the Sioux return to their own country, instructing him to do everything in his power to bring this about, despite the emphatic rejection of the Terry peace commission. Then Walsh turned his attention to recruiting.

* * *

While Walsh was in the east, new rumours circulated that a grand confederation of Indians and Métis was to be formed against the whites, to drive them out or kill them. These rumours pointed to a Cree chief, Big Bear, head of a band of disgruntled Indians from around Fort Pitt, a Hudson's Bay Company trading post on the North Saskatchewan River northwest of Battleford. Big Bear had moved his band south to the Cypress Hills, close to Fort Walsh. The American press picked up the rumours, eager to report anything even remotely connected with Sitting Bull.

Colonel Macleod ordered Inspector Crozier to investigate. Not long afterwards, Crozier heard yet another rumour. This one said that if he visited Big Bear's camp, he would not leave it alive. This was like waving a red flag in front of a bull, and Paddy Crozier left his Fort Walsh posting as soon as possible to ride to Big Bear's camp and confront him. Big Bear quickly denied any knowledge of such a threat and claimed to know nothing of the rumoured confederation.

The Mounted Police investigated the other stories of alliances, threatened attacks, and build-ups of Indian strength, but found little real substance to them. Blackfoot chief Crowfoot confirmed he and Sitting Bull had met briefly during a buffalo hunt in the summer of 1877. The meeting, Crowfoot said, had been cautiously friendly, but nothing of any real consequence had been discussed—certainly nothing about any alliance.

Nonetheless, Colonel Macleod thought it advisable to transfer NWMP headquarters to Fort Walsh to concentrate the strength of the force, such as it was, closer to the potential trouble spots. The transfer was carried out in

The Sioux headman Long Dog was one of the chiefs who crossed the medicine line after surviving Little Bighorn. He would share Sitting Bull's respect for Walsh after the Major gave them bullets to hunt and feed their families during their first winter in the Cypress Hills.

May 1878. Half of "B" Troop (the other half was at Wood Mountain), "E" Troop, and "F" Troop (except a sergeant and a few men who remained at Fort Calgary) moved to Fort Walsh. The stockade in the southeast corner of the fort was extended so quarters could be built for Major Irvine. Colonel Macleod remained at Fort Macleod and continued to fulfil his responsibilities as magistrate for the Fort Macleod-Fort Calgary region, a role he had been performing in addition to his duties as NWMP commissioner since he succeeded Colonel French in 1876. Fort Macleod was now reduced to a single troop—"C" Troop.

✳ ✳ ✳

Walsh, whom the American press had dubbed "Sitting Bull's Boss," had become a popular figure with journalists. He was news, and reporters sought him out, not only because of who he was, but also because he co-operated with them, forthrightly telling them what they wanted to know and sometimes more. On his way back to the west with his party of 65 recruits, a journalist from the *Chicago Times* caught up with him. Colonel Macleod had already reprimanded Walsh for giving unauthorized interviews to the press, and as he was travelling with Frederick White, head of the Mounted Police Branch at Ottawa, his answers to this interview may have been more circumspect than usual.

"Do you think Sitting Bull and his Sioux can be persuaded to return to the United States, Major?" the journalist asked.

"Yes, I believe they can, but it'll take time. They won't go back soon. A lot could be accomplished in a year. You can't get Indians to make up their minds right away, certainly not in a day or two. It could take months. You have to lay everything out in front of them. Then they'll debate it among themselves in a council of band chiefs. Objections will be put forth and they will then have to be resolved before any answer can be obtained. It's a slow business, but I believe it'll succeed in the end and do away with a dangerous element on the border between our two countries.

"Indians are independent of each other. If Sitting Bull had said to General Terry during the peace commission hearing at Fort Walsh, 'I'll go back,' he'd then have to go to his people and tell them the Americans had made an offer that he had accepted. They'd probably have replied, 'All right, you can go back.'

"If the Sioux start returning, they'll do so in small bands. They'll send a few families across the line first as feelers, then they'll wait to see how they're treated. If the return of the Sioux could be accomplished, it'll be good for them and it'll prove beneficial to the people on the frontier as well. It would turn out to be a happy end of the hostile question for both Canada and the United States. Should they return, they'll have to be dismounted and disarmed. Once dismounted, they will be conquered. That would be the best resolution of this matter. Canada doesn't want them. Our government believes the proper place for them is on a reservation in the United States."

"What do you think about the possibility of a confederation of all the tribes north of the line, Major?"

Walsh shook his head. "There are a lot of long-standing animosities between the various tribes. The Blackfoot and Bloods don't like the Crees, the Crees don't trust the Sioux. And given the hereditary enmity between the Sioux and the Blackfoot, it's not natural to presume they could become allies."

"What if the Nez Percés return to the United States and agree to go to a reservation?" the journalist asked, referring to White Bird and his followers, who were still with the Sioux.

"That would have a good effect on the Sioux."

Walsh and his party travelled on the Northern Pacific Railroad as far as Bismarck, Dakota Territory—across the Missouri River from Fort Abraham Lincoln, home of the U.S. 7th Cavalry—and boarded the flat-bottomed river steamer *Red Cloud*, continuing their journey along the Missouri. Fourteen days later they disembarked at the mouth of the Marias River, twelve miles east of Fort Benton, where they were met by two I.G. Baker Company three-wagon trains hauling supplies from Fort Benton to Fort Walsh. They loaded their baggage aboard the wagons, then walked alongside them the 148 miles to Fort Walsh, arriving there on June 16.

Here Frederick White, the civil servant responsible for Mounted Police financial management, began an inspection of Mounted Police posts, and Major Walsh resumed his regular duties.

One of the first things Walsh did was ride east toward the Sioux camps in the Wood Mountain region to size up conditions there and familiarize himself with any changes that might have occurred during his absence. He had been instructed to ascertain Sioux intentions for the future and particularly to learn if they had given any more thought to returning to their own country.

Walsh and his small escort were sitting on the bank of the upper White Mud, eating a meal, when three Indians appeared on the crest of a hill not far away and galloped toward them. Wondering what was up, Walsh and his men rose, their eyes on the oncoming Indians. As they drew closer, Walsh recognized Long Dog, the battle-scarred war chief of the Hunkpapas.

"*Wainga Tanka!*" Long Dog shouted. "It is *Wahonkeza!*"

Pulling his pony to a stop, Long Dog jumped down, bounded over to Walsh, and, with a wide smile, warmly embraced the redcoat chief. The next instant he pointed an arm to the sky and said, "*Wainga Tanka.* Look down on your son. If what I have done is not good, then strike me at the feet of *Wahonkeza.*"

Walsh visited all the Sioux camps, and everywhere he and his men went, they were welcomed with open arms. They were treated like brothers by Sitting Bull and his camp. Men, women, and children flocked around them wherever they went.

As to their intentions for the future, the Sioux told Walsh they wanted to remain in the White Mother's country, under the *Shaganosh* flag.

James Walsh knew in his heart that it was not to be.

Chapter 15

Riel in Montana

We were gathering to have a feast. Riel had a lot of rum ... He wanted me to raise all the men I could but I couldn't.

Big Bear recounting events at Riel's camp on the Missouri River, 1879

In the fall of 1878, the annual report of General Philip H. Sheridan, commander of the United States Army in the west, was published in American newspapers. He reported that the Indian situation was entirely unsatisfactory due to dishonesty on the part of Indian agents and a shortage of food among the tribes. Dishonest practices and corruption were rife among Indian agents, some of whom were known to have made fortunes in a few years while on relatively modest salaries. The food shortage in particular was contributing to unrest, resulting in hostilities by the tribes.

Bearing the brunt of these dishonest practices was the United States Army. The garrisons in Indian country were insufficient to preserve law and order and to meet the demands thrust upon them. General Sheridan paid tribute to the soldiers' energy in the face of many obstacles. He expected a general Indian uprising based on his belief that the tribes would fight before they would starve. Many were in a forlorn condition. Without exception, he reported, the management of the tribes had been inadequate and disastrous to peace. Some of the Sioux bands had been placed on reserves where the land was poor. Two reserves that were particularly bad were the Red Cloud and Spotted Tail agencies. Fighting would soon break out, General Sheridan predicted. He also expected trouble from the Crows. But he believed the situation could be remedied if food rations were handed out honestly. Until then, dishonest management by agents and traders would cause the deaths of more soldiers and cost the government needless millions of dollars. Sheridan foresaw more Sioux crossing the line and joining those in Canada.

This Indian unrest south of the border was creating unease north of it. Adding to the restlessness was a growing shortage of buffalo. Among Canadian tribes, the Blackfoot and Blood were becoming apprehensive about the precariousness of their food supply. The herds were no longer frequenting the high plains and rolling foothills of the Fort Macleod-Fort Calgary country. Once again the Blackfoot and Blood were

The charismatic Louis Riel seemed to withdraw to a quiet life in western Montana after James Walsh countered his attempts to recruit Métis and Indians to join him. But Riel would rise again.

forced eastward to the Cypress Hills and Wood Mountain, where the herds were more numerous, but where they were also closer to their ancient enemies. Volatile, violent people were brought together, adding to the danger of tribal clashes, even warfare. This also increased the possibility of troublemakers stirring up mischief and further talk of an Indian alliance.

Rumours of an alliance between Indians and Métis persisted as well, and many of these rumours mentioned the name Louis Riel, leader of the Red River Métis insurrection of 1869-70. Born at St. Boniface, across the Red River from Fort Garry (Winnipeg), in 1844, Riel had studied for the priesthood, but was too restless for a life in the church. His powers of oratory and charismatic personality propelled him to champion the cause of the Métis people against an unthinking and insensitive central government at Ottawa that had created the conditions for an insurrection in the first place. As a result of the Red River uprising, the federal government had created the province of Manitoba and granted land rights to the Métis people who lived there, but Riel was viewed by English-Canadians as a murderer. Twice the Métis elected Riel to the Parliament of Canada, but in Ottawa he had been expelled from the House and in 1875 exiled from Canada for five years. After recovering from a nervous breakdown, he had spent the last few years roaming from one Métis settlement to another in Dakota and Montana, eventually marrying and becoming a United States citizen, but his heart remained north of the border. From Dakota he wrote a long tirade against Sir John A. Macdonald, who had been prime minister at the time of the insurrection, berating him for what Riel termed the "hypocrisy and cowardice" of those responsible for his exile.

Shortly after Walsh returned to Wood Mountain from his trip east, he learned that Riel had secretly visited Wood Mountain's Métis community not long before. In the eyes of most of the Métis, many of whom had fled west from Red River following the insurrection, Riel was a demigod. They would do anything for him. Wood Mountain Métis began mixing with the Cree and Blackfoot, ostensibly to trade and hunt buffalo, but the Métis went out of their way to curry favour with the Blackfoot—with whom they had usually fought in the past—and suggested they should ride across the border and meet with Louis Riel, who they said was friendly with the American government and all the Indian tribes. As an inducement, the Métis told the Blackfoot that Montana was alive with buffalo. Although the Blackfoot were tempted by the story of buffalo, and some did ride south in search of them, the majority declined and gave the Métis a cool reception.

Angered by Riel's impudence in returning to Canada, Walsh moved to arrest him if he set foot across the border again. He sent his scouts to track him down and find out what he was up to. They found him at the Burnt Timber, a few miles south of the Montana border. While the scouts kept an eye on him, Walsh busied himself looking into Riel's activities. He found out that three Métis, including a man named Ambroise Lepine, had ridden from the South Saskatchewan, holding meetings at various Métis settlements and Indian camps before crossing into Montana to meet Riel at Fort Benton. They remained there two days, then rode back to the South Saskatchewan, while Riel had gone east to Fort Belknap, a trading post on the Milk River.

Walsh considered this information to be significant. Lepine had been Riel's right-hand man during the Red River insurrection and had been instrumental in the 1870 murder of Thomas Scott, who opposed Riel's provisional Métis government. After the insurrection was over, Lepine was charged with high treason and was sentenced to hang, but his death sentence had been commuted by the Governor General to two years' imprisonment and the permanent forfeiture of his political rights. Walsh was sure that Riel and Lepine were up to no good

Walsh learned Riel had persuaded the South Assiniboines to enter into a pact of the "Indian blood of the prairie" to liberate the western country and return it to the Indians and Métis. Riel had also tried to talk the Yankton Sioux of Medicine Bear and Black Horn—Walsh's friends, who were camped close to the Burnt Timber—into joining his pact, but they had refused.

Accompanied by one of his scouts, Walsh left Wood Mountain and rode 75 miles south, crossing into Montana and continuing until they reached the South Assiniboine camp of Red Stone. Following the

In Manitoba Ambroise Lepine had both captured Thomas Scott and headed the jury that senteced him to death in 1870, an event which would lead to Riel's escape and exile in the U.S.

normal preliminary conversation dear to the Indian heart, Walsh brought up the matter of Riel's pact. Red Stone showed him a paper on which Riel had written the articles of the pact, setting forth its purpose and listing the tribes that were to form it. It stated that the country belonged to the Indian blood and that the whites were taking it from them. Those of Indian blood were suffering from injustices inflicted upon them by the white man, but all this would be rectified.

According to John P. Turner's history of the NWMP, "Riel's document claimed the natives were being disposed of by the whites, while Riel himself had been driven into exile. The Indians and Métis were suffering from injustices, but the country would be redeemed through the proposed confederation, when all the tribes from the Saskatchewan to the Missouri joined as one people. He claimed that though other men ruled the country at present, he, Riel, was the true and rightful chief; that many of the whites in Canada and the United States admitted this and proposed to help him recover the country for his people. All that was needed was to establish his power through a loyal confederation of all the half-breeds and Indians." The paper was signed by Riel for the Métis and by Red Stone for the Assiniboines.

Walsh remained in Red Stone's camp that night and learned more about Riel's activities. Before leaving next morning, he talked Red Stone into withdrawing from Riel's pact. He asked Red Stone to give him the paper, which he wanted as proof of Riel's intentions, but Red Stone said he had given his word not to hand it over to anyone. Instead, he said he would burn it and send word to Riel that he had decided he was an impostor and that the Assiniboines would have nothing further to do with the pact.

When Riel learned of this, he was furious, swearing that someone would die because of it. He probably had James Walsh in mind.

Walsh returned to Wood Mountain, pleased he had struck a blow at Riel's planned uprising. But Riel wasn't finished. He had persuaded many of the Wood Mountain Métis to join him at his camp on the Big Bend of the Milk River. Walsh advised them to stay where they were lest Riel get them into trouble. Many followed Walsh's advice, but others, drawn by Riel's oratory and charisma, joined him. He inspired them as he had done before at Red River, his persuasive arguments and inflammatory speeches once again raising their hopes for a happy resolution of all their problems, a return to the old ways, removal of the white man's government, and an end to the threatened invasion of their hunting lands by thousands of white men as was happening below the border. Riel declared that with the coming of spring, he would be the ruler of the prairies and Crowfoot would be his right-hand man.

But he didn't have Crowfoot yet. He needed the help of the Sioux, claiming that if they joined him, the Blackfoot would follow. As 1878 went by, some Sioux in Canada slipped back across the border and joined Riel's camp. More Métis drifted in, but he needed more Indians—Crees, North Assiniboines (a Canadian tribe, distinct from the South Assiniboines of Montana), more Sioux. He needed Sitting Bull. While Riel held council meetings and discussed his spring uprising, Métis agitators rode back and forth between his camp on the Big Bend and Métis settlements and Indian camps as far away as the North Saskatchewan River.

Major Walsh was not idle either. His scouts had been watching Riel's camp and now Walsh decided the time was ripe to take counteraction. He ordered his men to seize all firearms and ammunition held by traders and to lock them up in the police posts to prevent Riel's supporters getting their hands on them. He wrote to the officer commanding Fort Walsh to do the same. Walsh was confident his standing with Sitting Bull, Spotted Eagle, Long Dog, Broad Trail, Dull Knife, Stone Dog, Black Bull, and the other Sioux in Canada would ensure their loyalty to him and the British flag. He was sure Red Stone of the Assiniboines would not go back on his word to have nothing further to do with Riel. He had the friendship of Medicine Bear of the Yanktons and his war chief, Black Horn. If it came down to it, Walsh believed, the Sioux veterans of the Little Bighorn would stand behind him. In his words, they "would have been sufficient to have walked over Riel's halfbreeds and Indians. Crowfoot and Big Bear knew that."

Walsh next moved to break up Riel's camp, to dislodge his supporters, split them up into small groups, and scatter them, removing them from Riel's influence and control and at the same time showing them Riel's claim that the Americans were sympathetic to him was false. Walsh rode down to the Indian reservation along the Big Bend, suggesting to the Indians that they complain to their agent that a large camp of troublesome Canadian Métis and Sioux hostiles was on their reserve. The Indians did as Walsh suggested. The agent informed Washington and the U.S. Army was ordered to take action against the intruders.

Before winter swept across the northern plains that year, a combined force of soldiers, U.S. marshals, and customs officers swooped on Riel's camp, seizing weapons and ammunition, rounding up Sioux hostiles, and ordering Canadian Métis and Indians back to their own country. The army moved those Métis who claimed to be American to more southerly regions of Montana.

Walsh had succeeded in scattering Riel's visionary scheme to the winds. To make sure it stayed that way, he sent word to Riel not to set foot north of the 49th parallel. If he did he would be arrested.

While Major Walsh had been quietly subduing unrest in the Cypress Hills and disrupting the plans of Louis Riel, Canada faced another election. Apparently tired of one dour but diligent Scot, Alexander Mackenzie, they opted to restore their faith in Old Tomorrow. John Alexander Macdonald, promising that his years of procrastination and hard boozing were behind him, started what would become a thirteen-year run as Canada's prime minister. Macdonald had a transcontinental railway to build, and trouble from that upstart Riel or the Native people was the last thing he needed.

Unfortunately, there was nobody to bear witness that Walsh was one of the best things Macdonald had going for his government in the North-West Territories. With the buffalo herds continuing to decline, the Indians restless, and settlers in constant fear of possible attack, Walsh made sure the seasons passed uneventfully.

Chapter 16

Hard Times

When all this is over I think we must dispense with his services in the Mounted Police.
Letter from John A. Macdonald to the governor general of the North-West Territories regarding Inspector James Walsh

Had Major Walsh remained at Fort Walsh, he might eventually have brought his wife, Mary Elizabeth, and their young daughter Cora out from Brockville to live with him. The quarters at both Fort Walsh and Fort Macleod had gradually been improved, and with budding villages adjacent to both forts, the country around was losing some of its wildness. Colonel Macleod had married Mary Isabella Drever of Winnipeg the year he became commissioner, and he brought her to Fort Macleod to live with him. Inspector Winder and Sub-Inspector Shurtliffe also brought their wives to Fort Macleod, but Wood Mountain was another matter. There were neither satisfactory quarters nor, it could be argued, a suitable environment for a Mounted Police officer's wife and daughter.

Although Major Walsh was still shown in the official records as officer commanding "B" Troop at Fort Walsh, he spent most of his time at Wood Mountain. Nonetheless, the officers and men of "B" Troop still at Fort Walsh continued to think of him as their OC. They celebrated Christmas 1878 as though he was still there. They hung his picture on the mess room wall facing the entrance, and then borrowed a page from the American media. Beneath the portrait were the words "Sitting Bull's Boss" formed by curb chains from bridles on a black cloth background. The picture was framed by evergreen branches, steel bits, and curb chains. The mess walls were decorated with lances, carbines, revolvers, and equestrian equipment. In large letters, on a dark cloth background, the words "Merry Christmas" were bordered by a set of lances and flags.

As for their honouree, Major Walsh and his 22 men at Wood Mountain celebrated Christmas in their more primitive quarters as best they could. Five days later Walsh wrote a year-end letter to Assistant Commissioner Irvine at Fort Walsh. He was still confident that the Sioux would enter the United States only to hunt or trade with tribes near the border. Walsh admired Siting Bull's lasting optimism, writing that Bull "was certain the Great Spirit would pity them and send buffalo."

The beginning of 1879 brought bitterly cold weather to the Canadian west. Deep snow often blocked the trails on the prairies. Fewer buffalo roamed the wind-swept plains or took protection in the coulees and valleys. Indians had to hunt farther and longer to obtain their barest needs. What Colonel Macleod had told Sitting Bull the day the Sioux chief turned down the U.S. peace commission offer—that the buffalo were becoming scarcer—was indeed happening, and faster than even Macleod had predicted. Indians all across the west were starving. The Mounted Police at Fort Macleod, Fort Calgary, Fort Walsh, and Battleford doled out beef and flour in limited quantities every other day to keep the hunger at bay.

Amid these food shortages, the rumours of Indian and Métis alliances were revived yet again. Although Louis Riel, from the safety of Montana, persisted in his efforts to get Sitting Bull to join him in his confederation of the Indian blood, Sitting Bull ignored the plea. He had set his heart on obtaining from the White Mother a reserve in Canada for himself and his people. She had given one to the Sisseton Sioux, who had fled across the medicine line years before. Why shouldn't she give him and his people a reserve also? His people had been *Shaganosh* Indians once. His ancestors had fought for a *Shaganosh* king. They would still be *Shaganosh* Indians if the king hadn't given their land to the Americans.

Increasing numbers of hungry Sioux began frequenting Wood Mountain and the Mounted Police post, looking for sustenance. The Mounties gave them what they could, even to the point of saving scraps of food from their mess tables and feeding it to hungry women and children. Many Sioux slipped across the border to hunt. Frequently they stole horses and brought them back to their camps. This resulted in a lot of extra work and long hours in the saddle for Walsh and his men. A typical investigation followed a complaint from a Montana rancher down near the Missouri, which sent Walsh's men on a week-long search without finding the stolen animals. Then Walsh took over the search personally,

Troops come out from under their canvas in the Cypress Hills to take in a NWMP band concert and pose against the backdrop of Fort Walsh.

leading three constables and a Métis scout to a Sioux camp south of the Pinto Horse Butte. They found the horses and returned them to the rancher. Justice prevailed, but the search took fifteen days and many miles.

Spring brought some relief to the Indian villages, but as summer approached, Sitting Bull's young warriors became more restless, more audacious. If the White Mother would not give them a reserve, why should they bother to obey her laws? A party of young bucks ran off some 50 horses belonging to a Métis named Pierre Poitras. Suspecting the Sioux, Poitras rode to Sitting Bull's camp and demanded his horses back. The young Sioux warriors laughed at him, telling him he could have them back provided he paid a ransom of ten of the best horses. Outraged, Poitras rode off and went to the Mounted Police post at Wood Mountain, complaining to Major Walsh. Walsh took a constable, Cajou Morin, Poitras, and several Métis herdsmen and rode to Sitting Bull's camp.

Unsuccessful in finding the horses among the Sioux pony herd, Walsh sought counsel with Sitting Bull. Normally diplomatic with the chief, Walsh, who was fed up with the young men and their horse-stealing antics, bluntly told Sitting Bull that he, Sitting Bull, knew damned well where the stolen horses were and that he'd better give them back or else Walsh would invite General Miles to cross the line with his soldiers and move the Sioux back to their own country.

In 1878 young James Schofield poses at Fort Walsh, but the star of the photograph seems to be the horse—possibly James Walsh's recently acquired Custer, a rare equine survivor of his namesake's last stand at the Little Bighorn.

Sitting Bull bristled at his friend's temper. He suspected a bluff, but could not be sure. He knew the lengths to which Walsh would go to enforce the law. He sent his braves to get the horses.

* * *

It was hot under the early summer sun at the Wood Mountain NWMP post as Major Walsh leaned his elbows on the top railing of the corral fence and raised a spurred boot to rest on the bottom rail. He closed his eyes for three or four seconds, opened them again, and shook his head. He raised a hand to touch his forehead. It felt warm, but he wasn't sure whether it was a fever or the day's heat. He hoped he wasn't getting another attack of erysipelas. He couldn't afford to be sick again, not now. Too much damned work to be done.

He ran his eyes over the dozen horses in the corral. All but one had been recovered by him and his men and had to be returned to their owners across the line. Despite his visit to Sitting Bull's camp a few weeks earlier, young Sioux men were still running off horses whenever they crossed the line hunting buffalo. Recovering stolen horses was a time-consuming task for the Mounted Police. What with that and checking into the persistent rumours of an Indian-Métis alliance Riel was still trying to stir up from Montana, Walsh and his men were seldom out of their saddles. This was hard on the men and harder on the horses. Good horses were difficult to come by, and the Mounted Police had never been able to make up the losses incurred on the march west five years before. Every post, every detachment, was short. Colonel Macleod had submitted a proposal to Ottawa suggesting that half the force be carried in regimental transport wagons. These wagons, each drawn by four horses, could carry twelve men and all the equipment and supplies they would require for a month. It was a well-known fact that men could be carried longer distances in a day in wagons than on horseback. Wagons could be taken practically anywhere in the west. All the posts used them to carry equipment and supplies from place to place. The only trouble was that by 1879, with the tendency to station more and more men out of the major posts on detached outpost duty, the ratio of men at the main posts to those on outpost duty was falling and the idea was losing some of its validity. Rarely did the outposts have more than four or five men.

Walsh's eyes surveyed the horses, then settled on the lone grey gelding. At the sound of Walsh's soft whistle, the grey perked his ears, then trotted over to him. "Hello, Custer, old trooper," Walsh said with a smile as he reached out his hand to stroke the twelve-year-old animal's nose. "How are you doing, old fellow?"

The horse nuzzled closer. Reaching into his breeches pocket, Walsh pulled out a handful of sugar and passed it through the railing. His eyes strayed to the brand on its rump.

The gelding had once belonged to the U.S. 7th Cavalry. Badly wounded, it had been left to die on the Little Bighorn battlefield. Two days after the tragic encounter the damaged horse was a rare sign of life when soldiers found it. No doubt desperate to salvage some survivor from the carnage, they rigged up a litter and carried the animal back to their camp. In time, the horse made an amazing recovery and was retired to live out the rest of its days in ease. As it turned out, the grey's Indian wars were not over. It was stolen by Sioux warriors and used in further fighting, this time mounted by the other side, and was finally brought north across the medicine line by one of Sitting Bull's warriors. A natural buffalo runner, the horse was stolen again but subsequently recovered, likely with Walsh's aid. Perhaps to buy food, the scout owner sold it to a Wood Mountain Métis. Walsh had noticed it in the Métis's yard one day, his eyes drawn to the 7th Cavalry brand. He saw signs of good breeding in the old trooper and bought it from the Métis. Then, lest he be accused of being in possession of stolen property, the Major had written to General

Terry, in command of the Military Department of Dakota at Fort Abraham Lincoln. Respectful of the history of the 7th Cavalry and their loss at Little Bighorn, Walsh explained how he came into possession of the grey gelding, described his affinity for the horse, and offered to turn it over to U.S. authorities if so instructed, but stated he would be most honoured to be allowed to keep it. In due course he received a reply from the adjutant-general of the United States Army informing him that the Secretary of War had personally authorized Walsh to keep the horse. Walsh was truly pleased and in honour of the 7th Cavalry's late commander had named the grey gelding "Custer."

Giving Custer the sugar remnants from his pocket and a final pat on the nose, Walsh left the corral fence and walked across the packed earth quadrangle to the collection of sod-roofed log cabins that made up the Wood Mountain post. It wasn't much of a place, lacking any but the barest comforts for the men. It didn't even have board floors. Walsh wanted it expanded to accommodate 75 men and as many horses, and he had submitted a report to Colonel Macleod recommending as much. He needed that many to carry out his duties properly and to handle any emergencies that might arise. Fortunately, no emergencies had arisen, nothing that Walsh hadn't been able to handle, but he could certainly have used extra men and horses. The Sioux were constantly crossing the border in search of buffalo. A few small ranches had sprung up on both sides of the line, run by brave and hopeful souls taking some encouragement from the fact that the predicted Indian uprising hadn't taken place, but they were presenting the Mounted Police with unwanted problems, for the Sioux, when they couldn't find buffalo, were running off horses instead. And Sitting Bull, damn his hide, wasn't doing anything to stop it.

Walsh reached his quarters, pushed the door open, and stepped inside. Taking off his pill-box hat, he sat down behind his desk, neatly covered with several stacks of paper. Too much time in the saddle had left his paperwork wanting, a not unusual situation. Picking up a report he had almost finished, he perused it to make sure he hadn't left anything out. It was his personal assessment of the continuing Sioux presence in Canada. He would forward it to Major Irvine, who would, in turn, read and forward it to Colonel Macleod with any comments he saw fit to add. Walsh wondered what impact the words would have. Macleod would then add his comments and send it to the Minister of the Interior at Ottawa. That portfolio, as fate would have it, belonged to the Right Honourable Sir John A. Macdonald. Almost immediately after defeating the Liberals on October 16, 1878, Macdonald had transferred the Mounted Police from the Department of the Secretary of State to the Department of the Interior, thereby giving himself ministerial control of the force. One of the first things he wanted to know was when Sitting Bull and the Sioux could be expected to leave Canada. Sir John was keen to rid the Dominion of such an expensive, potentially troublesome burden.

Major Walsh stated in his report that he was of the opinion the Sioux would eventually return to their own country. In fact, he had already prepared letters of introduction to the military authorities and Indian agents south of the line for the chiefs of 200 Sioux lodges. He suggested to the chiefs that the letters would facilitate their surrender and would help them get more favourable terms from the U.S. government. Driven by hunger, more Sioux were preparing to follow. Sitting Bull, though, was not one of them.

Major Walsh signed the report and leaned back. Just then, a blur of movement outside the window caught Walsh's attention. He looked out. Speak of the devil! Sitting Bull, Black Moon, and Four Horns were walking across the quadrangle toward Walsh's cabin. Walsh didn't like the look on Bull's face, on the faces of any of them for that matter. The blasted paperwork would again have to wait.

Getting up from his desk, Walsh moved to the door. He nodded to Sitting Bull, Black Moon, and Four Horns as they stepped into his cabin, addressing each by name. Walsh had a good knowledge of the Sioux language, although he still liked to have an interpreter around in case anything was missed. "Cajou!" he shouted across the quadrangle. Cajou Morin's head bobbed out from one of the log cabin's doorways. Walsh waved his arm, signalling the scout to come over to this office.

"Greetings, *Wahonkeza*," Sitting Bull said, his face solemn as he shook hands with the redcoat officer. The others also shook hands. Cajou joined them a moment later.

"Find out what they want, Cajou," Walsh directed gruffly, stepping back to his desk and sitting down.

The half-Sioux scout talked with the leaders, then looked at Walsh. "T'ey want provisions, Major, flour, tobacco, tea, bacon, an' bullets—'specially tea an' tobacco."

Walsh had already caught enough of what Sitting Bull said, particularly his demanding tone. The chief complained that there were no buffalo to hunt, the White Mother had no compassion for him or his people, and the Canadian government was letting his people starve. He did acknowledge that the Mounties had given them food from their own supplies, when they could spare it. Walsh listened to Sitting Bull's thinly veiled threats if provisions were not forthcoming.

The tirade was soon too much for Walsh. "What the bloody hell!" he exploded, jumping to his feet and slamming his clenched fist down so hard on the desk that the inkwell bounced. "Who in hell do they think they are? What gives them the right to barge in here and demand provisions from me, after all the god-damned trouble they've caused?" Walsh tore his angry eyes from Cajou to Sitting Bull. "You, Sitting Bull, you've been nothing but a bloody nuisance, you and your young men with their horse stealing! You've given me and my men no end of god-damned trouble! We've got enough to do without you and your mob adding to it! Have you forgotten that you're American Indians? You haven't any right to be in Canada. The only reason you're in this country is because the American soldiers chased you out of your own country. Now you come here and break our laws, even though you promised not to. You seem to think all white men are afraid of you! Well, they're not! Tell them that, Cajou!"

Sitting Bull had not learned any English, but he certainly understood the tone of Walsh's words. Walsh was known up and down the frontier for his colourful and sometimes intemperate language. Morin no sooner interpreted his words than Walsh added more. "Tell them to get their god-damned provisions at the trading store and get the hell out of here before I throw the whole damned lot of them in the guardroom!"

Sitting Bull's face remained expressionless, but his black eyes blazed in anger. "Be careful, *Wahonkeza*! You are talking to the leader of the mighty Sioux nation!"

Walsh didn't wait for Morin to translate this latest word of Sitting Bull. "I know damned well who I'm talking to. What I said still goes! Now get the hell out of here, and if there's any more horse stealing by any of your people, I'll clap irons on you too and toss you in the guardroom, you god-damned red son of a bitch!"

Sitting Bull stiffened. He raised his hand, shaking an angry brown finger at Walsh. "No man can speak to me like that!"

Walsh glared back at him. "Are you threatening me? Are you threatening the Mounted Police? Damn it all! Behave yourself or I'll throw you out of here!"

Walsh's words were too much for Sitting Bull. With an angry mutter, he reached for a revolver stuck in his waistband, but Walsh saw what he was about to do. Bounding around his desk, he grabbed Sitting Bull's wrist in a vise-like grip and twirled him around. Then he steered him toward the door and heaved him out of the cabin, sending him sprawling onto the ground outside. Snarling, Sitting Bull reached for the revolver again as he got to his feet. Walsh was too fast for him, raising his boot and kicking the Sioux chief in the buttocks, sending him sprawling into the dust again.

Black Moon and Four Horns pushed past Walsh out of the cabin. As Sitting Bull climbed to his feet, again reaching for the revolver, they grabbed him. Anxious to calm their ally, they held his arms, attempting to restrain him. Furious at Walsh, Sitting Bull struggled to free himself, determined to kill the white man—the only white man—to humiliate him so. In the ensuing struggle the two Sioux chiefs wrestled him against the log wall of Walsh's cabin, smashing his shoulder into the window in the process. Finally tiring, Sitting Bull gave in and sank to the ground, his hand releasing its grip on the revolver.

He sat there for several minutes, the other two standing beside him. Then rising again after regaining some composure, Sitting Bull stalked haughtily off without looking back. Black Moon and Four Horns followed him.

Walsh watched their retreating backs for a moment as they made their way along the settlement's street toward Jean Louis Legare's trading store, where a noisy mob of Sioux had gathered. Glancing at the barracks, Walsh shouted, "Turn out, men! Carbines and sidearms! There might be trouble!"

While the dozen or more NCOs and constables on the post tumbled out of barracks, buckling on sidearms and carrying carbines, Walsh stepped back into his cabin. He slid open a desk drawer, grabbed his Enfield and a box of ammunition, and broke the heavy service revolver open, stuffing six shiny brass-cased cartridges into the empty cylinder chambers. He snapped the revolver shut and slid it into its holster. Buckling the revolver belt around his waist, he stepped back outside and crossed the quadrangle to join his men.

"Weapons loaded, fellas?" he asked the men lined up in front of the scattering of log cabins.

"Yes, sir," Sergeant Henry Hamilton replied.

Walsh stood in front of his men and waited, watching the road from Legare's trading store. An outburst of shouting and ki-yiing erupted from the direction of the store. A moment later, Sioux horsemen appeared, moving toward the police post. Leading them was Sitting Bull riding his cream-coloured pony.

"Here they come," Walsh warned. He spoke to Morin. "Cajou, step over to the hay corral and pull out those two railing poles. Lay them end-to-end across the road in front of the barracks." He pointed to the roadway just beyond the entrance to the police grounds.

Morin hurried to the hay corral and dragged the rails over to the road where Walsh had indicated.

Shouting and jeering, the Sioux drew closer, young warriors shaking their rifles, tomahawks, and coup-sticks angrily at the thin red line in front of them.

"Tell them that's far enough, Cajou," Walsh said. "They're not to come any closer than those two poles on the ground. The first one who does will be shot."

Morin repeated Walsh's warning. The Mounties held their carbines ready.

Sitting Bull's gaze was locked on Walsh as he rode forward. Walsh stood his ground, staring back at the Sioux leader. Sitting Bull looked as though he would ride right over Walsh, but at the last moment he yanked hard on his reins. The cream-coloured pony stopped just as it was about to step over the poles. Sitting Bull's Sioux bunched up behind him.

"That's good," Walsh said. "You're wise not coming any closer. Now, you've caused enough trouble for one day. Go back to your camp."

Some of the young warriors growled and muttered among themselves. They knew there were enough of them to kill the few redcoats standing before them. Walsh continued staring up at Sitting Bull. Sitting Bull's face was expressionless, but his black eyes glittered. He had been poised to stab his dagger into the hearts of the White Mother's redcoats, but in the end he could not do it. He wheeled his pony around and rode away. Gradually the others turned their ponies and followed him back to their camp.

Chapter 17

Hunger By Design

The Mounted Police brought in wagonloads of food, a contravention of Dominion policy, courtesy of James Walsh.

John Finerty in *Warpath and Bivouac*

Heavy grey clouds drifted overhead, hiding the vast blue sky spread wide above the prairie grasslands. Sitting Bull cast his gaze upwards, back across the Milk River toward the bluish thunderheads in the northwest, over the Cypress Hills—the Thunder Breeding Hills. A fork of lightning lit up the summer sky. A look of contentment came onto his face as he smelled the rain in the air. Sitting Bull turned south, searching the horizon for smoke. The long-knives were burning land between the Milk and the Missouri to stop the buffalo from migrating north to the White Mother's land. Rains were the only hope to put out the fires.

As he rode south, Sitting Bull's eye remained keen. He was looking for buffalo. He was also watching for long-knives. You had to watch for long-knives south of the medicine line.

Sitting Bull was leading the forward line of hunters—the scouts or "wolves." There were twelve of them altogether, ten Sioux and two Nez Percés. Behind them at some distance the others were spread wide across the prairie, all looking for buffalo. They had already found one small herd and killed what they could, but there were many mouths and they needed a lot more. They would advance all the way to the Missouri if they had to, but hopefully there would be more buffalo before then.

Topping the next rise, Sitting Bull suddenly stiffened, focussing on a movement a quarter of a mile ahead. Coming down a hill toward them was a band of Indians and a *wasichu*! The *wasichu* wore blue. The Indians were Crow. There was a brief silence. Then the Crow started pointing and shouting, bringing their rifles to their shoulders.

The Sioux shouted warnings to one another. "*Absaraka!*"

A fusillade of rifle shots erupted from the rifles of the oncoming Indians. They were the despised Army scouts!

The twelve hunters snapped up their rifles and returned the fire as the Crow charged toward them. Wheeling their ponies around, the outnumbered Sioux raced back over the rise, threw themselves to the ground, and readied their weapons.

The Crow scattered, finding cover wherever they could—in shallow depressions, behind the occasional rock, burrowing into the ground. Some pulled their ponies around and galloped back over the hill they'd just come down. Once there they jumped out of their saddles, bellied down just below the crest of the hill, and returned the Sioux fire. The white soldier with them—Lieutenant William P. Clark of the 2nd Cavalry—turned his horse around and galloped back over the prairie in the direction he and his scouts had come from to notify General Nelson Miles that he'd made contact with hostile Indians and needed reinforcements.

Indian agents had complained to Washington that Canadian Métis and Sitting Bull's Sioux were crossing the border and hunting buffalo on agency land, denying agency Indians their share. Furthermore, the agents reported, the Sioux were also stealing horses from Montana ranchers and running them back to Canada, despite efforts by the North West Mounted Police to stop them. Washington had ordered General Miles, commanding the Military Department of the Yellowstone at Fort Keogh, to take the field and drive the intruders back across the border. With a force of approximately 500 cavalry, infantry, and scouts, General Miles left Fort Keogh, reaching Fort Buford on July 9. On the 15th he started marching north toward the Canadian border, and two days later Lieutenant Clark's scouts made contact with Sitting Bull and the first of his hunting party. Miles sent two companies of cavalry forward posthaste to reinforce the scouts, following with the rest of his force as fast as it could move.

Sitting Bull and his eleven Sioux and Nez Percé warriors continued to hold off the 50 Crow scouts, at the same time signalling the rest of the hunting party following to withdraw and get the women and children—who were following to skin and dress the kill—back across the Milk on their way to the White Mother's country. One woman and a child were killed, and they had to abandon some of the meat they'd been dressing from the earlier hunt and some of their camp equipment, such as drying racks for the hides.

Gradually Sitting Bull and his warriors retreated towards the Milk, fighting all the way to hold off the Crow scouts, who were duly reinforced by the two companies of cavalry Miles had sent forward. During the fighting, Sitting Bull saw some army officers on a hill just beyond rifle range, watching what was going on. It was easy to distinguish the tall, bearded figure of General Miles among them. Taking a few of his braves, Sitting Bull made his way forward to another hill and signalled that he wanted to parley. He didn't want to fight the soldiers, all he wanted to do was hunt buffalo. But Miles wasn't in the mood to discuss anything with his old adversary.

Seeing it was useless to try to talk to Bear Coat, Sitting Bull resumed fighting, taking up a position on top of a ridge a short distance from the river and firing at anything that moved. A Crow scout on top of a rise just above the solders' positions kept firing at the Sioux chieftain. One bullet ploughed into the grass a foot away from him. Sitting Bull spotted the Crow, watched him for a moment, then pulled his rifle into his shoulder, took careful aim, and squeezed the trigger. He saw the Crow throw up his rifle as his head snapped back. Sitting Bull smiled. "*Absaraka* dog!" he muttered.

But now General Miles, impatient at the way his advance was being checked, ordered up two Hotchkiss guns to blast away at the Sioux. Soldiers wheeled the guns into position, then Miles's artillery officer gave the order to fire. The next moment the guns rained down shells on the Sioux. At the same moment the heavens opened and the rain that had been sweeping across the hills and prairie from the northwest pelted down, drenching both sides. Under cover of the downpour, Sitting Bull and his warriors abandoned their positions and fell back across the Milk.

Realizing that Sitting Bull had got away from him once more, General Miles waited at the Milk for the rest of his troops to catch up with him, then crossed the river on July 21, continuing his advance. He followed the Sioux trail, finding more abandoned meat and camp equipment on the way. Two days later Miles camped along Rocky Creek, a few miles south of the border. His scouts continued north until they reached the stone cairns marking the medicine line. They could see Indians on the distant slopes of the lower reaches of Wood Mountain gazing calmly back at them.

✳ ✳ ✳

Riding out of the Wood Mountain NWMP post, Major Walsh, Cajou Morin, Corporal George O'Connor, three constables, and Lieutenant Tillson of General Miles's 5th Infantry headed toward Sitting Bull's camp. They met the Sioux on the trail to Wood Mountain. Sitting Bull was intent on moving closer to the settlement.

Walsh questioned him about the fight with the army south of the Milk River a few days earlier. His relationship with Sitting Bull was still somewhat strained as a result of the incident at Wood Mountain three weeks before. Uppermost in Walsh's mind was whether Sitting Bull had broken his pledge not to carry out raids across the American border. Sitting Bull, however, told Walsh that he and his people were hunting buffalo when Crow scouts came upon them and opened fire. He and his warriors had simply defended themselves and pulled back across the border.

Satisfied with Sitting Bull's explanation, Walsh then rode down to General Miles's camp just below the border to explain what had happened. Walsh thought well of the tall, bearded general in spite of some of his faulty reporting. They had already met and got along well together.

"Sitting Bull had no hostile intentions," Walsh said. "He and his people needed meat. Buffalo have been pretty scarce north of the line for the best part of a year now. Bull had heard there were buffalo around the Milk, so he took some of his band down there to look for them. If they hadn't been attacked, they would have returned peacefully after they'd shot enough buffalo. Bull told me that, in all sincerity, and I believe him. I've always found him to be a man of his word."

General Miles grunted. He did not share Major Walsh's confidence in Sitting Bull. "I've been ordered to drive all hostile Indians back across the line. We won't tolerate raids on our soil."

"Fair enough. I'm under orders myself to co-operate wherever I can, but I can't see that hunting buffalo can be considered a raid. The poor devils need food. They have to hunt."

"Orders are orders. Our own Indians need all the buffalo they can get. Anyway, the Sioux don't stop at hunting buffalo. They steal horses every chance they get."

"Whenever they do and it's brought to my attention, my men and I do everything we can to return them."

"Yes, and we appreciate that, Major, believe me."

General Miles spoke of the other matter that had brought him northward: parties of Canadian Métis were also crossing the border to hunt buffalo. "From now on, all property of any Canadian half-breeds we find trading ammunition with our Indians on our side of the line will be confiscated—wagons, contents, and horses."

"I don't have any instructions about our half-breeds trading ammunition to your Indians, General. But our traders sell ammunition to U.S. Indians living in Canada for hunting purposes only—and just enough for hunting. We keep a close watch on that, I can assure you."

Miles reminded Walsh that much of the country just south of the border was an Indian reservation and that his orders included keeping all non-reservation Indians as well as half-breeds off it for any purposes whatsoever. This may have been a reference to the big camp Louis Riel had set up on reservation land along the Big Bend of the Milk River the previous year, which the army had broken up. "If the Sioux want to cross the line, they'll have to surrender themselves, give up their horses and guns, and agree to go to a reservation. None of them will be harmed, and they'll be given enough food. I'd like you to pass that on to Sitting Bull."

Walsh nodded. "I'll give him your message, General." Walsh, however, knew the message would be wasted on Sitting Bull, who after this most recent encounter with Miles would be more determined than ever not to surrender to the army.

"And would you take John Finerty to Sitting Bull's camp with you? He's a newspaper correspondent for the *Chicago Times*. He's been with my column since we left Fort Buford, reporting on what's been going on. He'd love to get a look at that wily red devil and his Sioux."

Walsh smiled. "I'd be glad to, General."

Walsh spent a night in General Miles's camp, mixing with the army officers, exchanging pleasantries, and swapping stories. Next day he headed back to Wood Mountain, promising to return in a few days to take Finerty to the Sioux camp.

A day or two later, two Métis turned up at the post to report that General Miles had rounded up some 300 Métis families hunting buffalo in Montana. The Métis asked Walsh if he would speak to the general on their behalf.

Walsh and an escort returned to General Miles's camp. Upon vouching for the identity and good behaviour of most of the Métis hunters, Walsh was able to secure their release and then accompanied them back across the Canadian line. From there he took the American newspaperman, John Finerty, to Sitting Bull's camp. In charge of Walsh's escort was Sergeant-Major Joe Francis, who had been "B" Troop sergeant-major during the Dufferin days of 1874.

As Walsh's party approached Sitting Bull's camp, now enlarged with the addition of other Sioux bands that had joined him, Indians galloped to meet them. They gathered around, shaking Walsh's hand and the hands of his escort. They ignored Finerty at first, but their indifference turned to hostility, probably because his clothing was similar to the uniforms of the American soldiers. There was much excitement in the camp. A Métis had visited it a short time before with a story that Walsh had been killed in Miles's camp. The Sioux were all set to avenge *Wahonkeza* and were preparing to swoop down on the army in a mighty attack. Jubilant shouts arose when they saw Walsh was far from dead.

Chiefs, headmen, and councillors sat down on the ground in a big circle around Walsh and his party. Among those in the circle were Spotted Eagle; Gall, the war chief who had fought prominently at the Little Bighorn; Rain-In-The-Face, another prominent fighter at the Little Bighorn; Long Dog, Sitting Bull's war chief; One Bull, Sitting Bull's nephew; Pretty Bear, Long Dog's brother; Bad Soup, Sitting Bull's brother-in-law; Broad Trail; Stone Dog; and Iron Horse. Outside the circle, hundreds of warriors sat on their ponies, and beyond them stood women and children, all pressing in to see the visitors.

Then Sitting Bull appeared on his cream pony. The Sioux chief's expression was sober. He sat just outside the circle, staring fixedly at Finerty for several moments. Then he slid down from the pony and led it to one side. Finerty looked back at him, but dropped his eyes when he found Sitting Bull still staring at him.

When everyone was settled, Walsh addressed them through a Métis interpreter. "I have just come from Bear Coat's camp and he asked me to tell you that none of you are to cross the medicine line to hunt buffalo again, or for any other purpose except to surrender yourselves. It is my duty to remind you that you are safe on this side of the line as long as you behave yourselves. The White Mother will protect you as long as you do not break her laws. But you must understand that she will no longer protect you if you go back across the line to hunt buffalo while you are living on her land. Bear Coat told me there are buffalo heading this way, and I advise you to wait until they come. I saw them after I left Bear Coat's camp."

A babble of excited murmuring broke out among the Sioux. "*Washtay!*" Pleased looks covered their faces as they looked at one another. "*Washtay! Washtay!*"

At that moment an Indian galloped into the camp, rode up to the large circle, and breathlessly addressed the Sioux. The interpreter asked what had happened. He was told that two Sioux braves had been caught by the long-knives on the American side of the line, hunting buffalo. In the shooting that had followed, one of the braves had been killed, the other wounded.

When Walsh heard this, he said, "Your young men will not listen to me! If they had done as I told them, this would not have happened. As long as any of you turn a deaf ear to what I say, things like this will continue to happen."

One of the seated Indians, Bad Soup, pointed at Finerty. "Who is he?"

"He is what the Americans call a newspaperman," Walsh explained. "He tells the people what happens. He is not a soldier. He will do you no harm. His father and mine come from the same country across the sea. His heart is good."

The Hero, an Ogalala and Broad Trail's brother, stepped forward and shook hands with Walsh and Finerty, then began a long speech praising *Wainga Tanka* and the Great White Mother, but cursing the American soldiers who had killed women and children. He said it was strange that when his children cried for meat and he could see buffalo near the stone heaps, he was not allowed to kill them. "*Wainga Tanka* never meant to throw temptation in front of his people when they are so hungry." Then he looked directly at Finerty. "I would like to ask this *wasichu* to talk to my people. The Americans ask us to smoke with them today, yet they shoot us tomorrow." The Hero then sat down, his eyes riveted on Finerty.

The newspaperman looked at Walsh. "What should I do?"

"Talk to them. Tell them what your heart tells you."

Finerty looked around uneasily, but he was a journalist and words were his stock-in-trade. "I am not from the American government," he said, speaking slowly at first, then picking up speed, the Métis interpreter translating his words into the Lakota tongue. "I am from the American people, who live far from Indian land. I tell them what is happening, and that is why I have been riding with Bear Coat's soldiers. I do not have to tell you why the soldiers and their scouts fired on you a few days ago. The Americans will not deny you food if you don't make war on them. All Americans—all white men—don't have bad hearts for the Indians. I do not have a bad heart for you. I can only listen to what you have to say, then tell it to my people. Like you, my people do not always hear the truth."

A grumpy expression on his face, Bad Soup grunted. "Very few Americans speak the truth. It was the Americans who taught us to lie. I hope you are different." Bad Soup looked as though he had finished speaking, then he suddenly asked, "How long will Bear Coat stay beside the Milk River?"

Before Finerty could answer, Walsh said, "That's none of your business, Bad Soup. He'll probably stay there all summer if your young men keep on crossing the line. As long as you don't go down there, it shouldn't matter to you how long he stays. He won't cross over to harm you."

More Sioux rose to speak, most of them saying that it was not right for the long-knives to shoot down their young men who were only hunting buffalo across the line. Walsh repeated that they must not cross the line for any reason whatever, unless it was to surrender themselves.

Sitting Bull said nothing. Much of the time he didn't even appear to be listening to what was said. When the talking became heated, Spotted Eagle brought it to a stop by saying he would lead a buffalo hunting party to the White Mud the next day and watch for the buffalo said to be moving north.

Walsh nodded. "That is good, Spotted Eagle. Please make sure, though, that no one crosses the line."

"It will be done, *Wahonkeza*."

Walsh, his escort, and John Finerty remained in the Sioux camp for three days. RCMP historian Turner described that evening's gathering:

During [the] evening John Finerty gained a marked respect for the Sioux in general. Many came to shake his hand, though Bad Soup purposely stayed away. Though Sitting Bull adhered to his determination to have nothing to do with Americans, one of his wives, a nephew and several other members of his family turned up. The handsome young Lone Bull, his nephew, and Little Assiniboine proved to be friendly enough, while the great chieftain, the lord and master of the entire camp, amused himself by breaking young horses, at which he was very adept. During his conversation with Sitting Bull's relatives, Finerty gleaned that Sitting Bull had himself taken charge of the rear guard in the brush with Miles's scouts, in order to protect the women and children, and that Little Assiniboine, who was wounded, had later taken his place.

While jotting down his impressions the following day Finerty, accompanied by Superintendent Walsh, took himself to a nearby hillside and pictured the scene below him in the great camp:

"From that commanding elevation nearly every tepee of the tribes already mustered there was visible. Expecting as I did to see a great gathering of the Indian clans, I had no idea they were so formidable at that time in men and horses … I thought there were, at the lowest calculation, from 1,000 to 1,100 lodges in the encampment. There must have been at least 2,500 fighting men in the confederated tribes … They seemed to glory in their strength, and the young warriors wore an air of haughty hostility whenever I came near them. Their leaders, however, treated me respectfully. Sitting Bull stared at me occasionally, but was not rude, as was often his habit when brought in contact with people he supposed to be Americans, whom he hated with inconceivable rancour.

"The camp was placed in a lovely valley through which wound the crystal stream known as Mushroom Creek, and was shaped somewhat like the figure 8, the upper and larger side containing the Hunkpapas, Ogalalas and Sans Arcs, while the lower held the Yanktons, Santees and Nez Percés, not to mention the ferocious Minniconjous and the broken remnants of different tribes assembled there for protection … There were among them some of the greatest cutthroats on the plains, demons whose names are written in shame and the blood of the helpless and innocent … No matter in what direction we looked, there were ponies and war horses grazing on the thick buffalo grass…There could *not have been less than 15,000 animals ... My eyes were fascinated by this spectacle—wild horses and wilder men, constituting the lingering chivalry of the barbaric nations, against whom, from the days of Columbus to our own, the hand of advancing civilization has been steadily uplifted ... With all my confidence in General Miles as a soldier, and my high opinion of the men of his command, I declare frankly, although I was willing to take whatever chances might have come, I am glad it did not become a part of his duty to charge that nest of human hornets with the 500 available men of his command."*

Turner later wrote: "Despite Finerty's estimate that there were 1,000 lodges in the big Sioux camp, there were really not more than five or six hundred, representing a population of about 3,000."

The experience had a lasting impression on the Chicago newspaperman. Finerty later said: "I felt then, and I still feel, under great obligation to Major Walsh for having given me an opportunity that otherwise might never have fallen to my lot, or that could only be attained by the sacrifice of my hair. And a scalp once taken, like a neck once broken, is beyond all human aid."

After the three days in Sitting Bull's camp, Walsh said goodbye to the American newspaperman, then headed toward Wood Mountain, leaving Sergeant-Major Francis in charge of the escort of three constables and a Métis scout that would take the writer back to Miles's camp. Finerty was fascinated by Francis's past and the fact that he had ridden in the charge of the Light Brigade at Balaclava 25 years earlier.

On Finerty's return, Miles and the cavalry packed up and left the border, heading down to patrol the Missouri.

Chapter 18

Walsh Moves to Qu'Appelle

Walsh is, I fear, primarily responsible for the Indians' unwillingness to leave Canada.

John A. Macdonald to the Governor General,
November 1879

In early August 1879, the last of the great buffalo herds massed in the Milk River country. The virtual disappearance of the buffalo, and the resulting hunger, forced more Sioux to follow the trail of those who had already returned to the United States. A further 75 lodges went back across the line in November, making a total of more than 400 lodges that had surrendered to the army at Fort Keogh or at Fort Buford on the Missouri, just east of the Yellowstone in Dakota Territory. By the following April, more were on the way, the notable war chief Gall among them.

This was the way Walsh had predicted the Sioux would eventually return to their own country when newspaper reporters interviewed him in 1878. They would return in small numbers at first, as an experiment, with the others watching from the security of Canadian territory to see how they were treated. If satisfied the first of the returnees weren't being unduly punished, others would follow.

Sitting Bull, however, was another matter. His encounter with General Miles in the summer of 1879 was enough to make him fear, as he always had, that the bluecoats would be waiting for him to cross back over the line and that they would pounce on him, then pay him back for Custer's defeat.

During the winter of 1879–80, Walsh issued food to the Sioux to keep them from starving. The Sioux killed many of their weakened horses and ate them. Some of the horses had become diseased, so the Sioux suffered an epidemic of sickness. In a confidential report to Colonel Macleod—a report that subsequently found its way to Ottawa and, presumably, to the desk of Prime Minister Macdonald—Walsh praised the conduct and character of the Sioux, their general observance of law and order, their patience and endurance, the way they helped each other. Walsh pointed out that he and his men extended them every consideration, that they even divided their own rations among them. He also pointed out that the Métis went out of their way to help the Sioux. Jean Louis Legare, the Wood Mountain trader who was a friend to all Indians, used up just about everything in his store to help them, without any hope or expectation of payment.

Even so, at times there was little food to go around, and when the stores of the Mounted Police and of Legare had run out, the Sioux had to fall back on their own resources. There were four or five other trading stores now in Wood Mountain settlement. One of them, Kendall and Smith, was managed by a man named Allen. He had a bad reputation for short-changing the Indians, and the Sioux hated him. One evening after Allen had locked up for the night, some Sioux braves hammered on the door, demanding entry. Allen and his three employees, one of whom—Daniel "Peaches" Davis—was a 23-year-old former Mountie who had taken his discharge to seek better pay, barricaded the doors and windows while Mrs. Allen and her small child cowered in terror in the living quarters next door.

Eventually the Indians went away. But next morning when Allen opened the trading post door, they crowded in, shouting abuse and accusations, claiming he cheated them in the past and demanding food in payment for these past misdeeds. They said they were starving and needed flour, bacon, and tobacco. Allen demanded buffalo robes or other trade goods in payment, but the Indians claimed they had none. No one understood much of what the other said, but both the Indians and the trader comprehended enough to get the gist of their points across.

The Sioux were ranged in front of Allen, who was standing behind his counter, a loaded Winchester just out of sight beneath it. While all the shouting was going on, one Sioux brave pushed his way into the trader's house next to the trading post, where he confronted a terrified Mrs. Allen holding her baby. She tried to run into an adjacent room but the Indian bounded after her, grabbed the baby, and wrestled it from her grasp. He then pulled a hatchet from his belt and left the house, covering the short distance to the trading post in long strides with Mrs. Allen, crying hysterically and pleading for her baby, running after him.

Holding the hatchet threateningly over the baby's head, the Indian barged in through the trading post's front door and stood where Allen could see him plainly. The Sioux said, "You will not give us food, even though my children are starving. Well, if you don't, I'll kill your little one."

Screaming frantically, Mrs. Allen tried to grab the baby back, but the Indian shrugged her off his arm and kicked sideways at her. Mrs. Allen reached for the baby again, clinging to its clothes. Peaches Davis picked up a rifle and pointed it at the Indian's head, telling him to give the baby back to the mother or he'd shoot.

"Don't shoot, Peaches," Mr. Allen called out, picking up his loaded Winchester from beneath the counter. "I'll give 'em something to think about." He pointed his rifle at an open barrel of gunpowder sitting in a corner behind the counter. "One false move from anyone," he shouted, sweeping his eyes over the Indians, "and I'll blow the whole damn lot of us to hell!"

Everyone looked at one another, wide-eyed, not knowing what to do. Then Davis put down his rifle. "Don't do it, boss," he said. "I'm going to Major Walsh. I'll be back in a few minutes." Davis rushed for the door, pushing past the Indians, and ran down the street toward the Mounted Police post.

Major Walsh was sick in bed, but Sergeant Henry Hamilton hurried to the officers' quarters and told him what Davis had reported.

"Take some men and get over to that store, Sergeant," Walsh said. "Bring Mrs. Allen and her baby here and tell those Indians that if they are not all over here within fifteen minutes, I'll go over there and deal with them myself!"

Sergeant Hamilton took three constables—Allen (no relation to the trader), Thompson, and Dunn—and with Cajou Morin hurried along to the Kendall and Smith trading post. Constable Allen, a huge man, heaved Indians to left and right as he moved toward the one holding the baby. Grabbing him by the shoulder, Allen rammed the Indian in the back with his knee, then pulled him back until he released the baby into the arms of Mrs. Allen. The constable was about to throw the remaining Indians out of the trading post, but Sergeant Hamilton ordered otherwise. "Let's get Mrs. Allen and the baby to safety first!"

When they arrived back at the Mounted Police post, Major Walsh was sitting on an upturned box in front of his quarters, a blanket over his shoulders.

"Good," Walsh said when Sergeant Hamilton reported what had happened. "Now go back and take those Indians' names, then tell them to get back to their camp. Tell them they're lucky no harm came to the baby. And Sergeant," Walsh added, a glint in his eyes, "tell that trader I want to see him down here right away."

When the trader turned up at Walsh's quarters a few moments later, the steely glint was still in Walsh's eyes as he said, "Mr. Allen, you're damned lucky nothing else happened in that store this morning. If those Sioux had turned the place upside down, I wouldn't have blamed them. You would've got what you deserved. I know all about you, all about your shady trading practices. A buffalo robe for a pound of sugar, indeed! Or two robes for a lousy pound of tea! That's damned out-and-out robbery. You're lucky none of those Indians came to me with their complaints. You'd have wound up in the cells, believe me. I think it's high time you found employment elsewhere. Maybe someone over at Fort Walsh village will give you a job working as a clerk in their store. But you're not wanted around here. I advise you to get out of here smartly. I'll even hold the Sioux back from trailing after you."

Soon after, Allen, his wife, and the baby were aboard a wagon heading out on the Fort Walsh trail. They were not seen around Wood Mountain again.

✳ ✳ ✳

Many Americans accused the Canadians of being too soft on the Sioux, much to the annoyance of Sir John A. Macdonald. No one wanted Sitting Bull and his tribe off Canadian soil more than Old Tomorrow. Over time the prime minister concluded that one of his biggest problems wore a red coat. He decided that Major Walsh's handling of Sitting Bull was responsible for the Sioux leader's refusal to return to his own country. By late 1880 Macdonald's sources, and possibly Walsh's enemies, were exposed, and Walsh's future was defined in a letter sent from Indian Affairs Minister Edgar Dewdney to the prime minister (see page 190). Sir John had read the NWMP commissioner's reports and most of the relevant newspapers. He was well aware of Walsh's friendship with Sitting Bull and his sympathy for the Sioux. Ever since his re-election as prime minister in 1879 he had believed Walsh enjoyed the publicity he received and that he was purposely keeping Bull in Canada. As early as November of that year, Sir John confided his belief to the Governor General of Canada, the Marquess of Lorne: "Walsh undoubtedly has influence with Bull, which he tried to monopolize in order to make himself of importance." Macdonald added that he was considering having Walsh cashiered from the force.

Ironically Walsh, at almost the same time, was preparing the last year-end report he would ever forward to Commissioner Macleod from

Chicago Oct 23 1880

My Dear Sir John.

The day before I left Fort Walsh mail arrived from Wood Mountain and I was shown by Major Irvine a private & confidential letter from Capt. Crozier in which some references were made to Sitting Bull, and as I find the American Papers and some Canadians are publishing correspondences between the agent at Ft. Buford and the authorities at Washington in reference to a recent application said to have been made by Sitting Bull to surrender through a scout named Allison, I thought it better to advise you of the contents of Crozier's letter.

He states that in conversation with Sitting Bull, he informed him that Major Walsh ... promised to go to Washington and see the President of the United States and intercede for him & that he could not say what he would do in regard to surrendering until he heard from Major Walsh.

Capt. Crozier remarked that he thought it was unfortunate that any action of ours should delay the surrender and it would not look well at Washington if such an impression got abroad and advised that an official message from our government should be sent to Sitting Bull as soon as possible to let him know that Major Walsh had no authority from our government for leading the American Indians to believe that he was authorized to plead for them in Washington ...

Capt. Crozier's impression is that had it not been for this all the Sioux would have surrendered before this. At the time he wrote there were 140 lodges on our side of the line and some few were returning from the American agencies ...

Yours sincerely,
E Dewdney

A.G. Irvine's agenda regarding Walsh is made clear in the information he passed via Edgar Dewdney to Ottawa, as shown in this excerpt from a letter of Indian Affairs Minister Dewdney to Sir John A. Macdonald.

Wood Mountain. Walsh's words seemed more those of a pragmatist than an opportunist:

Within the last year very few buffalo have been in the section north of the line; consequently the Indians have camped the greater part of this time on the White Mud River ...

Considering the agitated state in which these people have been kept during the last year by Crow and other Indians stealing their horses and killing their young men while following the chase, and General Miles' expedition driving them from the hunting grounds and Milk River to the boundary line, their conduct has been extremely good; but this good conduct ... is only reached by their fear of being sent back to the United States ...

> There are some very good people in this tribe, people whose constant cry is for peace and rest, and who will make any sacrifice to maintain it, yet there are others who cannot be trusted.

Walsh had many times tried to talk Sitting Bull into returning to the United States. Sitting Bull, however, had it in his mind that he was a British Indian and was hopeful the White Mother would eventually give him a reserve in Canada. Walsh told Bull that she was unlikely to do this. He knew what the government's attitude was toward the Sioux. Sitting Bull was equally concerned, of course, about the treatment he would receive in the U.S. if he did go back.

In 1880, a new rumour arose that claimed Walsh was trying to talk Sitting Bull into accepting a promoter's scheme to make him part of a public exhibition touring eastern Canada, the implication being that Sitting Bull and Walsh would be paid handsomely. The rumour also named Sub-Inspector Edwin Allen in the plan, although Allen had resigned his commission two years earlier, in September 1878.

In a report to Colonel Macleod, Walsh admitted he had been approached to talk to Sitting Bull about such a proposal, but had refused. He also denied the rumour that Sitting Bull would have gone back to his own country by this time had Walsh not encouraged him to hold out for better conditions from the U.S. government.

Walsh no doubt had enemies in the Cypress Hills. In November 1878, a friend of Major Irvine's, using a pen name, had written a letter to the *Fort Benton Record* accusing Walsh of disloyalty to the assistant commissioner. The anonymous correspondent also accused him of trying to keep the Sioux in Canada so he could build up a "police empire" around Wood Mountain.

Finally, despite Walsh's denials, and even though none of the rumours were ever substantiated, the damage had been done. Prime Minister Macdonald, as minister in control of the NWMP, used his office to influence Colonel Macleod. He wanted Walsh transferred away from Wood Mountain to some place where he would no longer have any contact with Sitting Bull.

Although he had received his original appointment to the Mounted Police from Sir John, Macleod was not a pliable man, and during his period as commissioner he resisted the prime minister's attempts to appoint officers to the force whose main qualifications were their political connections. He may, however, have formed the opinion that it was not a good idea to keep officers in one place too long. And the possibility of friction between Walsh and Irvine, or, more specifically, of animosity

Walsh might hold for Major Irvine, was also a concern. In *Sitting Bull: The Years in Canada*, historian Grant MacEwan wrote: "The situation became serious when a letter appeared in the *Toronto Globe* sharply criticizing the Assistant Commissioner [Major Irvine] at Fort Walsh. Irvine's friends were incensed and blamed somebody close to Walsh."

In June 1880, Colonel Macleod ordered a general shifting of commands. He transferred Superintendent Walsh and "B" Division (the term "troop" had been replaced by "division") to Fort Qu'Appelle, a one-time Hudson's Bay Company trading centre that had become a growing farming community. It was 160 trail miles north and east of Wood Mountain. To replace them, Superintendent Crozier and part of "F" Division were moved from Fort Walsh to Wood Mountain. The officers and their commands at Fort Macleod, Fort Calgary, and Battleford were all caught up in these transfers. Grant MacEwan observed that "the Qu'Appelle assignment looked important, but for Walsh it did not hold the interest or the challenge of Wood Mountain ... He was not well and he was not happy." Fort Qu'Appelle might be a farming community of increasing importance to the economy of the west, but from a police point of view it offered far less than Wood Mountain. And in daily contact with "civilization," Walsh would not have enjoyed the free hand he had at his former post. He may well have thought his transfer was a punishment rather than a promotion. Macleod resigned from the NWMP shortly after the transfers were arranged.

* * *

Sitting Bull was devastated when he heard about Walsh's impending move. He immediately rode over to the Wood Mountain NWMP post to see his old friend. As the chief entered Walsh's quarters, the Major could not help but notice the old warrior's eagle-feathered war bonnet.

"Is it true," Sitting Bull asked, "that my friend the Major is going away?"

Walsh looked grave. "I'm afraid it is, Bull."

Walsh and Sitting Bull talked, pulling out their pipes. Walsh passed his tobacco across the desk, and Sitting Bull took it, filling his pipe, then returning the tobacco.

After they had been talking for some time, Walsh raised the matter of Sitting Bull returning to his own country. Time was running out. Walsh would not be able to help him much longer. There was no longer any belief the buffalo would return. Sitting Bull, however, said what he had said all along. He would never go back. Those who wanted could go, but he would not. He repeated the same fear that had held him from going back all along. "I know the Americans blame me for *Pahuska*'s death. It was a fair fight, and *Pahuska* carried the fight to us, as I have told you, but the Americans will hang me if I go back. The American people have not forgotten me."

As they talked on, though, Sitting Bull for the first time admitted that he might be prepared to go back and shake hands with the Americans. "If the White Mother is determined to drive me from her country into the arms of those waiting for me like hungry wolves, will you talk to the White Father and ask him whether I will be treated like a man and not like a dog if I go back? Will I get the same treatment others of the Lakota have received? Or will I be grabbed and hung up on a tree?"

"I will gladly speak with the White Father if the White Mother's government will allow me to," Walsh replied.

As they continued talking, Walsh became sentimental about leaving. "I won't forget you, Bull. We've had our differences, but they haven't been insurmountable. I hope some day we'll meet again." Walsh changed the subject. "By the way, when I ride out of here with the other redcoats in a few days, I'll be riding the old grey horse, the one your braves took down at the Little Bighorn. You remember? I bought him from a local mixed-blood. The one I call *Pahuska*."

Sitting Bull's eyes sparkled as he smiled, his face lighting up. "Yes, I remember. I hope you keep him always."

"I will."

"Before you go," Sitting Bull extended his arms, "I want you to take this." He handed the war bonnet across the desk to Walsh. It was his priceless possession. "Take it, my friend. And keep it. I won't need it again. Every feather marks a deed of bravery done in war when the Lakota were strong."

Walsh was deeply touched.

* * *

Later that week, Major Walsh rode out of the settlement on the old grey gelding Custer, at the head of the Wood Mountain half of "B" Division.

After four days of travel Walsh joined the rest of "B" Division at their camp on the north side of Qu'Appelle Lake opposite the old Hudson's Bay Company post. The Fort Qu'Appelle detachment was under the interim command of 31-year-old Inspector Samuel Benfield Steele. Steele had been sergeant-major under Walsh in the early days of the Mounted Police at Ottawa and Lower Fort Garry. They were old friends, often of like minds and rarely impressed by Ottawa.

Steele could see that the Major's spirits were low. And he knew that the one true Walsh rumour concerned his fleeting health. Walsh confessed that he already missed Wood Mountain and his Lakota and Métis friends. He would miss the moments of excitement, the occasional uncertainties, the independence of unfettered command. He could no longer ignore the fact that his health had deteriorated. He suffered from recurring bouts of erysipelas and the difficulties of Wood Mountain often aggravated the illness. The one bright spot on the horizon was a leave of absence awaiting him—a chance to spend time with his wife and daughter Cora, who was now eight years old.

Walsh spent five days reorganizing his command, arranging barrack accommodation, and stabling the division's horses. Then he turned over command to Inspector Steele and travelled to Winnipeg, then Fargo, where he entrained for St. Paul and Chicago, and finally reached Brockville, Ontario.

Chapter 19

Sitting Bull Waits

I wait for the return of White Forehead.
          Sitting Bull to Colonel Irvine, November 1880

Paddy Crozier wasn't fooling around. The prime minister's orders were to get rid of Sitting Bull, and that was what Crozier set out to do.

Irish-born Lief Newry Fitzroy Crozier's ambition was to command the North West Mounted Police one day. An infantry major before taking up his commission as a sub-inspector in the force at the age of 27 on November 4, 1873, he had gained valuable experience while stationed at Fort Macleod, Fort Calgary, and Fort Walsh. He had dealt with Bloods, Blackfoot, Peigans, Cree, North Assiniboines, and Sioux. He had as much experience dealing with Indians as any officer in the force, with the possible exception of James Morrow Walsh, and the two men had very different styles. Like Walsh, Crozier put up with no nonsense. Upon assuming command at Wood Mountain, he plunged in, intent on correcting his predecessor's "misguided" ways. There were a few old hands still at Wood Mountain: the scouts, Cajou Morin and Louis Daniels, and Sergeant Henry Hamilton had been left behind to help out with their knowledge of the country and the people.

In February 1880, Crozier began to visit Sitting Bull and the other Sioux chiefs. By this time, some 3,700 Sioux had returned to the United States, largely as a result of Walsh's efforts, leaving little more than 1,200 remaining on Canadian soil. A true sign of the continuing deterioration of the situation was renewed horse thievery. Only this year, rival tribes were stealing animals to eat.

Crozier sat down in Sitting Bull's lodge, hoping to convince him to return that summer before the weather turned cold with winter snow sweeping down on the prairie. One of his arguments was that if the

A dedicated, no-nonsense commander, Paddy Crozier never let compassion get in the way of managing the Sioux situation.

Sioux delayed any longer, they would jeopardize the favourable terms and conditions under which the U.S. government had promised to accept them.

Sitting Bull listened, but his lined face was like granite, showing no reaction, no feeling. He simply sat and smoked his pipe, looking back at this new redcoat chief sitting on a buffalo robe where his old friend used to sit. Sitting Bull was sure that Major Walsh would speak to the big chiefs in the east on his behalf, and he wasn't going anywhere until he had heard from Walsh.

Frustrated by Sitting Bull's unresponsiveness, Crozier got up and left the camp, determined to follow another course of action. If he could not persuade Sitting Bull to move back to his own country, he might be able to sway the other chiefs into returning without him, as Gall and others had already done. On his next visit to the Sioux camp, Crozier addressed the tribal council, speaking to them as a group, paying no attention to Sitting Bull as the chief, barely even looking at him. Crozier explained how much better off they would be in their own country, again pointing out to them that the Americans had not mistreated any of those who had already gone, telling them that nothing but starvation faced them in the White Mother's country, that the White Mother would continue to give them sanctuary but would no longer feed them. She had enough of her own Indians to look after. He reminded them that they could not hunt below the line without constant fear of attack from Colonel Miles's American soldiers.

The strategy of withdrawing food supplies came from Ottawa. Ignoring Sitting Bull was the Superintendent's idea. If Crozier's tactic worked, Bull would eventually be left with so few followers that he would have little choice but to go back, or he would be so weakened that the Canadian government could afford to risk moving him forcibly without fear of starting up an Indian war. Crozier's efforts had some success.

There were already 14,000 Sioux on reservations at Rosebud, Pine Ridge, and Standing Rock when Spotted Eagle and his Sans Arcs decided to leave Sitting Bull's camp, subsequently surrendering to Miles at Fort Keogh.

Sitting Bull soon realized what was happening, and his soldier society warriors—his "camp police"—resorted to force to discourage others who wanted to go back. Most of the remaining Sioux were camped fairly close to each other, and it wasn't difficult for Sitting Bull's warriors to exercise enough vigilance to keep them where they were.

Conditions on both sides of the border were in a state of unrest. Food was as scarce in northern Montana as it was in the southern North-West Territories. War parties of Crows, Gros Ventres, and South Assiniboines dashed across the line to run off horses they found loosely guarded. Canadian Crees and Bloods struck back in retaliation just as quickly. The few buffalo that found their way into the Milk River country were swooped upon from all sides. The Sioux in Canada, regardless of rumours of long-knives hovering just below the border, hunted buffalo as always. Intertribal killings were common. The relative calm that Walsh had long maintained grew more fragile. The Mounted Police at both Fort Walsh and Wood Mountain were seldom out of their saddles.

* * *

Superintendent Crozier worked incessantly to resolve the Sioux problem and see the last of Sitting Bull. As Major Walsh had done, he recommended to his superiors that a force of at least 50 men be stationed at Wood Mountain to ensure order along the American border and to provide protection for any settlers arriving in the area. He also favoured locating reserves far from the border to reduce contact between opposing Indian tribes and the temptation of making raids into each other's territory. In particular, he said that Sioux reserves in Montana should be a considerable distance from the border to diminish the temptation to cross over to Canadian territory. Crozier simply wanted the Sioux gone. He cited instances of Sioux headed for agencies south of the border who stole horses as a departing act of "gratitude" to a country that took them in. Crozier also warned of the probability of war parties:

> In fact, should they come, they would do so in all probability as "war parties," which means horse stealing, or when necessary or when convenient, killing people as well. Threats to that effect have, I understand, been already made by those who have gone to the American agencies. Then in addition to hostile Sioux, there are,

covering our frontier from Fort Assiniboine to Buford, thousands of American Indians who, though agency Indians, roam about the country seemingly without restraint, and are altogether unreliable. Therefore, for the present at least, if a force is to be maintained here at all, it should be a strong one.

* * *

Between his skin disease and the prime minister, Walsh was having a frustrating time. His home at Brockville was a relatively short train ride from Ottawa, and once he had attended to family, his thoughts turned back to Wood Mountain. Although he was on sick leave, the Major persisted and finally obtained an interview with the prime minister.

Sir John A. Macdonald gave Walsh as much consideration as he gave Sitting Bull's request for a reservation in Canada. Macdonald had been highly displeased at what he saw as Walsh's inability to persuade Sitting Bull and the Sioux to return to their own country, though he *was* aware of the service Walsh had performed in general with regard to the Sioux. Now he listened silently while Walsh outlined Sitting Bull's plight, pointing out the reasons Sitting Bull was reluctant to return to the United States. Walsh made no secret of his sympathies for the Sioux. He told Sir John he was willing to go to Washington and speak to Rutherford Hayes, noting that he had been extended an invitation to call on the White House whenever he was in Washington.

Macdonald flinched at Walsh's mention of going to see Hayes. Mounted Police officers had no business calling on U.S. presidents. That was for prime ministers and ambassadors, not a Mounted Police superintendent. And to hell with Sitting Bull's personal safety! Sir John didn't give a damn what happened to Sitting Bull. He'd been a nuisance to the Canadian government for far too long already. Macdonald had heard enough from the Sioux sympathizer in front of him. He assured Walsh that he was well aware that many Sioux had gone back to the U.S. reserves. Handled properly, Macdonald knew it would only be a matter of time before Sitting Bull would leave as well. Macdonald wanted to see the last of him, but he wasn't going to risk allowing Walsh to go to Washington. Sitting Bull, Macdonald figured, would eventually get so damned hungry he'd be only too glad to go back. Macdonald not only refused Walsh's overture to Washington, he insisted Walsh extend his sick leave. Walsh left Ottawa suspicious that Macdonald was less concerned about his health then he was intent on keeping the Major out of the action indefinitely.

Deeply disappointed by the prime minister's attitude, Walsh returned to Brockville and resigned himself to a well-earned rest. For one of the rare times in his life he surely felt he had failed a friend.

* * *

Sitting Bull could not understand why he had not heard from his good friend. He was now isolated from any sense of moral support among the redcoats. The Sioux chief had no confidence in Superintendent Crozier, whose blunt, blustery, impatient manner was a contrast to Walsh's more diplomatic personality. Bull even missed Walsh's explosive temper; Bull always knew where he stood with Walsh, and the Major had never let him down.

Crozier was ready to try anything when Major David Brotherton, commanding the U.S. Army at Fort Buford, contacted him in autumn 1880 and asked to send an army scout to Sitting Bull's camp. Although Crozier frowned upon army scouts entering the Sioux camps with inducements for them to return south, one such visit would soon change his opinion. Scout Edwin Allison was sent to visit Sitting Bull, who was still on the White Mud. Allison, a long-time fixture in the Montana territory, was well aware of the Sioux plight. He had won the trust of the Sioux headman, Gall, through a chance meeting while delivering cattle from the Sun River toward North Dakota.

Gall had returned to the U.S. but was still in contact with Sitting Bull's camp, intent on convincing his spiritual leader to give up his self-imposed exile.

Allison, who would later write a book on the events that were about to unfold, had no affinity for Sitting Bull, but he did see an opportunity for himself. With provisions provided by Major Brotherton, Allison soon found himself at Wood Mountain. After a three-day visit, Allison reported back to Fort Buford where General Terry heard his story and encouraged a second meeting.

He carried a renewed offer from Washington of a full pardon in exchange for the Sioux's surrender. These were the same conditions that had applied when General Terry met Bull at Fort Walsh three years earlier.

Allison approached Sitting Bull's camp, leading pack horses loaded with presents, which he distributed to Sitting Bull's band. The Sioux greeted him warmly—something they wouldn't have done earlier. They appreciated the presents of tobacco, tea, flour, and meat. Sitting Bull invited Allison to spend the night in his lodge with his family of two wives, sisters, twin sons, and two daughters.

That evening Sitting Bull unburdened himself of all his troubles, the history of his complaints about the U.S. government, and the reasons he stood up for the rights of his people and refused to give up Sioux land in the Black Hills. The Americans had driven him from his country. Sitting Bull told Allison, however, that his heart was no longer bad toward the American government or the people.

Allison repeated the U.S. government offer. He pointed out that it meant Sitting Bull and his people would no longer go hungry. Sitting Bull replied that he would think it over. Although he was conscious of the approach of winter and the certainty that food would be hard to find, Sitting Bull was still determined not to make a move until the Major returned from the east with good news.

Allison departed for Fort Buford. He had not persuaded Sitting Bull to return, but he had given many of his followers something to think about.

Before winter snows descended over the Cypress Hills-Wood Mountain region, Lieutenant-Colonel Irvine, who on November 1, 1880, succeeded Colonel Macleod as commissioner of the NWMP, rode over to Wood Mountain with his acting adjutant and a small escort to inspect the post. (Macleod had resigned to devote his full time to judicial duties in the Bow River judicial district, which now took in the country as far north as Edmonton.) While at Wood Mountain, Colonel Irvine visited Sitting Bull and the other Sioux chiefs. Irvine was anxious to hear what Sitting Bull thought of the American offer put to him by Allison, hopeful that he could pass on good news to the prime minister. Irvine told Sitting Bull he should accept the American offer, adding that it was unlikely the White Mother's government would grant him a reserve in Canada. Irvine urged Sitting Bull not to wait for Walsh to return but to take up the American offer right away, before the onslaught of winter.

Colonel Irvine had impressed Sitting Bull when they first met three years before. The chief liked Irvine and would listen to him before he would listen to Crozier. Irvine met the Sioux headmen at Wood Mountain on November 23 and left four days later, believing that Sitting Bull would soon return to his own country.

Meanwhile, Crozier continued his efforts to sway the other Sioux chiefs. He got a positive response from Low Dog, a chief of the Ogalalas. Displaying unusual patience, Crozier talked of Low Dog's prospects in Canada for the coming winter. When Low Dog asked him what the White Mother thought about his situation, Crozier explained that she was a compassionate woman with a big heart and that it distressed her to see so many of the Sioux suffering in her land because of the stubbornness of a few selfish chiefs. She believed the Sioux should act in their own best interests.

Low Dog told Crozier there were many in the Sioux camps who wanted to accept the American government's offer, including himself. He told Crozier to visit the other Sioux camps and repeat the White Mother's belief. Low Dog said that if he started out with his band, others would follow. Crozier followed Low Dog's suggestion, visiting other camps and explaining the situation.

Little more than a week later, Low Dog and his band pulled up camp and started south for the medicine line. A day later he was across the border. To Crozier's amazement, Sitting Bull went with him. But it was too soon to rejoice. Before many days passed, Sitting Bull and his band came trudging back across the snow-swept plains, seeking once more the sanctuary north of the line. He had changed his mind.

Many attempts have been made to interpret Sitting Bull's actions in those difficult November days. Certainly, fewer Sioux headmen were willing to risk starvation through the winter as time passed. Edwin Allison would later identify Gall as the driving force behind the schism with Sitting Bull. In a final showdown, Allison wrote, Gall "publicly called upon all who acknowledged him as their chief to … prepare immediately to follow him to Fort Buford."

It wasn't part of Crozier's character to accept defeat. Throughout the winter of 1880–81 he tried to persuade the Sioux leader to take his few hundred remaining Sioux and return to their own country. Jean Louis Legare assisted him, promising to ride with the Sioux down to Fort Buford and feed them along the way. Crozier invited a hungry Sitting Bull and his chiefs and headmen to a big feast. During the dinner, Crozier talked about the advantages to the Sioux of going back to their own country, contrasting it to the starkness of winter on the Canadian plains and emphasizing the scarcity of buffalo north of the border. Sitting Bull was receptive and admitted that a letter from Major Brotherton guaranteeing they would be given the best of treatment would tempt him to go.

Crozier lost no time following this up. He sent Inspector Macdonell and two constables, a Métis scout, and three Sioux warriors across the line to Fort Buford to see Major Brotherton. A fortnight later they returned carrying a letter from the major and a reassuring report from the three warriors who had gone to see for themselves how well they would be treated. Another big feast was thrown for the outwardly grateful Sitting Bull, at which he sat down and ate his fill. Then Major Brotherton's letter was interpreted to him. Crozier and Inspector Macdonell waited with bated breath.

Unknown to Crozier, or most at the feast, was the latest tragedy. At Poplar Creek on December 31, one of General Terry's officers, Major Guido Ilges, had insulted Gall and then attacked the Sioux encampment, killing eight. Sitting Bull had learned of the bluecoats' latest deceit only hours before.

Sitting Bull turned his eyes to Superintendent Crozier. "The Americans lie!" he said. "I don't believe them!" Then he stood up, tossed his blanket over his shoulder, and stalked out.

Crozier was momentarily dumbfounded. Then he stood up, shaking a fist at the departing backs of the Sioux chiefs and headmen. "Damn you—all of you! I don't want to see any of you again. You can all go to hell!"

Chapter 20
Sitting Bull Hears from His Friend

A warrior I have been
Now it is all over
A hard time I have.
　　　　　Sitting Bull's surrender song

If the eastern chiefs would not let Walsh return to Wood Mountain, if no message from him was forthcoming, Sitting Bull would go to Fort Qu'Appelle to see him. With his immediate following of a little less than a hundred people, including women and children, he set out on the 160-mile trail as soon as the winter snows had melted.

When they arrived in the Qu'Appelle valley, Sitting Bull found the Mounted Police post and asked for his friend. But instead of finding Major Walsh, he was confronted by Inspector Sam Steele, still acting in command of "B" Division. Steele told him Walsh had not yet returned from eastern Canada.

Sitting Bull was deeply disappointed. He told Steele that Canada was his country and the *Shagalasha* were his friends, and that he had been given to understand he would be given a reservation in Canada. He did not want to go back to the United States. He was a British Indian, and the fact that the British gave the part of the country he was born in to the United States did not bind him to the Americans.

Steele replied that the Canadian government considered the Sioux to be American Indians, and the government's policy was for them to return to their own country. Steele told him it was highly unlikely the government would give him a reservation in Canada. According to the White Father, he had long ago become a citizen of the United States and that was where he would have to return eventually, where he and his people would receive the benefits of being United States citizens, such as food and a reservation.

Sitting Bull argued that he had always been given to understand that he could ask for a reservation in Canada and that it would be given to him. Steele said he did not have the authority to make a decision of that sort, but he agreed to send a rider to notify the Indian commissioner, who was at Shoal Lake, 160 miles farther east, and he could perhaps resolve the question.

Indian Commissioner Edgar Dewdney arrived a few days later. He was unsympathetic. He told Sitting Bull the White Mother's government wanted him to return to his own country. He told the Indians to go back to Wood Mountain, secretly hoping they could be persuaded to continue on and surrender to the U.S. Army at Fort Buford. As an

Sam Steele had risen to the rank of superintendent when this photo was taken. In the long run he fared better at conforming to the constraints placed on frontier policemen by their political masters than James Walsh did.

inducement, he offered to provide enough food to last them until they reached Wood Mountain. Steele offered to send a Mounted Police escort with them to take charge of the food and issue it along the way.

Sitting Bull, however, was in no hurry to return to a life of hunger, and he still hoped Walsh would return with good news. The Qu'Appelle valley was pleasant to behold, with Métis cabins dotting the landscape, the Hudson's Bay Company post nearby, and a Métis settlement and a mission four miles away. Sitting Bull and his warriors moved their camp from place to place, begging food here, scrounging food there, trading some worn-out saddles, clothing, and old American army uniforms taken from the dead at the Little Bighorn. Fear of the Sioux spread throughout the peaceful valley at the sight of the forlorn but still dangerous warriors. Finally Inspector Steele and the local Indian agent persuaded them to move back to Wood Mountain, renewing the offer to provide food along the way. When they set out on the return journey, Sitting Bull's disappointment that he had not heard anything from Walsh grew.

As soon as Sitting Bull and his followers arrived back at Wood Mountain, their Mounted Police escort turned around and headed out on the return ride to Fort Qu'Appelle. The Sioux had eaten all the food and now found themselves with nothing to eat. Sitting Bull was in a belligerent mood. He went to the Mounted Police post and demanded rations. Superintendent Crozier had left a short time before to take command at Fort Macleod, and Inspector Macdonell was now in command at Wood Mountain.

"We want rations," Sitting Bull told him. "The same as you give the Crees and Assiniboines. If you don't give them to us, we'll take them."

He was threatening the wrong man. Inspector Macdonell glowered back at him. "I'll ration you with bullets!"

Sitting Bull was taken aback. The Scottish-born NWMP officer reminded him of Walsh. "I am thrown away," Sitting Bull said.

"No you're not," Macdonell replied. "You've been given good advice to go back where you came from, where you can get all the food you need. Take it and go back."

* * *

The following spring, Walsh was still on indefinite sick leave at Brockville. He was free to enjoy the comforts of his family and home life, but he was also anxious to return to duty, though his health had not improved sufficiently to allow him to go back. At least, that was Sir John A. Macdonald's stance. The prime minister didn't want Walsh going anywhere near Sitting Bull. Macdonald was committed to his starvation tactics and he had made it clear to the NWMP chain of command that they were to be followed until Sitting Bull left. Walsh's tactics of persuasion took too long, so he had become part of the problem. Rumour already had it that Walsh had written Sitting Bull and sent him presents via the well-regarded trader, Jean Louis Legare. Macdonald wanted to cashier Walsh, to remove him from the force completely, but he was afraid that if he did this, Walsh might go back to the west on his own and undo the progress others had made in getting the Sioux to return to their own country. So the prime minister kept the Major in Ontario on sick leave, where he could rest in ignorance of what was going on out west until Sitting Bull was safely back across the border and so far removed that he would never cause any trouble for the Canadian government again.

Ironically, Walsh and Macdonald wanted the same thing, and Walsh was only too ready to help resolve Sitting Bull's primary fear—that the

American government would retaliate against him for Custer's defeat. However, Sir John had forbidden him to go to Washington to see the president on Sitting Bull's behalf. Luckily for all concerned, James Morrow Walsh had a mind of his own.

Walsh took a train to Chicago, where he went to see General Hammond of the Indian Bureau, whom he had met previously. General Hammond agreed with him that Sitting Bull should not be singled out for unfair treatment over the Custer incident. He assured Walsh that Sitting Bull could proceed to Fort Buford and surrender there without any fear. General Hammond told Walsh he had influential friends in cabinet positions in Washington who would, if necessary, intercede on Sitting Bull's behalf.

Returning to Ontario, Walsh resolved to send a message to Sitting Bull. He decided, though, to avoid official channels. He wrote to Louis Daniels, one of his former scouts at Fort Walsh and Wood Mountain, who was in Manitoba looking into the prospects of farming. He could trust Daniels. Walsh asked him to go to Sitting Bull's camp at Wood Mountain and assure him that he could proceed to Fort Buford and surrender to the army, that the U.S. government would extend to him the same treatment it had given to the other Sioux chiefs such as Spotted Eagle and Gall.

Grant MacEwan wrote: "Daniels carried out the instructions faithfully. Sitting Bull had heard similar assurances from other people but was not convinced. If Walsh said it, however, it was … all [Bull] needed."

* * *

Sitting Bull surrendered to Major Brotherton at Fort Buford on July 19, 1881. The Sioux chief was accompanied by Jean Louis Legare and several Wood Mountain Métis who went along to help. Legare gave Sitting Bull and his followers food along the way and provided wagons for those who no longer had ponies to ride. When they arrived at Fort Buford, Inspector Macdonell joined them, assisting in the negotiations for the surrender of Sitting Bull and his followers, in all about 238 Indians. Under house arrest, Sitting Bull started his new life by composing a surrender song.

There were many sighs of relief in Canada when word got around that Sitting Bull had left Canadian soil for good. Colonel Irvine reported:

> I cannot refrain from again placing on record my appreciation of the services rendered by Superintendent Crozier who was in command at Wood Mountain during the past winter. I also wish to bring to the

After finally returning to the U.S. in 1881, Sitting Bull was held at Fort Randall, South Dakota for two years. These photographs were taken at Sitting Bull's winter camp in 1882.

favourable notice of the Dominion Government the loyal and good service rendered by Mr. Legare, trader, who at all times used his influence with the Sioux in a manner calculated to further the policy of the government, his disinterested and honourable course being decidedly marked, more particularly when compared with that of other traders and individuals. At the time of surrender of the Sioux Mr. Legare must have been put to considerable personal expense, judging from the amount of food and other aid supplied by him.

Although a great deal of praise from both sides of the border was accorded Major Walsh for his work and courage and endurance in helping to resolve the Sitting Bull situation, Colonel Irvine did not even mention him in his report to Prime Minister Macdonald.

Historian Grant MacEwan describes how an "American editor nominated Commissioner Irvine for the distinction, saying: 'There is no doubt whatever that Sitting Bull's surrender is attributable to the great exertions shown by Col. Irvine.' But Irvine did not see much of Sitting Bull. Colonel James Macleod carried more influence with the Chief but, in his case as in Irvine's, he was only occasionally among the Sioux."

Following Sitting Bull's surrender, Walsh returned to his command of "B" Division at Fort Qu'Appelle. He remained there for two years. On September 1, 1883, after almost exactly ten years of service, he retired from the NWMP with a gratuity of $1,166.66 per annum, consistent with pensions granted to other retired officers based on their rank and service.

According to R.C. Macleod in his book *The North-West Mounted Police and Law Enforcement 1873-1905*, Macdonald "had found a scapegoat and Walsh, although not summarily dismissed, was forced to resign in 1883, after Sitting Bull was safely back in the United States … It is equally certain that Walsh did not deliberately prolong the [Sitting Bull's return] crisis. He was understandably bitter about the way he had been treated and in later years wrote several drafts of a book justifying his conduct."

Walsh was human enough to feel sympathy for an oppressed people. He had a sense of destiny and faith in his ability, as well as the courage, to acquit himself with distinction in the situations his duty took him into. It was no sin to enjoy publicity, and there is little proof that he went out of his way to court it. He served his country well and was rewarded poorly for it. He deserved better.

Chapter 21

The After Years

He looked death in the face, his bright keen eyes
without a tremor.

Brockville Times obituary July 25, 1905

After his return to the U.S., Walsh's old friend Sitting Bull was confined at Fort Randall until 1883, then moved to Standing Rock. In the summer of 1885, just after Riel's failed North-West Rebellion ended the dream of an Indian–Métis alliance regaining control of the west, Bull joined "Buffalo Bill" Cody's Wild West Show as one of its main attractions, touring the United States and eastern Canada. A false rumour persists to this day that he was seen camped in Walsh's backyard at Brockville, Ontario. In an interview with a journalist from the *Toronto Globe* in August that year, Sitting Bull admitted to having been approached five times by Louis Riel or one of his Métis agitators to join Riel's army of the Indian blood. He would not bear arms against his trusted friend White Forehead and the Mother Walsh represented.

Sitting Bull continued to fight for Sioux rights and against the continuing assault on their lands. At Standing Rock he often remained at odds with his old ally Gall, who befriended local Indian agent James McLauglin. Gall was appointed a judge over Indian offences in 1889 by McLauglin who, a year later, was intent on stamping out a new source of optimism amongst his Sioux charges. Sitting Bull, although there was no proof of his participation, was associated with the Ghost Dance religion, which promised that an Indian messiah was coming who would drive the whites from their lands. Sitting Bull was shot and killed with his seventeen-year-old son Crowfoot and six followers in a fight with tribal police and soldiers at Grant River, South Dakota, on December 14, 1890, aged 54. It is said that Sitting Bull, ever the visionary, had forecast his death at the hands of his own people. In one sense Sitting Bull's death was a blessing that saved him from a final heartbreak. Two weeks after the great chief was buried, his old nemesis Nelson Miles triggered one of the great atrocities of the era when he ordered the arrest of Sioux Chief Big Foot in South Dakota. Over 200 Sioux, followers of the Ghost Dance religion, were slaughtered at Wounded Knee Creek. The holocaust was conducted by the 7th Cavalry, formerly led by George Armstrong Custer.

Sitting Bull's appearance with Buffalo Bill Cody in Montreal in 1885 fuelled rumours of a visit to Major Walsh's home in nearby Brockville. As Walsh was preoccupied with his coal business in Manitoba that year, such a meeting was unlikely.

* * *

In 1884 a delegation of Métis from the Saskatchewan River country rode down to Sun River, Montana, where Louis Riel was teaching school. They persuaded him to return with them to the North-West Territories to lead them in their fight for redress of their land claims. In March 1885 the North-West Rebellion broke out with a Métis–Indian attack on a Mounted Police party from Fort Carlton that was out to recover abandoned food and ammunition supplies from a store at Duck Lake, halfway between Prince Albert and Battleford. The NWMP troop, led by Paddy Crozier, encountered an ambush. At the end of the skirmish, five Métis and twelve Mounties were dead. Hastily mobilized troops from eastern Canada were carried west on the almost-completed Canadian Pacific Railway line, arriving within marching distance of the rebellion to assist the Mounted Police in suppressing it. Riel surrendered to the force's commander in mid-May. He was charged with treason-felony, tried, and convicted, and was hanged at the Mounted Police barracks at Regina on November 16, 1885.

In spite of his retirement years earlier, Major Walsh's legacy lived on in the spirit and style of some of his "B" Troop men. Here his former sub-inspector, John McIllree (on the white horse), is seen sporting an imperial beard, similar to Walsh's, and symbolic of "B" Troop at Fort Walsh. McIllree is leading a NWMP patrol in 1885 at the time of the Riel Rebellion.

Paddy Crozier's career suffered as a result of his ill-advised confrontation at Duck Lake, and he resigned from the force in 1886 after he was overlooked by John A. Macdonald for appointment as the new commissioner.

* * *

If Inspector Walsh was to gain only one admirer in his brief command at Fort Qu'Appelle, he impressed the right man. After Walsh returned from his extended leave of absence, he took back from Sam Steele the task of maintaining order along the new rail lines crossing the prairie.

A letter from William Cornelius Van Horne, then the 39-year-old general manager of the Canadian Pacific Railway construction project, addressed to NWMP Commissioner Irvine praises Walsh and his detachment. Van Horne was not given to effusiveness, so his words, which marked the beginning of Walsh's last year of service, are therefore significant.

Lt. Col. A.G. Irvine, Commissioner,
North West Mounted Police,
Regina.

Dear Sir,—Our work of construction for the year 1882 has just closed, and I cannot permit the occasion to pass without acknowledging the obligations of the company to the North West Mounted Police, whose zeal and industry in preventing traffic in liquor and preserving order along the line of construction have contributed so much to the successful prosecution of the work. Indeed, without the assistance of the officers and men of the splendid Force under your command it would have been impossible to have accomplished as much as we did. On no great work within my knowledge, where so many men have been employed, has such perfect order prevailed. On behalf of the company and of all their officers, I wish to return thanks and to acknowledge particularly our obligations to yourself and Major Walsh.

I am, sir,
    Yours very truly,
        W.C. Van Horne, General Manager.

The expression of gratitude was extended a few months later when two siding sites east and west of Maple Creek were designated "Walsh" and "Irvine."

Walsh's association with Van Horne would prove fortuitous. Trains need fuel. Upon leaving the NWMP, Walsh established the Dominion Coal, Coke and Transportation Company in Brandon and helped open up coal mining in Manitoba's Souris River district. Soon his largest customer was the CPR and his good friend was W.C. Van Horne, the company president at the time. With his new-found wealth, Walsh bought a grand home in central Brockville for his beloved daughter Cora and her mother in 1884 and named it "Indian Cliff."

Walsh prospered in business and nurtured his social standing, becoming a friend of Clifford Sifton, a Liberal politician who rose to the position of Minister of the Interior in Prime Minister Sir Wilfrid Laurier's cabinet. His business demands often found him in Winnipeg and it was there that he first heard that Sitting Bull had been killed at his reservation. One of Walsh's regrets thereafter was his failure to visit his old friend.

During his association with Van Horne, one act more than any other demonstrated the affection and respect he held for Cornelius Van Horne. Sitting Bull's war bonnet, a friendship gift given to the Major by the Sioux chief, was presented in turn to Van Horne by Walsh. The treasured symbol of the great Sioux leader was eventually donated by the Van Horne family to the Royal Ontario Museum.

No doubt inspired by his shoddy treatment at the hands of Old Tomorrow and his Tory colleagues, Walsh gravitated to Liberal politics. In the decade after he left the force, Walsh became a strong critic of the direction politics seemed to take the NWMP.

Although it was not his intent, a letter he wrote Liberal Prime Minister Wilfrid Laurier after his 1896 election win almost led to dissolution of the force. Regarding a bill introduced in Parliament to amend the Mounted Police Act, Walsh wrote an introduction outlining aspects of his personal career, "five years of which I had charge of … the Territory of Cypress [sic] and Wood Mountains, fronting for a distance of 250 miles on the home of the most hostile Indian Country of the United States."

Walsh recounted Sitting Bull's arrival, the plight of the Nez Percé, and ultimately, in 1879, placating Sitting Bull's camp of 2,500, keeping them from crossing the border and "destroying [General Miles's] command for had the Indians attacked Miles his fate would have been that of Custer."

As he had during his tenure in the force, Walsh harshly criticized government misspending. In 1896 he recommended that the Liberals "cut the force in two … 500 men were sufficient to … maintain law and order quite as well as it was being done … Extravagance has been rampant in the Public Departments and it is the duty of our Party to put a stop to it if we can."

Walsh was a reluctant recruit the following year when his friend, cabinet minister Clifford Sifton, came knocking. Sifton appointed Walsh, then aged 54, Commissioner (Administrator) of the Yukon during the Gold Rush of 1897. Although opposition newspapers would cry foul, it was the old Mountie who was doing the favour. His was not a political appointment, although much was made of his $5,000 annual salary. Most agreed with the *Winnipeg Tribune*'s assessment: "It might be difficult to find a man possessed of more of the essential qualifications." Walsh crossed the country by rail to Victoria, B.C. and sailed north on the steamer *Quadra* destined for the Klondike.

He was also superintendent in charge of the NWMP in the Yukon, reporting directly to the Minister of the Interior rather than the commissioner of the NWMP. Ironically, in the Yukon Walsh had 250 Mounties under his command, almost the same number as had embarked from Fort Dufferin as part of the original NWMP column 25 years earlier.

Although Walsh strove to establish and maintain an efficient and effective government administration in the Yukon, he was caught up in political controversy and happily resigned his appointment after slightly

Some historians claim Walsh's passing was largely ignored. Surviving photos of his funeral procession suggest otherwise.

less than a year. All the same, he left his mark. As if by fate the NWMP officer who took over much of the role was his old comrade of 1873. Superintendent Sam Steele, who commanded the North West Mounted Police in the Yukon during the gold rush, wrote in this book *Forty Years in Canada*: "… each [man] having to bring into the Yukon district at least 1,150 pounds of solid food besides tents, cooking utensils, prospectors' and carpenters' tools, or he would not be permitted to enter the country. This order given by the commissioner of the territory [Walsh] was one of the wisest given in the Yukon and was the means of preventing much trouble and privation; needless to say it was strictly enforced."

While much of his adult life was spent far from his roots, James Morrow Walsh made Brockville, Ontario, his final home; Indian Cliff honoured his favourite rock outcropping in the Cypress Hills. He died there at age 65, survived by Mary and their only daughter, Cora. His funeral was held on July 25, 1905 and the *Brockville Times* wrote, "It is long since Brockville has beheld so solemn and impressive a spectacle as the funeral of Major Walsh under the military auspices of the 41st Regiment, Brockville Rifles … His courage like his convictions was strong and intense. A prominent feature of his life was unselfishness."

If Canada had evolved as a country to cherish such thing, he could have been a national hero.

* * *

The last word on Walsh's relationship with the great Sioux chief belongs to James Morrow Walsh himself, quoted in Grant MacEwan's book *Sitting Bull: The Years in Canada*. "Major Walsh wrote of Sitting Bull the day after learning of his death: 'I am glad to hear that Sitting Bull is relieved of his miseries, even if it took the bullet to do it. A man who wielded such power as Sitting Bull once did, that of a king, and over a wild and spirited people, cannot endure abject poverty ... without suffering a great mental pain, and death is a relief. I regret now that I had not gone to Standing Rock and seen him. Bull has been misrepresented. He was not the bloodthirsty man reports made him out to be. He asked for nothing but justice. He was not a cruel man. He was king. He was not dishonest. He was truthful. He loved his people and was glad to give his hand in friendship to any man who was honest with him'."

Almost 100 years after his death, Major James Morrow Walsh is kindly remembered in Brockville, Ontario. Walsh, his wife Mary, and daughter Cora rest in their own private corner of the community graveyard on the outskirts of town. The lower half of this composite photograph shows the front of the three gravestones that face the Walsh monument.

Walsh built this house in Brockville, Ontario for his wife, Mary, and his daughter, Cora. He named it Indian Cliff in honour of his favourite place in the Cypress Hills. The attractive commemorative plaque shown on the back cover was placed in front of his home to pay tribute to the man and his deeds.

Appendix

There is ample evidence that James Morrow Walsh held ideas and values that clashed with perspectives that surrounded him. By all accounts Major Walsh was a humanitarian placed on a frontier where hardship, starvation and death were common. From the time Walsh lead the first NWMP recruits across an unfriendly Dawson Route, to the day he left Wood Mountain, no proof exists that Walsh purposely acted to the detriment of his country, the loyal members of "B" Division or the Native peoples under his supervision.

Walsh was asked to accomplish the impossible, then to defend his actions when he had reduced this task to the improbable. Correspondence from Walsh's days in the force until his retirement fifteen years later suggests that Walsh was far less influenced by personal aspirations than he was by the plight of the Sioux people and of Sitting Bull, a man he greatly respected.

Walsh saw that Sitting Bull was a man of wisdom, vision, and generosity. In James Walsh, Sitting Bull had found a man he could, and would, trust. At an unfortunate time, in a remote place, an invisible bond grew between these two men. The NWMP Major would later recall, "No man ever left Bull's camp hungry." That is, if there was any food to be had. And whether it was against orders or not, James Walsh and his men willingly went without in order to share their rationed food supply with the Sioux.

Frontier reporter John Finerty witnessed the NWMP delivering a wagonload of Wood Mountain foodstuffs to Sitting Bull's people, but the act was for the benefit of the Sioux, not the visiting newspaperman. Yet politicians in Ottawa and Washington cringed when the *Chicago Times* wrote, "It was only the intense humanity of Major Walsh that kept the wretched people from eating their horses."

James Walsh earned the wrath of John A. Macdonald, largely through circumstances beyond his control, but the Major also seemed to operate beyond the government's authority.

Ottawa not only condemned Walsh's handling of Indian matters in his territory, but it also took him to task for his actions against the exiled Louis Riel. In a letter to commissioner J.F. Macleod typed on six pages of legal-size paper, Walsh defended his efforts to upset the plans of the Métis he called "Reil."

At this time, the impassioned Riel, recently released from psychiatric care in Montreal, was preaching insurrection and seeking Indian allies to wipe out any white influence on the Canadian prairie, including the NWMP. The following excerpts from Walsh's letter summarize his time at Fort Walsh and have been edited for clarity and grammar.

> Returned from leave of absence in July 1876 with instructions from Hon. Mr. Mills to use every exertion to persuade the half-breeds and Indians of the plains to return to reservations and instructions from Hon. Mr. Scott to keep a urgent watch on the hostile Sioux and to try and persuade them to return to the United States on my arrival to Wood Mountain ...
>
> About the first intelligence I received was that Louis Riel had but a short time previous visited the half-breeds of Wood Mountain and was now located at a place known as the Burnt Timber a few miles south of the 49th parallel. I immediately sent scouts to hunt up Riel's whereabouts and was not long in locating him. I knew pretty nearly every move he made ... I learned that during my absence in the east Sitting Bull had met Crowfoot and I obtained a pretty full account of how the meeting was brought about, the object of it and the result of it. The next information I received was that Ambroise Lepine is in company with one or two other influential half-breeds...after holding meetings at several places crossed to Montana and met Riel at Benton ... The next information I received was that Riel had got the promise from the Wolf Point Assiniboines to support his confederation scheme and that he endeavoured to secure the Yankton Sioux also but failed.
>
> I at once started for the Assiniboine camp seventy miles away. I found it north of the Milk River. Red Stone ... on my request produced the articles of agreement binding the Assiniboine to Riel's confederation. The agreement and signatures attached thereto were written with red ink or blood as the Indians were told. This document set forth that the country belonged to the Indian blood of the prairie, the Indians and their brethren the half-breeds ... That all the tribes from the Saskatchewan to the Missouri would be joined as one people and again they would here live. That although other men ruled the country at present, he Riel, was the true and rightful chief. That ... all that was necessary to establish this power was the loyal confederation of the half-breeds and Indian tribes ... The document was signed by Riel for the half-breeds and by Red Stone for the Assiniboines and

witnessed by a man, a half-breed whose name I do not want to give. The affair is all gone by and it would be no pleasure to me to injure this poor man who allowed himself to be hoodwinked. I remained overnight in Red Stone's camp and had several hours conversation on the subject from which I received a good deal of information regarding Riel's conduct.

Before leaving [the] Assiniboine camp I succeeded in undoing all Riel had done. I asked Red Stone to give me a copy of his agreement but he declined, saying that he had sworn not to give it to any man, but that he would destroy it and send a message informing Riel that the Assiniboine found him to be an imposter [and] that they withdrew from the agreement they entered into with him and burnt the document. Riel received the Assiniboine message of withdrawal, this I had proof of. So enraged was he ... that he declared someone should die for the part I was playing. This ... was the first substantial proof I had of Riel's trying to raise insurrection.

In September I was informed that it was the intention of many of the half breeds in the Wood Mountain district to join the Riel camp and Big Bend on the Milk Rive condemned ... I advised their people to remain where they were or that Riel would lead them into trouble. Quite a number remained, a number went and joined Riel's camp ...

In October I was fully informed as to Riel's intention and his hopes. In a few months the opening of spring he would be the dictator of the prairie and loyal Crowfoot who always loved the Queen and the British was to be his Great Lieutenant ... Not one word of all this information ... has ever before been told. Not even to the Government and why it was not communicated to the Government at the time or after I will tell you before I finish my story. I ... adopted the policy that I felt would defeat Riel without costing the Canadian people a dollar ... With the knowledge that I possessed ... I could destroy Riel's plans and scatter to the winds the great confederation that his visionary mind led him to believe was waiting for him ... One of the reasons why I did not communicate the affair to the Government ... the facts as they really stood would alarm it unnecessarily and ... the influence I possessed over many of the Indians among the plains, and particularly the Sioux, would be sufficient to crush Riel out. Sensational, exaggerated and exciting reports would be flying throughout the land at a great expense to the people, an expedition would have been sent into the territories for what—for nothing but to learn on arrival that the affairs had burst like a bubble and disappeared.

I ordered the sale of arms and ammunition discontinued and wrote Fort Walsh requesting the Commander there to do the same. Subsequently I had all the arms and ammunition in the possession of traders for sale, collected and placed in a post for security. I had the promise of Red Stone that the Assiniboines would not join Riel. I had a sworn pledge of fidelity of Sitting Bull, Long Dog of the Uncpapas, Broad Trail, Bull Knife, and Stone Dog of the Ogallalls, Spotted Eagle of the Robows and Black Bull of the Bruels. I had the friendship and the promise of Black Horn, the war chief of the Yankton, that he would forever remain true to me. The force of the

Teton Sioux alone, which numbers over 3000 warriors, veterans of the Custer battle, would have been sufficient alone to have walked over Riel's half-breeds ... Riel, Crowfoot and Big Bear knew it, and I knew there would be no attempt at hostility without Bull and the Sioux ... Between the months of September and December nearly all the Teton Sioux moved their camp to the Milk River and settled for the winter a short distance from Reil's headquarters ... From this point a movement north was to be made in the spring, although 75 miles away I was in constant communication with the camp, receiving a message from it almost daily. By the middle of December Riel found himself surrounded by a large camp of half-breeds, Cree and Sioux Indians. I do not suppose he was ever more happy in his life ...

The time had now arrived ... to annoy his camp and dislodge him from the Milk River. For this there were two reasons: the first to show the Indians and half-breeds that the report Riel made that the Americans being in sympathy with him was false and deceiving. The second to break up the camp and make the northern band that composed part of it move north and separate into small parties ... [T]his would separate them from the influence of Riel who would not dare come north of the 49th Parallel as he had been informed, then I would arrest him. My force to accomplish this end was the Assiniboines and Yankton Sioux American Indians whom I convinced it was not to their interest that this camp should be allowed to remain on the Milk River.

It was my suggestion and the Yanktons made complaints to their agents ... against northern half-breeds ... upon the Assiniboine and Yankton reserve ... United States marshals and Customs officials commenced to visit the camp in search of ammunition or contraband goods. From the military orders were received that the Canadian Indians and half-breeds must move north. Riel's power was melting away. The Indians commenced to see that Riel's statements regarding the friendship of the Americans was not reliable. My prophecies were about to be realized: part of the Sioux withdrew from the main camp and moved to Wood Mountain.

February brought us the information that Miles in all probability would take the field in the spring and occupy Milk River. When this news reached the camp, delegations came from every quarter to ask us who Miles was taking the field and to ask me to stop him. Riel had told the Indians it was my work; they thought I could stop Miles and pled hard for me to do so. The only reason I gave them for Miles' movements was that the conduct of Riel and of the half-breeds was not approved of and the Indians who associated with him would receive the same punishment as they did ... By the month of March the confederation had become so derailed that a postponement for another year was thought necessary [so] ... Miles arrived at Milk River in July, drove any Sioux there out of it, and took into custody a great number of half-breeds, Riel having disappeared before his arrival.

This ended his influence with the southern Indians. The severest communication I ever received from the Government during my whole term of service was in February 1879 when I was working night and day to save the country the trouble and expense of an insurrection. I was told that the minister condemned my conduct in trying to disturb the camp in Milk River. I only make mention of this to illustrate to you how thoroughly ignorant the Government was of things in that quarter. Some people think I liked notoriety, but Sir if I did I had in the winter of 1878 and 1879 and the summer of 1879 such opportunities as was never offered man before. But I valued the life of the people and the peace of my country too much to sacrifice either for my aggrandizement.

James Morrow Walsh.

Bibliography

Ahrens, Merv. "The First NWMP Trek: From Ottawa to the Stone Fort, 1873." *The Beaver* June/July 1998, 78(3): 4-12.

Alan, Iris. *White Sioux*. Sidney, B.C.: Gray's Publishing, 1969.

Anderson, Frank W. *Fort Walsh and the Cypress Hills*. Saskatoon: Frank Anderson, 1980.

Andrist, Ralph K. *The Long Death: The Last Days of the Plains Indians*. New York: Collier Books, 1964.

Calloway, Colin, ed. *Our Hearts Fell to the Ground: Plains Indian Views of How the West Was Lost*. Boston: Bedford Books of St. Martin's Press, 1996.

Capps, Benjamin. *The Indians*. In "The Old West Series." Alexandria: Time-Life Books, 1973.

Chambers, Ernest J. *The Royal North-West Mounted Police: A Corps History 1906*. Toronto: Coles Publishing, 1972.

Cruise, David and Alison Griffiths. *The Great Adventure: How the Mounties Conquered the West*. Toronto: Penguin Books Canada, 1996.

Czech, Kenneth. "Warriors and Chiefs." *Wild West Magazine* February 1993, n.p.

Dempsey, Hugh A. "A Mountie's Diary—1875." *The Early West*. Hugh A. Dempsey, ed. Edmonton: Historical Society of Alberta, 1957.

Denny, Sir Cecil E. *March of the Mounties* (1939). Surrey: Heritage House, 1994.

Downs, Art. "March of the Mounties." *Outlaws and Lawmen of Western Canada*, Vol. 1. Art Downs, ed. Surrey: Heritage House, 1983.

Fardy, B.D. *Jerry Potts: Paladin of the Plains*. Langley: Mr. Paperback, 1984.

Grindle, Lucretia. "Pride and Prejudice." *Canadian Geographic* November 1999, 59-68.

Haydon, A.L. *The Riders of the Plains: A Record of the Royal North-West Mounted Police of Canada, 1873-1910*. Edmonton: Hurtig Books, 1971.

Horrall, S.W. *The Pictorial History of the Royal Canadian Mounted Police.* Toronto: McGraw-Hill Ryerson, 1973.

Johnston, Terry C. *Seize the Sky.* New York: Bantam Books, 1991.

———. *A Cold Day in Hell.* New York: Bantam Books, 1996.

MacEwan, Grant. *Sitting Bull: The Years in Canada.* Edmonton: Hurtig Publishers, 1973.

Macleod, R.G. *The North-West Mounted Police and Law Enforcement: 1873-1905.* Toronto: University of Toronto, 1976.

Manzione, Joseph. *I Am Looking to the North for My Life: Sitting Bull, 1876-1881.* Salt Lake City: University of Utah, 1991.

Michno, Greg. "Lakota Noon at the Greasy Grass." *Wild West Magazine* June 1996, n.p.

Nuefeld, Dr. Peter. "Brisebois: Forgotten Mountie Pioneer." *Canadian Frontier Annual.* Surrey: Antonson Publishing, 1977.

Primrose, Tom. *The Cypress Hills.* [location unknown]: Frontier Publishing, 1969.

Rasky, Frank. *The Taming of the Canadian West.* Toronto: McClelland & Stewart, 1967.

Steele, Samuel B. *Forty Years In Canada.* Toronto: McGraw-Hill Ryerson, 1972.

Stegner, Wallace. *Wolf Willow: A History, a Story and a Memory of the Last Prairie Frontier.* Toronto: Macmillan of Canada, 1955.

Stewart, Robert. *Sam Steele: Lion of the Frontier.* Toronto: Nelson Canada, 1981.

Tannee, Olga. *The Canadians.* Alexandria, Virginia: Time-Life Books, 1977.

Turner, John Peter. *The North-West Mounted Police: 1873-1893.* Vol. 1. Ottawa: King's Printer, 1950.

Utley, Robert M. *The Lance and the Shield: The Life and Times of Sitting Bull.* New York: Henry Holt, 1993.

Newspapers, Reports and Journals

    Brockville Times. August 13, 1897

    ———. August 16. 1897.

    ———. August 20, 1897

    ———. September 6, 1898

    ———. July 25, 1905.

    NWMP Commissioner's Report, 1877.

    ———. 1879.

Letters from the Brockville Museum

    Walsh to Commissioner Macleod, NWMP. undated [1879].

    Walsh to Prime Minister Wilfrid Laurier. September 15, 1896.

    Dewdney to John A. Macdonald.

Photo Credits

The Beaver (Lakehead University)—B
Glenbow Archives—GA
Heritage House Collection—HH
Hudson's Bay Co. Library—HBCL
Library of Congress —LC
Manitoba Archives—MA
Montana Historical Society—MH
National Archives of Canada—NA
RCMP Museum—RM
Saskatchewan Archives—SA
Smithsonian Institution—SI

Index

Great RCMP Stories

Then ...   ## ... and Now

March of the Mounties Sir Cecil E. Denny, one of the original 275 Mounties, recounts the demanding 800-mile westward trek completed in 1874, and profiles the men who made it.
ISBN 1-895811-06-6 $12.95

Red Serge & Stetsons Donovan Saul collected these recollections by members of the RCMP: gripping, tragic, and funny stories about pioneer outposts, prohibition, rum-runners, bachelor housekeeping, and more.
ISBN 0-920663-21-4 $15.95

Outlaws & Lawmen, Vols. 1-3 Enjoy Western Canada's most shocking tales of pioneer murder and mayhem from the safety of your armchair! These anthologies of dramatic crimes and the men that solved them are full of historical photos and maps.
Vol. 1 ISBN 1-895811-79-1 $9.95
Vol. 2 ISBN 0-919214-54-1 $10.95
Vol. 3 ISBN 0-919214-88-6 $11.95

Where Shadows Linger Bruce Northrop and Les Holmes go behind the crime scene—the most controversial RCMP investigation of the past 50 years—and erase the questions that still linger around the Olson murders.
ISBN 1-895811-92-9 $27.95 Cn $22.95 US

Mountie Makers Bob Teather's story brings you close to six young men, who learned from their RCMP recruitment and training that if it hurts you "just tape an aspirin to it."
ISBN 1-895811-41-4 $14.95

Scarlet Tunic, Vol. 1 & 2 After surviving RCMP training, Bob Teather shares the joys and frustrations of being a cop in these two volumes that reveal the emotional side of his work. By popular demand, Volume One includes, "The Deck," Bob Teather's current selection of adage cards that have helped him stay true to his job for three decades.
Vol. 1 ISBN 1-895811-52-X $11.95
Vol. 2 ISBN 1-895811-01-5 $11.95

The Author

Ian Anderson left Australia as a lad of eighteen, intent on fulfilling his dream in Canada—to become a Mountie. He visited the RCMP museum in Regina and found a hero in the history of the force—James Morrow Walsh. With police careers in both Canada and Australia behind him, Ian has retained his interest in RCMP history and is the author of a fiction series called *The Scarlet Riders*. "As for Major James Walsh, I feel as though I knew him personally," says Anderson.